THE COMMUNIST MANIFESTO & OTHER SELECTED WRITINGS

Karl Marx and Friedrich Engels

COLLINS
CLASSICS

William Collins
An imprint of HarperCollins*Publishers*
1 London Bridge Street
London SE1 9GF

WilliamCollinsBooks.com

HarperCollinsPublishers
Macken House
39/40 Mayor Street Upper
Dublin 1
D01 C9W8, Ireland

This William Collins paperback edition published in Great Britain in 2024

2

A catalogue record for this book is available from the British Library

ISBN 978-0-00-861997-8

Set in HC Arc by HarperCollins*Publishers* India

Printed and Bound in the UK using 100%
Renewable Electricity at CPI Group (UK) Ltd

MIX
Paper | Supporting responsible forestry
FSC™ C007454
FSC
www.fsc.org

This book contains FSC™ certified paper and other controlled sources to ensure responsible forest management.

For more information visit: www.harpercollins.co.uk/green

History of William Collins

In 1819, millworker William Collins from Glasgow, Scotland, set up a company for printing and publishing pamphlets, sermons, hymn books and prayer books. That company was Collins and was to mark the birth of HarperCollins Publishers as we know it today. The long tradition of Collins dictionary publishing can be traced back to the first dictionary William co-published in 1825, *Greek and English Lexicon*. Indeed, from 1840 onwards, he began to produce illustrated dictionaries and even obtained a licence to print and publish the Bible.

Soon after, William published the first Collins novel; however, it was the time of the Long Depression, where harvests were poor, prices were high, potato crops had failed and violence was erupting in Europe. As a result, many factories across the country were forced to close down and William chose to retire in 1846, partly due to the hardships he was facing.

Aged 30, William's son, William II, took over the business. A keen humanitarian with a warm heart and a generous spirit, William II was truly 'Victorian' in his outlook. He introduced new, up-to-date steam presses and published affordable editions of Shakespeare's works and *The Pilgrim's Progress*, making them available to the masses for the first time.

A new demand for educational books meant that success came with the publication of travel books, scientific books, encyclopedias and dictionaries. This demand to be educated led to the later publication of atlases, and Collins also held the monopoly on scripture writing at the time.

In the 1860s Collins began to expand and diversify and the idea of 'books for the millions' was developed, although the phrase wasn't coined until 1907. Affordable editions of classical literature were published, and in 1903 Collins introduced 10 titles in their Collins Handy Illustrated Pocket Novels. These proved so popular that a few years later this had increased to an output of 50 volumes, selling nearly half a million in their year of publication. In the same year, The Everyman's Library was also instituted, with the idea of publishing an affordable library of the most important classical works, biographies, religious and philosophical treatments, plays, poems, travel and adventure books. This series eclipsed all competition at the time, and the introduction of paperback books in the 1950s helped to open that market and marked a high point in the industry.

HarperCollins is and has always been a champion of the classics, and the current Collins Classics series follows in this tradition – publishing classical literature that is affordable and available to all. Beautifully packaged, highly collectible and intended to be reread and enjoyed at every opportunity.

Life and Times

Inscribed upon the tomb of Karl Marx in London's Highgate Cemetery are the words: 'The philosophers have only interpreted the world, in various ways; the point, however, is to change it.' Writing over many years with his friend and collaborator Friedrich Engels, their lifelong association resulted in the development and dissemination of Marxism, whose influence on modern intellectual, economic and political history and theory is difficult to overstate. Indeed, it cannot be refuted that the pair succeeded in this endeavour to make a lasting impact.

Karl Marx: Radical Rebel

Karl Marx was born on 5 May 1818 to an upper-middle-class Prussian family. After an academic yet liberal education, Marx studied at the universities of Bonn, Berlin and Jena, falling in with a vibrant community of political radicals and thinkers, including the leftist intellectual group the Young Hegelians, who set him on the path towards socialism. An active participant of the rowdy Trier Tavern Club, he also became known for his reckless carousing, troublemaking and disdain for the conservative establishment.

After attaining his doctorate in 1841, Marx turned to journalism. While working for the anti-government newspaper *Die Rheinische Zeitung*, he continued to develop and expound his views on socialism and economics, writing on issues such as poor housing conditions and press freedoms. It was here that he crossed paths with Engels for the first time, though they would not become firm friends until 1844.

Marx married his fiancée of seven years Jenny von Westphalen in 1843, and when *Die Rheinische Zeitung* was finally banned they moved to Paris, where Marx became co-editor of another radical left-wing newspaper, deepening his acquaintance with Engels and their shared socialist ideology, and embarking on a collaboration that would last a lifetime.

Life and Work in Exile

Hounded out of Paris for his political activities, Marx moved to the more liberal Brussels in 1845, where he and Engels would spend three years working on the pamphlet that would become *The Communist Manifesto*. As revolution spread throughout Europe in 1848 in a series of workers' uprisings, Marx continued to publish his political writings, eventually forcing him to seek exile in London. While there, he founded his own newspaper, the *Neue Rheinische Zeitung*, and, alongside Engels, developed and disseminated his social, political and economic theory – Marxism – which, above all, was concerned with the struggle between the labouring classes and the bourgeoisie. It was during this time that he wrote the critique of capitalism that would become his magnum opus – *Das Kapital*.

Despite his prolific output, Marx was destitute for much of his adult life. He and his wife Jenny had seven children, though only three survived, in part due to their poor living conditions in London. He relied on the financial support of Engels, recalling in a letter to his friend a statement his mother had once made:

'If only Karl made capital instead of just writing about it.' He was a heavy drinker, and also suffered from poor health which worsened significantly in his final years. He died in London in 1883.

Friedrich Engels: Political Industrialist

Friedrich Engels was born on 28 November 1820 into the heart of the European industrial revolution: his family owned large cotton mills in Prussia and Salford, and his bourgeois beginnings exposed Engels to the human cost of industrialisation, providing an outlook that would shape his life's work. Like Marx, he fell in with the Young Hegelians at the University of Berlin, writing inflammatory articles critiquing labour exploitation that were published in none other than Marx's *Rheinische Zeitung* – anonymously, to avoid the ire of his family.

In 1842, Engels was sent to work in the family mill in Salford in the hope he would reconsider his revolutionary principles, but instead he fell in love with Mary Burns, an Irish factory worker, who showed him the darker side of Manchester's slums. Confronted by the child labour, squalor and extreme poverty he found there, Engels was drawn ever more to socialism, and in 1845 he published his masterpiece, *The Condition of the Working Class in England*. In it he described 'the grim future of capitalism and the industrial age', writing of 'women made unfit for childbearing, children deformed, men enfeebled, limbs crushed, whole generations wrecked, afflicted with disease and infirmity, purely to fill the purses of the bourgeoisie.'

Engels returned to Germany to take part in the 1848 revolutions, writing and editing revolutionary articles for the *Neue Rheinische Zeitung* and volunteering in an armed uprising in southern Germany. Upon his unit's defeat, he escaped via Switzerland as a refugee back to England.

Double Life

Engels was forced to return to his family's cotton mills in order to provide Marx with financial support, but he led something of a double life, continuing his involvement with socialist politics and journalism, associating with the English Labour and Chartist movements, even enduring police scrutiny and surveillance for his radical activity. After Marx's death in 1883, Engels destroyed some 1,500 of their letters, to conceal the details of their secretive lifestyle.

Though both were opposed to the institution of marriage, Engels' relationship with Mary Burns continued until her death in 1863. Engels continued to live in London until his death in 1895, with much of his remaining years dedicated to editing and publishing Marx's major works, and expanding Marx's theories into new areas such as private property, family and the state. In his biography of Engels, Vladimir Lenin wrote that, after Marx, 'Engels was the finest scholar and teacher of the modern proletariat in the whole civilised world.'

The Communist Manifesto

From 1845 to 1848, amid the political unrest spreading throughout Europe, Marx and Engels sought refuge in Brussels. Commissioned by the Communist League – an underground movement promoting socialist values and an egalitarian society – to write a pamphlet setting forth the movement's principles and goals, the pair began work on what would eventually become *The Communist Manifesto*.

The *Manifesto* advocated for the abolition of bourgeois property and the establishment of a classless, communist society with collective ownership over the means of production. It emphasised the role of class struggle in historical development, making the claim that capitalism would necessarily collapse and lead to communism. Its stirring closing words read: 'Let the ruling classes tremble at a Communistic revolution. The proletariat have nothing to lose but their chains. They have a world to win. Working men of all countries, unite!'

First published on 21 February 1848, the initial reaction to the *Manifesto* was mixed. It gained attention among socialists, but faced strong opposition from government and the bourgeoisie. But with the advent of the uprisings of 1848, it increased ever more in significance, and it had established the basis for Marxist ideology, whose effects would ripple into the twentieth century and beyond.

A Collaborative Approach

Although Engels described himself as 'second fiddle' to Marx's political and economic prowess ('Marx was a genius; we others were at best talented'), his contribution was no less crucial. While Marx may have developed the complex theory that bears his name, it was Engels' endeavours that shaped it into an accessible philosophy. He provided not only the funding that allowed Marx to continue his work, but also real-world insights from the textile trade, as well as valuable publicity in the form of clear, accessible interpretations and practical applications that popularised many of his colleague's insights. Thanks to Engels' contribution, Marxism was able to reach mainstream audiences and gain supporters across the world.

A Remarkable Legacy

Karl Marx and Friedrich Engels left an intellectual and political legacy as extensive as it is enduring. *The Communist Manifesto* and Marxism exerted major influence on socialist thought, providing a catalyst for twentieth-century revolutionary movements across the world, and the pair's combined output is still integral to economic and political discourse and ideology today. Their work continues to be of utmost relevance to any critique of capitalism and economic inequality, and their collaboration has been lauded as one of the most influential in modern history.

CONTENTS

THE COMMUNIST MANIFESTO & OTHER SELECTED WRITINGS

THE COMMUNIST MANIFESTO

Karl Marx and Friedrich Engels

A spectre is haunting Europe – the spectre of Communism. All the Powers of old Europe have entered into a holy alliance to exorcise this spectre: Pope and Czar, Metternich and Guizot, French Radicals and German police-spies.

Where is the party in opposition that has not been decried as Communistic by its opponents in power? Where the Opposition that has not hurled back the branding reproach of Communism, against the more advanced opposition parties, as well as against its reactionary adversaries?

Two things result from this fact.

I. Communism is already acknowledged by all European Powers to be itself a Power.

II. It is high time that Communists should openly, in the face of the whole world, publish their views, their aims, their tendencies, and meet this nursery tale of the Spectre of Communism with a Manifesto of the party itself.

To this end, Communists of various nationalities have assembled in London, and sketched the following Manifesto, to be published in the English, French, German, Italian, Flemish and Danish languages.

I BOURGEOIS AND PROLETARIANS

The history of all hitherto existing society is the history of class struggles.

Freeman and slave, patrician and plebeian, lord and serf, guild-master and journeyman, in a word, oppressor and oppressed, stood in constant opposition to one another, carried on an uninterrupted, now hidden, now open fight, a fight that each time ended, either in a revolutionary re-constitution of society at large, or in the common ruin of the contending classes.

In the earlier epochs of history, we find almost everywhere a complicated arrangement of society into various orders, a manifold gradation of social rank. In ancient Rome we have patricians, knights, plebeians, slaves; in the Middle Ages, feudal lords, vassals, guild-masters, journeymen, apprentices, serfs; in almost all of these classes, again, subordinate gradations.

The modern bourgeois society that has sprouted from the ruins of feudal society has not done away with class antagonisms. It has but established new classes, new conditions of oppression, new forms of struggle in place of the old ones.

Our epoch, the epoch of the bourgeoisie, possesses, however, this distinctive feature: it has simplified the class antagonisms. Society as a whole is more and more splitting up into two great hostile camps, into two great classes, directly facing each other: Bourgeoisie and Proletariat.

From the serfs of the Middle Ages sprang the chartered burghers of the earliest towns. From these burgesses the first elements of the bourgeoisie were developed.

The discovery of America, the rounding of the Cape, opened up fresh ground for the rising bourgeoisie. The East-Indian and Chinese markets, the colonisation of America, trade with the colonies, the increase in the means of exchange and in commodities generally, gave to commerce, to navigation, to industry, an impulse never before known, and thereby, to the revolutionary element in the tottering feudal society, a rapid development.

The feudal system of industry, under which industrial production was monopolised by closed guilds, now no longer sufficed for the growing wants of the new markets. The manufacturing system took its place. The guild-masters were pushed on one side by the manufacturing middle class; division of labour between the different corporate guilds vanished in the face of division of labour in each single workshop.

Meantime the markets kept ever growing, the demand ever rising. Even manufacture no longer sufficed. Thereupon, steam and machinery revolutionised industrial production. The place of manufacture was taken by the giant, Modern Industry, the place of the industrial middle class, by industrial millionaires, the leaders of whole industrial armies, the modern bourgeois.

Modern industry has established the world-market, for which the discovery of America paved the way. This market has given an immense development to commerce, to navigation, to communication by land. This development has, in its turn, reacted on the extension of industry; and in proportion as industry, commerce, navigation, railways extended, in the same proportion the bourgeoisie developed, increased its capital, and pushed into the background every class handed down from the Middle Ages.

We see, therefore, how the modern bourgeoisie is itself the product of a long course of development, of a series of revolutions in the modes of production and of exchange.

Each step in the development of the bourgeoisie was accompanied by a corresponding political advance of that class. An oppressed class under the sway of the feudal nobility, an armed and self-governing association in the mediaeval commune; here independent urban republic (as in Italy and Germany), there taxable "third estate" of the monarchy (as in France), afterwards, in the period of manufacture proper, serving either the semi-feudal or the absolute monarchy as a counterpoise against the nobility, and, in fact, corner-stone of the great monarchies in general, the bourgeoisie has at last, since the establishment of Modern Industry and of the world-market, conquered for itself, in the modern representative State, exclusive political sway. The executive of the modern State is but a committee for managing the common affairs of the whole bourgeoisie.

The bourgeoisie, historically, has played a most revolutionary part.

The bourgeoisie, wherever it has got the upper hand, has put an end to all feudal, patriarchal, idyllic relations. It has pitilessly torn asunder the motley feudal ties that bound man to his "natural superiors", and has left remaining no other nexus between man and man than naked self-interest, than callous "cash payment". It has drowned the most heavenly ecstasies of religious fervour, of chivalrous enthusiasm, of philistine sentimentalism, in the icy water of egotistical calculation. It has resolved personal worth into exchange value, and in place of the numberless and indefeasible chartered freedoms, has set up that single, unconscionable freedom – Free Trade. In one word, for exploitation, veiled by religious and political illusions, naked, shameless, direct, brutal exploitation.

The bourgeoisie has stripped of its halo every occupation hitherto honoured and looked up to with reverent awe. It has converted the physician, the lawyer, the priest, the poet, the man of science, into its paid wage-labourers.

The bourgeoisie has torn away from the family its sentimental veil, and has reduced the family relation to a mere money relation.

The bourgeoisie has disclosed how it came to pass that the brutal display of vigour in the Middle Ages, which Reactionists so much admire, found its fitting complement in the most slothful indolence. It has been the first to show what man's activity can bring about. It has accomplished wonders far surpassing Egyptian pyramids, Roman aqueducts, and Gothic cathedrals; it has conducted expeditions that put in the shade all former Exoduses of nations and crusades.

The bourgeoisie cannot exist without constantly revolutionising the instruments of production, and thereby the relations of production, and with them the whole relations of society. Conservation of the old modes of production in unaltered form, was, on the contrary, the first condition of existence for all earlier industrial classes. Constant revolutionising of production, uninterrupted disturbance of all social conditions, everlasting uncertainty and agitation distinguish the bourgeois epoch from all earlier ones. All fixed, fast-frozen relations, with their train of ancient and venerable prejudices and opinions, are swept away, all new-formed ones become antiquated before they can ossify. All that is solid melts into air, all that is holy is profaned, and man is at last compelled to face with sober senses, his real conditions of life, and his relations with his kind.

The need of a constantly expanding market for its products chases the bourgeoisie over the whole surface of the globe. It must nestle everywhere, settle everywhere, establish connexions everywhere.

The bourgeoisie has through its exploitation of the world-market given a cosmopolitan character to production and consumption in every country. To the great chagrin of Reactionists, it has drawn from under the feet of industry the national ground on which it stood. All old-established national industries have been destroyed or are daily being destroyed. They are dislodged by new industries, whose introduction becomes a life and death question for all civilised nations, by industries that no longer work up indigenous raw material, but raw material drawn from the remotest zones; industries whose products are consumed, not only at home, but in every quarter of the globe. In place of the old wants, satisfied by the productions of the country, we find new wants, requiring for their satisfaction the products of distant lands and climes. In place of the old local and national seclusion and self-sufficiency, we have intercourse in every direction, universal inter-dependence of nations. And as in material, so also in intellectual production. The intellectual creations of individual nations become common property. National one-sidedness and narrow-mindedness become more and more impossible, and from the numerous national and local literatures, there arises a world literature.

The bourgeoisie, by the rapid improvement of all instruments of production, by the immensely facilitated means of communication, draws all, even the most barbarian, nations into civilisation. The cheap prices of its commodities are the heavy artillery with which it batters down all Chinese walls, with which it forces the barbarians' intensely obstinate hatred of foreigners to capitulate. It compels all nations, on pain of extinction, to adopt the bourgeois mode of production; it compels them to introduce what it calls civilisation into their midst, i.e., to become bourgeois themselves. In one word, it creates a world after its own image.

The bourgeoisie has subjected the country to the rule of the towns. It has created enormous cities, has greatly increased the urban population as compared with the rural, and has thus rescued a considerable part of the population from the idiocy of rural life. Just as it has made the country dependent on the towns, so it has made barbarian and semi-barbarian countries dependent on the civilised ones, nations of peasants on nations of bourgeois, the East on the West.

The bourgeoisie keeps more and more doing away with the scattered state of the population, of the means of production, and of property. It has agglomerated population, centralised means of production, and has concentrated property in a few hands. The necessary consequence of this was political centralisation. Independent, or but loosely connected provinces, with separate interests, laws, governments and systems of taxation, became lumped together into one nation, with one government, one code of laws, one national class-interest, one frontier and one customs-tariff.

The bourgeoisie, during its rule of scarce one hundred years, has created more massive and more colossal productive forces than have all preceding generations together. Subjection of Nature's forces to man, machinery, application of chemistry to industry and agriculture, steam-navigation, railways, electric telegraphs, clearing of whole continents for cultivation, canalisation of rivers, whole populations conjured out of the ground – what earlier century had even a presentiment that such productive force lumbered in the lap of social labour?

We see then: the means of production and of exchange, on whose foundation the bourgeoisie built itself up, were generated in feudal society. At a certain stage in the development of these means of production and of exchange, the conditions under which feudal society produced and exchanged, the feudal organisation of agriculture and manufacturing industry, in one word, the feudal relations of property became no longer compatible with the already developed productive forces; they became so many fetters. They had to be burst asunder; they were burst asunder.

Into their place stepped free competition, accompanied by a social and political constitution adapted to it, and by the economical and political sway of the bourgeois class.

A similar movement is going on before our own eyes. Modern bourgeois society with its relations of production, of exchange and of property, a society that has conjured up such gigantic means of production and of exchange, is like the sorcerer, who is no longer able to control the powers of the nether world whom he has called up by his spells. For many a decade past the history of industry and commerce is but the history of the revolt of modern productive forces against modern conditions of production, against the property relations that are the conditions for the existence of the bourgeoisie and of its rule. It is enough to mention the commercial crises that by their periodical return put on its trial, each time more threateningly, the existence of the entire bourgeois society. In these crises a great part not only of the existing products, but also of the previously created productive forces, are periodically destroyed. In these crises there breaks out an epidemic that, in all earlier epochs, would have seemed an absurdity – the epidemic of overproduction. Society suddenly finds itself put back into a state of momentary barbarism; it appears as if a famine, a universal war of devastation had cut off the supply of every means of subsistence; industry and commerce seem to be destroyed; and why? Because there is too much civilisation, too much means of subsistence, too much industry, too much commerce. The productive forces at the disposal of society no longer tend to further the development of the conditions of bourgeois property; on the contrary, they have become too powerful for these conditions, by which they are fettered, and so soon as they overcome these fetters, they bring disorder into the whole of bourgeois society, endanger the existence of bourgeois property. The conditions of bourgeois society are too narrow to comprise the wealth created by them. And how does the bourgeoisie get over these crises? On the one hand by enforced destruction of a mass of productive forces; on the other, by the conquest of new markets, and by the more thorough exploitation of the old ones. That is to say, by paving the way for more extensive and more destructive crises, and by diminishing the means whereby crises are prevented.

The weapons with which the bourgeoisie felled feudalism to the ground are now turned against the bourgeoisie itself.

But not only has the bourgeoisie forged the weapons that bring death to itself; it has also called into existence the men who are to wield those weapons – the modern working class – the proletarians.

In proportion as the bourgeoisie, i.e., capital, is developed, in the same proportion is the proletariat, the modern working class, developed – a class of labourers, who live only so long as they find work, and who find work only so long as their labour increases capital. These labourers, who must sell themselves piecemeal, are a commodity, like every other article of commerce, and are consequently exposed to all the vicissitudes of competition, to all the fluctuations of the market.

Owing to the extensive use of machinery and to division of labour, the work of the proletarians has lost all individual character, and consequently, all charm for the workman. He becomes an appendage of the machine, and it is only the most simple, most monotonous, and most easily acquired knack, that is required of him. Hence, the cost of production of a workman is restricted, almost entirely, to the means of subsistence that he requires for his maintenance, and for the propagation of his race. But the price of a commodity, and therefore also of labour, is equal to its cost of production. In proportion therefore, as the repulsiveness of the work increases, the wage decreases. Nay more, in proportion as the use of machinery and division of labour increases, in the same proportion the burden of toil also increases, whether by prolongation of the working hours, by increase of the work exacted in a given time or by increased speed of the machinery, etc.

Modern industry has converted the little workshop of the patriarchal master into the great factory of the industrial capitalist. Masses of labourers, crowded into the factory, are organised like soldiers. As privates of the industrial army they are placed under the command of a perfect hierarchy of officers and sergeants. Not only are they slaves of the bourgeois class, and of the bourgeois State; they are daily and hourly enslaved by the machine, by the overlooker, and, above all, by the individual bourgeois manufacturer himself. The more openly this despotism proclaims gain to be its end and aim, the more petty, the more hateful and the more embittering it is.

The less the skill and exertion of strength implied in manual labour, in other words, the more modern industry becomes developed, the more is the labour of men superseded by that of women. Differences of age and sex have no longer any distinctive social validity for the working class. All are instruments of labour, more or less expensive to use, according to their age and sex.

No sooner is the exploitation of the labourer by the manufacturer, so far, at an end, and he receives his wages in cash, than he is set upon by the other portions of the bourgeoisie, the landlord, the shopkeeper, the pawnbroker, etc.

The lower strata of the middle class – the small tradespeople, shopkeepers, and retired tradesmen generally, the handicraftsmen and peasants – all these sink gradually into the proletariat, partly because their diminutive capital does not suffice for the scale on which Modern Industry is carried on, and is swamped in the competition with the large capitalists, partly because their specialised skill is rendered worthless by the new methods of production. Thus the proletariat is recruited from all classes of the population.

The proletariat goes through various stages of development. With its birth begins its struggle with the bourgeoisie. At first the contest is carried on by individual labourers, then by the workpeople of a factory, then by the operatives of one trade, in one locality, against the individual bourgeois who directly exploits them. They direct their attacks not against the bourgeois conditions of production, but against the instruments of production themselves; they destroy imported wares that compete with their labour, they smash to pieces machinery, they set factories ablaze, they seek to restore by force the vanished status of the workman of the Middle Ages.

At this stage the labourers still form an incoherent mass scattered over the whole country, and broken up by their mutual competition. If anywhere they unite to form more compact bodies, this is not yet the consequence of their own active union, but of the union of the bourgeoisie, which class, in order to attain its own political ends, is compelled to set the whole proletariat in motion, and is moreover yet, for a time, able to do so. At this stage, therefore, the proletarians do not fight their enemies, but the enemies of their enemies, the remnants of absolute monarchy, the landowners, the non-industrial bourgeois, the petty bourgeoisie. Thus the whole historical movement is concentrated in the hands of the bourgeoisie; every victory so obtained is a victory for the bourgeoisie.

But with the development of industry the proletariat not only increases in number; it becomes concentrated in greater masses, its strength grows, and it feels that strength more. The various interests and conditions of life within the ranks of the proletariat are more and more equalised, in proportion as machinery obliterates all distinctions of labour, and nearly everywhere reduces wages to the same low level. The growing competition among the bourgeois, and the resulting commercial crises, make the wages of the workers ever more fluctuating. The unceasing improvement of machinery, ever more rapidly developing, makes their livelihood more and more precarious; the collisions between individual workmen and individual bourgeois take more and more the character of collisions between two classes. Thereupon the workers begin to form combinations (Trades, Unions) against the bourgeois; they club together in order to keep up the rate of wages; they found permanent associations in order to make provision beforehand for these occasional revolts. Here and there the contest breaks out into riots.

Now and then the workers are victorious, but only for a time. The real fruit of their battles lies, not in the immediate result, but in the ever-expanding union of the workers. This union is helped on by the improved means of communication that are created by modern industry and that place the workers of different localities in contact with one another. It was just this contact that was needed to centralise the numerous local struggles, all of the same character, into one national struggle between classes. But every class struggle is a political struggle. And that union, to attain which the burghers of the Middle Ages, with their miserable highways, required centuries, the modern proletarians, thanks to railways, achieve in a few years.

This organisation of the proletarians into a class, and consequently into a political party, is continually being upset again by the competition between the workers themselves. But it ever rises up again, stronger, firmer, mightier. It compels legislative recognition of particular interests of the workers, by taking advantage of the divisions among the bourgeoisie itself. Thus the ten-hours' bill in England was carried.

Altogether collisions between the classes of the old society further, in many ways, the course of development of the proletariat. The bourgeoisie finds itself involved in a constant battle. At first with the aristocracy; later on, with those portions of the bourgeoisie itself, whose interests have become antagonistic to the progress of industry; at all times, with the bourgeoisie of foreign countries. In all these battles it sees itself compelled to appeal to the proletariat, to ask for its help, and thus, to drag it into the political arena. The bourgeoisie itself, therefore, supplies the proletariat with its own instruments of political and general education, in other words, it furnishes the proletariat with weapons for fighting the bourgeoisie.

Further, as we have already seen, entire sections of the ruling classes are, by the advance of industry, precipitated into the proletariat, or are at least threatened in their conditions of existence. These also supply the proletariat with fresh elements of enlightenment and progress.

Finally, in times when the class struggle nears the decisive hour, the process of dissolution going on within the ruling class, in fact within the whole range of old society, assumes such a violent, glaring character, that a small section of the ruling class cuts itself adrift, and joins the revolutionary class, the class that holds the future in its hands. Just as, therefore, at an earlier period, a section of the nobility went over to the bourgeoisie, so now a portion of the bourgeoisie goes over to the proletariat, and in particular, a portion of the bourgeois ideologists, who have raised themselves to the level of comprehending theoretically the historical movement as a whole.

Of all the classes that stand face to face with the bourgeoisie today, the proletariat alone is a really revolutionary class. The other classes decay and finally disappear in the face of Modern Industry; the proletariat is its special and essential product.

The lower middle class, the small manufacturer, the shopkeeper, the artisan, the peasant, all these fight against the bourgeoisie, to save from extinction their existence as fractions of the middle class. They are therefore not revolutionary, but conservative. Nay more, they are reactionary, for they try to roll back the wheel of history. If by chance they are revolutionary, they are so only in view of their impending transfer into the proletariat, they thus defend not their present, but their future interests, they desert their own standpoint to place themselves at that of the proletariat.

The "dangerous class", the social scum, that passively rotting mass thrown off by the lowest layers of old society, may, here and there, be swept into the movement by a proletarian revolution; its conditions of life, however, prepare it far more for the part of a bribed tool of reactionary intrigue.

In the conditions of the proletariat, those of old society at large are already virtually swamped. The proletarian is without property; his relation to his wife and children has no longer anything in common with the bourgeois family-relations; modern industrial labour, modern subjection to capital, the same in England as in France, in America as in Germany, has stripped him of every trace of national character. Law, morality, religion, are to him so many bourgeois prejudices, behind which lurk in ambush just as many bourgeois interests.

All the preceding classes that got the upper hand, sought to fortify their already acquired status by subjecting society at large to their conditions of appropriation. The proletarians cannot become masters of the productive forces of society, except by abolishing their own previous mode of appropriation, and thereby also every other previous mode of appropriation. They have nothing of their own to secure and to fortify; their mission is to destroy all previous securities for, and insurances of, individual property.

All previous historical movements were movements of minorities, or in the interests of minorities. The proletarian movement is the self-conscious, independent movement of the immense majority, in the interests of the immense majority. The proletariat, the lowest stratum of our present society, cannot stir, cannot raise itself up, without the whole superincumbent strata of official society being sprung into the air.

Though not in substance, yet in form, the struggle of the proletariat with the bourgeoisie is at first a national struggle. The proletariat of each country must, of course, first of all settle matters with its own bourgeoisie.

In depicting the most general phases of the development of the proletariat, we traced the more or less veiled civil war, raging within existing society, up to the point where that war breaks out into open revolution, and where the violent overthrow of the bourgeoisie lays the foundation for the sway of the proletariat.

Hitherto, every form of society has been based, as we have already seen, on the antagonism of oppressing and oppressed classes. But in order to oppress a class, certain conditions must be assured to it under which it can, at least, continue its slavish existence. The serf, in the period of serfdom, raised himself to membership in the commune, just as the petty bourgeois, under the yoke of feudal absolutism, managed to develop into a bourgeois. The modern labourer on the contrary, instead of rising with the progress of industry, sinks deeper and deeper below the conditions of existence of his own class. He becomes a pauper, and pauperism develops more rapidly than population and wealth. And here it becomes evident, that the bourgeoisie is unfit any longer to be the ruling class in society, and to impose its conditions of existence upon society as an over-riding law. It is unfit to rule because it is incompetent to assure an existence to its slave within his slavery, because it cannot help letting him sink into such a state, that it has to feed him, instead of being fed by him. Society can no longer live under this bourgeoisie, in other words, its existence is no longer compatible with society.

The essential condition for the existence, and for the sway of the bourgeois class, is the formation and augmentation of capital; the condition for capital is wage-labour. Wage-labour rests exclusively on competition between the labourers. The advance of industry, whose involuntary promoter is the bourgeoisie, replaces the isolation of the labourers, due to competition, by their revolutionary combination, due to association. The development of Modern Industry, therefore, cuts from under its feet the very foundation on which the bourgeoisie produces and appropriates products. What the bourgeoisie, therefore, produces, above all, is its own grave-diggers. Its fall and the victory of the proletariat are equally inevitable.

II PROLETARIANS AND COMMUNISTS

In what relation do the Communists stand to the proletarians as a whole?

The Communists do not form a separate party opposed to other working-class parties.

They have no interests separate and apart from those of the proletariat as a whole.

They do not set up any sectarian principles of their own, by which to shape and mould the proletarian movement.

The Communists are distinguished from the other working-class parties by this only: (1) In the national struggles of the proletarians of the different countries, they point out and bring to the front the common interests of the entire proletariat, independently of all nationality. (2) In the various stages of development which the struggle of the working class against the bourgeoisie has to pass through, they always and everywhere represent the interests of the movement as a whole.

The Communists, therefore, are on the one hand, practically, the most advanced and resolute section of the working-class parties of every country, that section which pushes forward all others; on the other hand, theoretically, they have over the great mass of the proletariat the advantage of clearly understanding the line of march, the conditions, and the ultimate general results of the proletarian movement.

The immediate aim of the Communists is the same as that of all the other proletarian parties: formation of the proletariat into a class, overthrow of the bourgeois supremacy, conquest of political power by the proletariat.

The theoretical conclusions of the Communists are in no way based on ideas or principles that have been invented, or discovered, by this or that would-be universal reformer.

They merely express, in general terms, actual relations springing from an existing class struggle, from a historical movement going on under our very eyes. The abolition of existing property relations is not at all a distinctive feature of Communism.

All property relations in the past have continually been subject to historical change consequent upon the change in historical conditions.

The French Revolution, for example, abolished feudal property in favour of bourgeois property.

The distinguishing feature of Communism is not the abolition of property generally, but the abolition of bourgeois property. But modern bourgeois private property is the final and most complete expression of the system of producing and appropriating products, that is based on class antagonisms, on the exploitation of the many by the few.

In this sense, the theory of the Communists may be summed up in the single sentence: Abolition of private property.

We Communists have been reproached with the desire of abolishing the right of personally acquiring property as the fruit of a man's own labour, which property is alleged to be the groundwork of all personal freedom, activity and independence.

Hard-won, self-acquired, self-earned property! Do you mean the property of the petty artisan and of the small peasant, a form of property that preceded the bourgeois form? There is no need to abolish that; the development of industry has to a great extent already destroyed it, and is still destroying it daily.

Or do you mean modern bourgeois private property?

But does wage-labour create any property for the labourer? Not a bit. It creates capital, i.e., that kind of property which exploits wage-labour, and which cannot increase except upon condition of begetting a new supply of wage-labour for fresh exploitation. Property, in its present form, is based on the antagonism of capital and wage-labour. Let us examine both sides of this antagonism.

To be a capitalist, is to have not only a purely personal, but a social *status* in production. Capital is a collective product, and only by the united action of many members, nay, in the last resort, only by the united action of all members of society, can it be set in motion.

Capital is, therefore, not a personal, it is a social power.

When, therefore, capital is converted into common property, into the property of all members of society, personal property is not thereby transformed into social property. It is only the social character of the property that is changed. It loses its class-character.

Let us now take wage-labour.

The average price of wage-labour is the minimum wage, i.e., that quantum of the means of subsistence, which is absolutely requisite in bare existence as a labourer. What, therefore, the wage-labourer appropriates by means of his labour, merely suffices to prolong and reproduce a bare existence. We by no means intend to abolish this personal appropriation of the products of labour, an appropriation that is made for the maintenance and reproduction of human life, and that leaves no surplus wherewith to command the labour of others. All that we want to do away with, is the miserable character of this appropriation, under which the labourer lives merely to increase capital, and is allowed to live only in so far as the interest of the ruling class requires it.

In bourgeois society, living labour is but a means to increase accumulated labour. In Communist society, accumulated labour is but a means to widen, to enrich, to promote the existence of the labourer.

In bourgeois society, therefore, the past dominates the present; in Communist society, the present dominates the past. In bourgeois society capital is independent and has individuality, while the living person is dependent and has no individuality.

And the abolition of this state of things is called by the bourgeois, abolition of individuality and freedom! And rightly so. The abolition of bourgeois individuality, bourgeois independence, and bourgeois freedom is undoubtedly aimed at.

By freedom is meant, under the present bourgeois conditions of production, free trade, free selling and buying.

But if selling and buying disappears, free selling and buying disappears also. This talk about free selling and buying, and all the other "brave words" of our bourgeoisie about freedom in general, have a meaning, if any, only in contrast with restricted selling and buying, with the fettered traders of the Middle Ages, but have no meaning when opposed to the Communistic abolition of buying and selling, of the bourgeois conditions of production, and of the bourgeoisie itself.

You are horrified at our intending to do away with private property. But in your existing society, private property is already done away with for nine-tenths of the population; its existence for the few is solely due to its non-existence in the hands of those nine-tenths. You reproach us, therefore, with intending to do away with a form of property, the necessary condition for whose existence is the non-existence of any property for the immense majority of society.

In one word, you reproach us with intending to do away with your property. Precisely so; that is just what we intend.

From the moment when labour can no longer be converted into capital, money, or rent, into a social power capable of being monopolised, i.e., from the moment when individual property can no longer be transformed into bourgeois property, into capital, from that moment, you say individuality vanishes.

You must, therefore, confess that by "individual" you mean no other person than the bourgeois, than the middle-class owner of property. This person must, indeed, be swept out of the way, and made impossible.

Communism deprives no man of the power to appropriate the products of society; all that it does is to deprive him of the power to subjugate the labour of others by means of such appropriation.

It has been objected that upon the abolition of private property all work will cease, and universal laziness will overtake us.

According to this, bourgeois society ought long ago to have gone to the dogs through sheer idleness; for those of its members who work, acquire nothing, and those who acquire anything, do not work. The whole of this objection is but another expression of the tautology: that there can no longer be any wage-labour when there is no longer any capital.

All objections urged against the Communistic mode of producing and appropriating material products, have, in the same way, been urged against the Communistic modes of producing and appropriating intellectual products. Just as, to the bourgeois, the disappearance of class property is the disappearance of production itself, so the disappearance of class culture is to him identical with the disappearance of all culture.

That culture, the loss of which he laments, is, for the enormous majority, a mere training to act as a machine.

But don't wrangle with us so long as you apply, to our intended abolition of bourgeois property, the standard of your bourgeois notions of freedom, culture, law, etc. Your very ideas are but the outgrowth of the conditions of your bourgeois production and bourgeois property, just as your jurisprudence is but the will of your class made into a law for all, a will, whose essential character and direction are determined by the economical conditions of existence of your class.

The selfish misconception that induces you to transform into eternal laws of nature and of reason, the social forms springing from your present mode of production and form of property – historical relations that rise and disappear in the progress of production – this misconception you share with every ruling class that has preceded you. What you see clearly in the case of ancient property, what you admit in the case of feudal property, you are of course forbidden to admit in the case of your own bourgeois form of property.

Abolition of the family! Even the most radical flare up at this infamous proposal of the Communists.

On what foundation is the present family, the bourgeois family, based? On capital, on private gain. In its completely developed form this family exists only among the bourgeoisie. But this state of things finds its complement in the practical absence of the family among the proletarians, and in public prostitution.

The bourgeois family will vanish as a matter of course when its complement vanishes, and both will vanish with the vanishing of capital.

Do you charge us with wanting to stop the exploitation of children by their parents? To this crime we plead guilty.

But, you will say, we destroy the most hallowed of relations, when we replace home education by social.

And your education! Is not that also social, and determined by the social conditions under which you educate, by the intervention, direct or indirect, of society, by means of schools, etc.? The Communists have not invented the intervention of society in education; they do but seek to alter the character of that intervention, and to rescue education from the influence of the ruling class.

The bourgeois clap-trap about the family and education, about the hallowed co-relation of parent and child, becomes all the more disgusting, the more, by the action of Modern Industry, all family ties among the proletarians are torn asunder, and their children transformed into simple articles of commerce and instruments of labour.

But you Communists would introduce community of women, screams the whole bourgeoisie in chorus.

The bourgeois sees in his wife a mere instrument of production. He hears that the instruments of production are to be exploited in common, and, naturally, can come to no other conclusion than that the lot of being common to all will likewise fall to the women.

He has not even a suspicion that the real point aimed at is to do away with the status of women as mere instruments of production.

For the rest, nothing is more ridiculous than the virtuous indignation of our bourgeois at the community of women which, they pretend, is to be openly and officially established by the Communists. The Communists have no need to introduce community of women; it has existed almost from time immemorial.

Our bourgeois, not content with having the wives and daughters of their proletarians at their disposal, not to speak of common prostitutes, take the greatest pleasure in seducing each other's wives.

Bourgeois marriage is in reality a system of wives in common and thus, at the most, what the Communists might possibly be reproached with, is that they desire to introduce, in substitution for a hypocritically concealed, an openly legalised community of women. For the rest, it is self-evident that the abolition of the present system of production must bring with it the abolition of the community of women springing from that system, i.e., of prostitution both public and private.

The Communists are further reproached with desiring to abolish countries and nationality.

The working men have no country. We cannot take from them what they have not got. Since the proletariat must first of all acquire political supremacy, must rise to be the leading class of the nation, must constitute itself *the* nation, it is, so far, itself national, though not in the bourgeois sense of the word.

National differences and antagonisms between peoples are

daily more and more vanishing, owing to the development of the bourgeoisie, to freedom of commerce, to the world-market, to uniformity in the mode of production and in the conditions of life corresponding thereto.

The supremacy of the proletariat will cause them to vanish still faster. United action, of the leading civilised countries at least, is one of the first conditions for the emancipation of the proletariat.

In proportion as the exploitation of one individual by another is put an end to, the exploitation of one nation by another will also be put an end to. In proportion as the antagonism between classes within the nation vanishes, the hostility of one nation to another will come to an end.

The charges against Communism made from a religious, a philosophical, and, generally, from an ideological standpoint, are not deserving of serious examination.

Does it require deep intuition to comprehend that man's ideas, views and conceptions, in one word, man's consciousness, changes with every change in the conditions of his material existence, in his social relations and in his social life?

What else does the history of ideas prove, than that intellectual production changes its character in proportion as material production is changed? The ruling ideas of each age have ever been the ideas of its ruling class.

When people speak of ideas that revolutionise society, they do but express the fact, that within the old society, the elements of a new one have been created, and that the dissolution of the old ideas keeps even pace with the dissolution of the old conditions of existence.

When the ancient world was in its last throes, the ancient religions were overcome by Christianity. When Christian ideas succumbed in the eighteenth century to rationalist ideas, feudal society fought its death battle with the then revolutionary bourgeoisie. The ideas of religious liberty and freedom of conscience merely gave expression to the sway of free competition within the domain of knowledge.

"Undoubtedly", it will be said, "religious, moral, philosophical and juridical ideas have been modified in the course of historical development. But religion, morality philosophy, political science, and law, constantly survived this change".

"There are, besides, eternal truths, such as Freedom, Justice, etc. that are common to all states of society. But Communism abolishes eternal truths, it abolishes all religion, and all morality, instead of constituting them on a new basis; it therefore acts in contradiction to all past historical experience".

What does this accusation reduce itself to? The history of all past society has consisted in the development of class antagonisms, antagonisms that assumed different forms at different epochs.

But whatever form they may have taken, one fact is common to all past ages, *viz.*, the exploitation of one part of society by the other. No wonder, then, that the social consciousness of past ages, despite all the multiplicity and variety it displays, moves within certain common forms, or general ideas, which cannot completely vanish except with the total disappearance of class antagonisms.

The Communist revolution is the most radical rupture with traditional property relations; no wonder that its development involves the most radical rupture with traditional ideas.

But let us have done with the bourgeois objections to Communism.

We have seen above, that the first step in the revolution by the working class, is to raise the proletariat to the position of ruling class, to win the battle of democracy.

The proletariat will use its political supremacy to wrest, by degrees, all capital from the bourgeoisie, to centralise all instruments of production in the hands of the State, i.e., of the proletariat organised as the ruling class; and to increase the total of productive forces as rapidly as possible.

Of course, in the beginning, this cannot be effected except by means of despotic inroads on the rights of property, and on the conditions of bourgeois production; by means of measures, therefore, which appear economically insufficient and untenable, but which, in the course of the movement, outstrip themselves, necessitate further inroads upon the old social order, and are unavoidable as a means of entirely revolutionising the mode of production.

These measures will of course be different in different countries.

Nevertheless in the most advanced countries, the following will be pretty generally applicable.

1. Abolition of property in land and application of all rents of land to public Purposes
2. A heavy progressive or graduated income tax.
3. Abolition of all right of inheritance.
4. Confiscation of the property of all emigrants and rebels.
5. Centralisation of credit in the hands of the State, by means of a national bank with State capital and an exclusive monopoly.
6. Centralisation of the means of communication and transport in the hands of the State.
7. Extension of factories and instruments of production

owned by the State; the bringing into cultivation of waste-lands, and the improvement of the soil generally in accordance with a common plan.

8. Equal liability of all to labour. Establishment of industrial armies, especially for agriculture.
9. Combination of agriculture with manufacturing industries; gradual abolition of the distinction between town and country, by a more equable distribution of the population over the country.
10. Free education for all children in public schools. Abolition of children's factory labour in its present form. Combination of education with industrial production, &c., &c.

When, in the course of development, class distinctions have disappeared, and all production has been concentrated in the hands of a vast association of the whole nation, the public power will lose its political character. Political power, properly so called, is merely the organised power of one class for oppressing another. If the proletariat during its contest with the bourgeoisie is compelled, by the force of circumstances, to organise itself as a class, if, by means of a revolution, it makes itself the ruling class, and, as such, sweeps away by force the old conditions of production, then it will, along with these conditions, have swept away the conditions for the existence of class antagonisms and of classes generally, and will thereby have abolished its own supremacy as a class.

In place of the old bourgeois society, with its classes and class antagonisms, we shall have an association, in which the free development of each is the condition for the free development of all.

III SOCIALIST AND COMMUNIST LITERATURE

1 REACTIONARY SOCIALISM

A *Feudal Socialism*

Owing to their historical position, it became the vocation of the aristocracies of France and England to write pamphlets against modern bourgeois society. In the French revolution of July 1830, and in the English reform agitation, these aristocracies again succumbed to the hateful upstart. Thenceforth, a serious political contest was altogether out of question. A literary battle alone remained possible. But even in the domain of literature the old cries of the restoration period had become impossible.

In order to arouse sympathy, the aristocracy were obliged to lose sight, apparently, of their own interests, and to formulate their indictment against the bourgeoisie in the interest of the exploited working class alone. Thus the aristocracy took their revenge by singing lampoons on their new master, and whispering in his ears sinister prophecies of coming catastrophe.

In this way arose Feudal Socialism: half lamentation, half lampoon; half echo of the past, half menace of the future; at times, by its bitter, witty and incisive criticism, striking the bourgeoisie to the very heart's core; but always ludicrous in its effect, through total incapacity to comprehend the march of modern history.

The aristocracy, in order to rally the people to them, waved the proletarian alms-bag in front for a banner. But the people, so often as it joined them, saw on their hindquarters the old feudal coats of arms, and deserted with loud and irreverent laughter.

One section of the French Legitimists and "Young England" exhibited this spectacle.

In pointing out that their mode of exploitation was different to that of the bourgeoisie, the feudalists forget that they exploited under circumstances and conditions that were quite different, and that are now antiquated. In showing that, under their rule, the modern proletariat never existed, they forget that the modern bourgeoisie is the necessary offspring of their own form of society.

For the rest, so little do they conceal the reactionary character of their criticism that their chief accusation against the bourgeoisie amounts to this, that under the bourgeois *régime* a class is being developed, which is destined to cut up root and branch the old order of society.

What they upbraid the bourgeoisie with is not so much that it creates a proletariat, as that it creates a *revolutionary* proletariat.

In political practice, therefore, they join in all coercive measures against the working class; and in ordinary life, despite their high falutin phrases, they stoop to pick up the golden apples dropped from the tree of industry, and to barter truth, love, and honour for traffic in wool, beetroot-sugar, and potato spirits.

As the parson has ever gone hand in hand with the landlord, so has Clerical Socialism with Feudal Socialism.

Nothing is easier than to give Christian asceticism a Socialist tinge. Has not Christianity declaimed against private property, against marriage, against the State? Has it not preached in the place of these, charity and poverty, celibacy and mortification of the flesh, monastic life and Mother Church? Christian Socialism is but the holy water with which the priest consecrates the heart-burnings of the aristocrat.

B *Petty-Bourgeois Socialism*

The feudal aristocracy was not the only class that was ruined by the bourgeoisie, not the only class whose conditions of existence pined and perished in the atmosphere of modern bourgeois society. The mediaeval burgesses and the small peasant proprietors were the precursors of the modern bourgeoisie. In those countries which are but little developed, industrially and commercially, these two classes still vegetate side by side with the rising bourgeoisie.

In countries where modern civilisation has become fully developed, a new class of petty bourgeois has been formed, fluctuating between proletariat and bourgeoisie and ever renewing itself as a supplementary part of bourgeois society. The individual members of this class, however, are being constantly hurled down into the proletariat by the action of competition, and, as modern industry develops, they even see the moment approaching when they will completely disappear as an independent section of modern society, to be replaced, in manufactures, agriculture and commerce, by overlookers, bailiffs and shopmen.

In countries like France, where the peasants constitute far more than half of the population, it was natural that writers who sided with the proletariat against the bourgeoisie, should use, in their criticism of the bourgeois *régime*, the standard of the peasant and petty bourgeois, and from the standpoint of these intermediate classes should take up the cudgels for the working class. Thus arose petty-bourgeois Socialism. Sismondi was the head of this school, not only in France but also in England.

This school of Socialism dissected with great acuteness the contradictions in the conditions of modern production. It laid bare the hypocritical apologies of economists. It proved, incontrovertibly, the disastrous effects of machinery and division of labour; the concentration of capital and land in a few hands; overproduction and crises; it pointed out the inevitable ruin of the petty bourgeois and peasant, the misery of the proletariat, the anarchy in production, the crying inequalities in the distribution of wealth, the industrial war of extermination between nations, the dissolution of old moral bonds, of the old family relations, of the old nationalities.

In its positive aims, however, this form of Socialism aspires either to restoring the old means of production and of exchange, and with them the old property relations, and the old society, or to cramping the modern means of production and of exchange, within the framework of the old property relations that have been, and were bound to be, exploded by those means. In either case, it is both reactionary and Utopian.

Its last words are: corporate guilds for manufacture, patriarchal relations in agriculture.

Ultimately, when stubborn historical facts had dispersed all intoxicating effects of self-deception, this form of Socialism ended in a miserable fit of the blues.

C *German, or "True", Socialism*

The Socialist and Communist literature of France, a literature that originated under the pressure of a bourgeoisie in power, and that was the expression of the struggle against this power, was introduced into Germany at a time when the bourgeoisie, in that country, had just begun its contest with feudal absolutism.

German philosophers, would-be philosophers, and *beaux esprits*, eagerly seized on this literature, only forgetting, that when these writings immigrated from France into Germany,

French social conditions had not immigrated along with them. In contact with German social conditions, this French literature lost all its immediate practical significance, and assumed a purely literary aspect. Thus, to the German philosophers of the eighteenth century, the demands of the first French Revolution were nothing more than the demands of "Practical Reason" in general, and the utterance of the will of the revolutionary French bourgeoisie signified in their eyes the law of pure Will, of Will as it was bound to be, of true human Will generally.

The world of the German *literati* consisted solely in bringing the new French ideas into harmony with their ancient philosophical conscience, or rather, in annexing the French ideas without deserting their own philosophic point of view.

This annexation took place in the same way in which a foreign language is appropriated, namely, by translation.

It is well known how the monks wrote silly lives of Catholic Saints *over* the manuscripts on which the classical works of ancient heathendom had been written. The German *literati* reversed this process with the profane French literature. They wrote their philosophical nonsense beneath the French original. For instance, beneath the French criticism of the economic functions of money, they wrote "Alienation of Humanity", and beneath the French criticism of the bourgeois State they wrote "dethronement of the Category of the General", and so forth.

The introduction of these philosophical phrases at the back of the French historical criticisms they dubbed "Philosophy of Action", "True Socialism", "German Science of Socialism", "Philosophical Foundation of Socialism", and so on.

The French Socialist and Communist literature was thus completely emasculated. And, since it ceased in the hands of the

German to express the struggle of one class with the other, he felt conscious of having overcome "French one-sidedness" and of representing, not true requirements, but the requirements of Truth; not the interests of the proletariat, but the interests of Human Nature, of Man in general, who belongs to no class, has no reality, who exists only in the misty realm of philosophical fantasy.

This German Socialism, which took its schoolboy task so seriously and solemnly, and extolled its poor stock-in-trade in such mountebank fashion, meanwhile gradually lost its pedantic innocence.

The fight of the German, and, especially, of the Prussian bourgeoisie, against feudal aristocracy and absolute monarchy, in other words, the liberal movement, became more earnest.

By this, the long wished-for opportunity was offered to "True" Socialism of confronting the political movement with the Socialist demands, of hurling the traditional anathemas against liberalism, against representative government, against bourgeois competition, bourgeois freedom of the press, bourgeois legislation, bourgeois liberty and equality, and of preaching to the masses that they had nothing to gain, and everything to lose, by this bourgeois movement. German Socialism forgot, in the nick of time, that the French criticism, whose silly echo it was, presupposed the existence of modern bourgeois society, with its corresponding economic conditions of existence, and the political constitution adapted thereto, the very things whose attainment was the object of the pending struggle in Germany.

To the absolute governments, with their following of parsons, professors, country squires and officials, it served as a welcome scarecrow against the threatening bourgeoisie.

It was a sweet finish after the bitter pills of floggings and bullets with which these same governments, just at that time, dosed the German working-class risings.

While this "True" Socialism thus served the governments as a weapon for fighting the German bourgeoisie, it, at the same time, directly represented a reactionary interest, the interest of the German Philistines. In Germany the *petty-bourgeois* class, a *relic* of the sixteenth century, and since then constantly cropping up again under various forms, is the real social basis of the existing state of things.

To preserve this class is to preserve the existing state of things in Germany. The industrial and political supremacy of the bourgeoisie threatens it with certain destruction; on the one hand, from the concentration of capital; on the other, from the rise of a revolutionary proletariat. "True" Socialism appeared to kill these two birds with one stone. It spread like an epidemic.

The robe of speculative cobwebs, embroidered with flowers of rhetoric, steeped in the dew of sickly sentiment, this transcendental robe in which the German Socialists wrapped their sorry "eternal truths", all skin and bone, served to wonderfully increase the sale of their goods amongst such a public.

And on its part, German Socialism recognised, more and more, its own calling as the bombastic representative of the petty-bourgeois Philistine.

It proclaimed the German nation to be the model nation, and the German petty Philistine to be the typical man. To every villainous meanness of this model man it gave a hidden, higher, Socialistic interpretation, the exact contrary of its real character. It went to the extreme length of directly opposing the "brutally destructive" tendency of Communism, and of proclaiming its supreme and impartial contempt of all class struggles. With very few exceptions, all the so-called Socialist and Communist publications that now (1847) circulate in Germany belong to the domain of this foul and enervating literature.

2 CONSERVATIVE, OR BOURGEOIS, SOCIALISM

A part of the bourgeoisie is desirous of redressing social grievances, in order to secure the continued existence of bourgeois society.

To this section belong economists, philanthropists, humanitarians, improvers of the condition of the working class, organisers of charity, members of societies for the prevention of cruelty to animals, temperance fanatics, hole-and-corner reformers of every imaginable kind. This form of Socialism has, moreover, been worked out into complete systems.

We may cite Proudhon's *Philosophie de la Misère* as an example of this form.

The Socialistic bourgeois want all the advantages of modern social conditions without the struggles and dangers necessarily resulting therefrom. They desire the existing state of society minus its revolutionary and disintegrating elements. They wish for a bourgeoisie without a proletariat. The bourgeoisie naturally conceives the world in which it is supreme to be the best; and bourgeois Socialism develops this comfortable conception into various more or less complete systems. In requiring the proletariat to carry out such a system, and thereby to march straightway into the social New Jerusalem, it but requires in reality, that the proletariat should remain within the bounds of existing society, but should cast away all its hateful ideas concerning the bourgeoisie.

A second and more practical, but less systematic, form of this Socialism sought to depreciate every revolutionary movement in the eyes of the working class, by showing that no mere political reform, but only a change in the material conditions of existence, in economic relations, could be of any advantage to them. By changes in the material conditions of existence, this form of Socialism, however, by no means understands abolition of the bourgeois relations of production, an abolition that can be effected only by a revolution, but administrative reforms, based on the continued existence of these relations; reforms, therefore, that in no respect affect the relations between capital and labour, but, at the best, lessen the cost, and simplify the administrative work, of bourgeois government.

Bourgeois Socialism attains adequate expression, when, and only when, it becomes a mere figure of speech.

Free trade: for the benefit of the working class. Protective duties: for the benefit of the working class. Prison Reform: for the benefit of the working class. This is the last word and the only seriously meant word of bourgeois Socialism.

It is summed up in the phrase: the bourgeois is a bourgeois – for the benefit of the working class.

3 CRITICAL-UTOPIAN SOCIALISM AND COMMUNISM

We do not here refer to that literature which, in every great modern revolution, has always given voice to the demands of the proletariat, such as the writings of Babeuf and others.

The first direct attempts of the proletariat to attain its own ends, made in times of universal excitement, when feudal society was being overthrown, these attempts necessarily failed, owing to the then undeveloped state of the proletariat, as well as to the absence of the economic conditions for its emancipation, conditions that had yet to be produced, and could be produced by the impending bourgeois epoch alone. The revolutionary literature that accompanied these first movements of the proletariat had necessarily a reactionary character. It inculcated universal asceticism and social levelling in its crudest form.

The Socialist and Communist systems properly so called, those of Saint-Simon, Fourier, Owen and others, spring into existence in the early undeveloped period, described above, of the struggle between proletariat and bourgeoisie (see Section 1, Bourgeois and Proletarians).

The founders of these systems see, indeed, the class antagonisms, as well as the action of the decomposing elements, in the prevailing form of society. But the proletariat, as yet in its infancy, offers to them the spectacle of a class without any historical initiative or any independent political movement.

Since the development of class antagonism keeps even pace with the development of industry, the economic situation, as they find it, does not as yet offer to them the material conditions for the emancipation of the proletariat. They therefore search after a new social science, after new social laws, that are to create these conditions.

Historical action is to yield to their personal inventive action, historically created conditions of emancipation to fantastic ones, and the gradual, spontaneous class-organisation of the proletariat to the organisation of society specially contrived by these inventors. Future history resolves itself, in their eyes, into the propaganda and the practical carrying out of their social plans.

In the formation of their plans they are conscious of caring chiefly for the interests of the working class, as being the most suffering class. Only from the point of view of being the most suffering class does the proletariat exist for them.

The undeveloped state of the class struggle, as well as their own surroundings, causes Socialists of this kind to consider themselves far superior to all class antagonisms. They want to improve the condition of every member of society, even that of the most favoured. Hence, they habitually appeal to society at large, without distinction of class; nay, by preference, to the ruling class. For how can people, when once they understand their system, fail to see in it the best possible plan of the best possible state of society?

Hence, they reject all political, and especially all revolutionary, action; they wish to attain their ends by peaceful means, and endeavour, by small experiments, necessarily doomed to failure, and by the force of example, to pave the way for the new social Gospel.

Such fantastic pictures of future society, painted at a time when the proletariat is still in a very undeveloped state and has but a fantastic conception of its own position, correspond with the first instinctive yearnings of that class for a general reconstruction of society.

But these Socialist and Communist publications contain also a critical element. They attack every principle of existing society. Hence they are full of the most valuable materials for the enlightenment of the working class. The practical measures proposed in them – such as the abolition of the distinction between town and country, of the family, of the carrying on of industries for the account of private individuals, and of the wage system, the proclamation of social harmony, the conversion of the functions of the State into a mere superintendence of production, all these proposals point solely to the disappearance of class antagonisms which were, at that time, only just cropping up, and which, in these publications, are recognised in their earliest, indistinct and undefined forms only. These proposals, therefore, are of a purely Utopian character.

The significance of Critical-Utopian Socialism and Communism bears an inverse relation to historical development. In proportion as the modern class struggle develops and takes definite shape, this fantastic standing apart from the contest, these fantastic attacks on it, lose all practical value and all theoretical justification. Therefore, although the originators of these systems were, in many respects, revolutionary, their disciples have, in every case, formed mere reactionary sects. They hold fast by the original views of their masters, in opposition to the progressive historical development of the proletariat. They, therefore, endeavour, and that consistently, to deaden the class struggle and to reconcile the class antagonisms. They still dream of experimental realisation of their social Utopias, of founding isolated "*phalanstères*", of establishing "Home Colonies", of setting up a "Little Icaria" – duodecimo editions of the New Jerusalem – and to realise all these castles in the air, they are compelled to appeal to the feelings and purses of the bourgeois. By degrees they sink into the category of the reactionary conservative Socialists depicted above, differing from these only by more systematic pedantry, and by their fanatical and superstitious belief in the miraculous effects of their social science.

They, therefore, violently oppose all political action on the part of the working class; such action, according to them, can only result from blind unbelief in the new Gospel.

The Owenites in England, and the Fourierists in France, respectively, oppose the Chartists and the "*Réformistes*".

IV POSITION OF THE COMMUNISTS IN RELATION TO THE VARIOUS EXISTING OPPOSITION PARTIES

Section II has made clear the relations of the Communists to the existing working-class parties, such as the Chartists in England and the Agrarian Reformers in America.

The Communists fight for the attainment of the immediate aims, for the enforcement of the momentary interests of the working class; but in the movement of the present, they also represent and take care of the future of that movement. In France the Communists ally themselves with the Social-Democrats, against the conservative and radical bourgeoisie, reserving, however, the right to take up a critical position in regard to phrases and illusions traditionally handed down from the great Revolution.

In Switzerland they support the Radicals, without losing sight of the fact that this party consists of antagonistic elements, partly of Democratic Socialists, in the French sense, partly of radical bourgeois.

In Poland they support the party that insists on an agrarian revolution as the prime condition for national emancipation, that party which fomented the insurrection of Cracow in 1846.

In Germany they fight with the bourgeoisie whenever it acts in a revolutionary way, against the absolute monarchy, the feudal squirearchy, and the petty bourgeoisie.

But they never cease, for a single instant, to instil into the working class the clearest possible recognition of the hostile antagonism between bourgeoisie and proletariat, in order that the German workers may straightaway use, as so many weapons against the bourgeoisie, the social and political conditions that the bourgeoisie must necessarily introduce along with its supremacy, and in order that, after the fall of the reactionary classes in Germany, the fight against the bourgeoisie itself may immediately begin.

The Communists turn their attention chiefly to Germany, because that country is on the eve of a bourgeois revolution that is bound to be carried out under more advanced conditions of European civilisation, and with a much more developed proletariat, than that of England was in the seventeenth, and of France in the eighteenth century, and because the bourgeois revolution in Germany will be but the prelude to an immediately following proletarian revolution.

In short, the Communists everywhere support every revolutionary movement against the existing social and political order of things.

In all these movements they bring to the front, as the leading question in each, the property question, no matter what its degree of development at the time.

Finally, they labour everywhere for the union and agreement of the democratic parties of all countries.

The Communists disdain to conceal their views and aims. They openly declare that their ends can be attained only by the forcible overthrow of all existing social conditions. Let the ruling classes tremble at a Communistic revolution. The proletarians have nothing to lose but their chains. They have a world to win.

WORKING MEN OF ALL COUNTRIES, UNITE!

WAGE-LABOUR AND CAPITAL

Karl Marx

INTRODUCTION TO KARL MARX'S 'WAGE-LABOUR AND CAPITAL'

This pamphlet first appeared in the form of a series of leading articles in the *Neue Rheinische Zeitung*, beginning on April 4, 1849. The text is made up of from lectures delivered by Marx before the German Workingmen's Club of Brussels in 1847. The series was never completed. The promise "to be continued", at the end of the editorial in Number 269 of the newspaper, remained unfulfilled in consequence of the precipitous events of that time: the invasion of Hungary by the Russians, and the uprisings in Dresden, Iserlohn, Elberfeld, the Palatinate, and in Baden, which led to the suppression of the paper on May 19, 1849. And among the papers left by Marx no manuscript of any continuation of these articles has been found.

"Wage-Labour and Capital" has appeared as an independent publication in several editions, the last of which was issued by the Swiss Co-operative Printing Association, in Hottingen-Zurich, in 1884. Hitherto, the several editions have contained the exact wording of the original articles. But since at least 10,000 copies of the present edition are to be circulated as a propaganda tract, the question necessarily forced itself upon me, would Marx himself, under these circumstances, have approved of an unaltered literal reproduction of the original?

Marx, in the 40s, had not yet completed his criticism of political economy. This was not done until towards the end of the fifties. Consequently, such of his writings as were published before the first installment of his Critique of Political Economy was finished, deviate in some points from those written after 1859, and contain expressions and whole sentences which, viewed from the standpoint of his later writings, appear inexact, and even incorrect. Now, it goes without saying that in ordinary editions, intended for the public in general, this earlier standpoint, as a part of the intellectual development of the author, has its place; that the author, as well as the public, has an indisputable right to an unaltered reprint of these older writings. In such a case, I would not have dreamed of changing a single word in it. But it is otherwise when the edition is destined almost exclusively for the purpose of propaganda. In such a case, Marx himself would unquestionably have brought the old work, dating from 1849, into harmony with his new point of view, and I feel sure that I am acting in his spirit when I insert in this edition the few changes and additions which are necessary in order to attain this object in all essential point.

Therefore, I say to the reader at once: this pamphlet is not as Marx wrote it in 1849, but approximately as Marx would have written it in 1891. Moreover, so many copies of the original text are in circulation, that these will suffice until I can publish it again unaltered in a complete edition of Marx's works, to appear at some future time.

My alterations centre about one point. According to the original reading, the worker sells his labour for wages, which he receives from the capitalist; according to the present text, he sells his labour-power. And for this change, I must render an explanation: to the workers, in order that they may understand that we are not dealing here with a quibble and word-juggling, but with one of the most important points in the whole range of political economy; to the bourgeois, in order that they may convince themselves how greatly the uneducated workers, who can be easily made to grasp the most difficult economic analyses, excel our supercilious "cultured" folk, for whom such ticklish problems remain insoluble their whole life long.

Classical political economy borrowed from the industrial practice the current notion of the manufacturer, that he buys and pays for the labour of his employees. This conception had been quite serviceable for the business purposes of the manufacturer, his bookkeeping and price calculation. But naively carried over into political economy, it there produced truly wonderful errors and confusions.

Political economy finds it an established fact that the prices of all commodities, among them the price of the commodity which it calls "labour", continually change; that they rise and fall in consequence of the most diverse circumstances, which often have no connection whatsoever with the production of the commodities themselves, so that prices appear to be determined, as a rule, by pure chance. As soon, therefore, as political economy stepped forth as a science, it was one of its first tasks to search for the law that hid itself behind this chance, which apparently determined the prices of commodities, and which in reality controlled this very chance. Among the prices of commodities, fluctuating and oscillating, now upward, now downward, the fixed central point was searched for around which these fluctuations and oscillations were taking place. In short, starting from the price of commodities, political economy sought for the value of commodities as the regulating law, by means of which all price fluctuations could be explained, and to which they could all be reduced in the last resort.

And so, classical political economy found that the value of

a commodity was determined by the labour incorporated in it and requisite to its production. With this explanation, it was satisfied. And we too may for the present, stop at this point. But, to avoid misconceptions, I will remind the reader that today this explanation has become wholly inadequate. Marx was the first to investigate thoroughly into the value-forming quality of labour and to discover that not all labour which is apparently, or even really, necessary to the production of a commodity, imparts under all circumstances to this commodity a magnitude of value corresponding to the quantity of labour used up. If, therefore, we say today in short, with economists like Ricardo, that the value of a commodity is determined by the labour necessary to its production, we always imply the reservations and restrictions made by Marx. Thus much for our present purpose; further information can be found in Marx's *Critique of Political Economy*, which appeared in 1859, and in the first volume of *Capital*.

But so soon as the economists applied this determination of value by labour to the commodity "labour", they fell from one contradiction into another. How is the value of "labour" determined? By the necessary labour embodied in it. But how much labour is embodied in the labour of a labourer of a day, a week, a month, a year. If labour is the measure of all values, we can express the "value of labour" only in labour. But we know absolutely nothing about the value of an hour's labour, if all that we know about it is that it is equal to one hour's labour. So thereby, we have not advanced one hair's breadth nearer our goal; we are constantly turning about in a circle.

Classical economy, therefore, essayed another turn. It said: the value of a commodity is equal to its cost of production. But, what is the cost of production of "labour"? In order to answer this question, the economists are forced to strain logic just a little. Instead of investigating the cost of production of labour itself, which, unfortunately, cannot be ascertained, they now investigate the cost of production of the labourer. And this latter can be ascertained. It changes according to time and circumstances, but for a given condition of society, in a given locality, and in a given branch of production, it, too, is given, at least within quite narrow limits. We live today under the regime of capitalist production, under which a large and steadily growing class of the population can live only on the condition that it works for the owners of the means of production – tools, machines, raw materials, and means of subsistence – in return for wages. On the basis of this mode of production, the labourer's cost of production consists of the sum of the means of subsistence (or their price in money) which on the average are requisite to enable him to work, to maintain in him this capacity for work, and to replace him at his departure, by reason of age, sickness, or death, with another labourer – that is to say, to propagate the working class in required numbers.

Let us assume that the money price of these means of subsistence averages 3 shillings a day. Our labourer gets, therefore, a daily wage of 3 shillings from his employer. For this, the capitalist lets him work, say, 12 hours a day. Our capitalist, moreover, calculates somewhat in the following fashion: Let us assume that our labourer (a machinist) has to make a part of a machine which he finishes in one day. The raw material (iron and brass in the necessary prepared form) costs 20 shillings. The consumption of coal by the steam-engine, the wear-and-tear of this engine itself, of the turning-lathe, and of the other tools with which our labourer works, represent, for one day and one labourer, a value of 1 shilling. The wages for one day are, according to our assumption, 3 shillings. This makes a total of 24 shillings for our piece of a machine.

But the capitalist calculates that on an average he will receive for it a price of 27 shillings from his customers or 3 shillings over and above his outlay.

Whence do the 3 shillings pocketed by the capitalist come? According to the assertion of classical political economy, commodities are in the long run sold at their values, that is, they are sold at prices which correspond to the necessary quantities of labour contained in them. The average price of our part of a machine – 27 shillings – would therefore equal its value, i.e., equal the amount of labour embodied in it. But, of these 27 shillings, 21 shillings were values were values already existing before the machinist began to work; 20 shillings were contained in the raw material, 1 shilling in the fuel consumed during the work and in the machines and tools used in the process and reduced in their efficiency to the value of this amount. There remains 6 shillings, which have been added to the value of the raw material. But according to the supposition of our economists, themselves, these 6 shillings can arise only from the labour added to the raw material by the labourer. His 12 hours' labour has created, according to this, a new value of 6 shillings. Therefore, the value of his 12 hours' labour would be equivalent to 6 shillings. So we have at last discovered what the "value of labour" is.

"Hold on there!" cries our machinist. "Six shillings? But I have received only 3 shillings! My capitalist swears high and dry that the value of my 12 hours' labour is no more than 3 shillings, and if I were to demand 6, he'd laugh at me. What kind of a story is that?"

If before this we got with our value of labour into a vicious circle, we now surely have driven straight into an insoluble contradiction. We searched for the value of labour, and we found more than we can use. For the labourer, the value of the 12 hours' labour is 3 shillings; for the capitalist, it is 6 shillings, of which he pays the workingman 3 shillings as wages, and pockets the remaining 3 shilling himself. According to this, labour has not one but two values, and, moreover, two very different values!

As soon as we reduce the values, now expressed in money, to labour-time, the contradiction becomes even more absurd. By the 12 hours' labour, a new value of 6 shillings is created. Therefore, in 6 hours, the new value created equals 3 shilling – the amount which the labourer receives for 12 hours' labour. For 12 hours' labour, the workingman receives, as an equivalent, the product of 6 hours' labour. We are thus forced to one of two conclusions: either labour has two values, one of which is twice as large as the other, or 12 equals 6! In both cases we get pure absurdities. Turn and twist as we may, we will not get out of this contradiction as long as we speak of the buying and selling of "labour" and of the "value of labour". And just so it happened to the political economists. The last offshoot of classical political economy – the Ricardian school – was largely wrecked on the insolubility of this contradiction. Classic political economy had run itself into a blind alley. The man who discovered the way out of this blind alley was Karl Marx.

What the economists had considered as the cost of production of "labour" was really the cost of production, not of "labour", but of the living labourer himself. And what this labourer sold to the capitalist was not his labour. "So soon as his labour really begins", says Marx, "it ceases to belong to him, and therefore can no longer be sold by him". At the most, he could sell his future labour – i.e., assume the obligation of executing a certain piece of work in a certain time. But, in this way, he does not sell labour (which would first have to be performed), but not for a stipulated payment he places his labour-power at the disposal of the capitalist for a certain time (in case of time-wages), or for the performance of a certain task (in case of piece-wages). He hires out or sells his labour-power. But this labour-power has grown up with his person and is inseparable from it. Its cost of production, therefore, coincides with his own cost of production; what the economist called the cost of production of labour is really the cost of production of the labourer, and therewith of his labour-power. And, thus, we can also go back from the cost of production of labour-power to the value of labour-power, and determine the quantity of social labour that is required for the production of a labour-power of a given quantity, as Marx has done in the chapter on "The Buying and Selling of Labour Power". [*Capital*, Volume 1]

Now what takes place after the worker has sold his labour-power, i.e., after he has placed his labour-power at the disposal of the capitalist for stipulated wages – whether time-wages or piece-wages? The capitalist takes the labourer into his workshop or factory, where all the articles required for the work can be found – raw materials, auxiliary materials (coal, dyestuffs, etc.), tools and machines. Here the worker begins to toil. His daily wages are, as above, 3 shillings, and it makes no difference whether he earns them as day-wages or piece-wages. We again assume that in 12 hours the worker adds by his labour a new value of 6 shillings to the value of the raw materials consumed, which new value the capitalist realises by the sale of the finished piece of work. Out of this new value, he pays the worker his 3 shillings, and the remaining 3 shillings he keeps for himself. If, now the labourer creates in 12 hours a value of 6 shillings, in 6 hours he creates a value of 3 shillings. Consequently, after working 6 hours for the capitalist, the labourer has returned to him the equivalent of the 3 shillings received as wages. After 6 hours' work, both are quits, neither one owing a penny to the other.

"Hold on there!" now cries out the capitalist. "I have hired the labourer for a whole day, for 12 hours. But 6 hours are only half a day. So work along lively there until the other 6 hours are at an end – only then will we be even". And, in fact, the labourer has to submit to the conditions of the contract upon which he entered of "his own free will", and according to which he bound himself to work 12 whole hours for a product of labour which cost only 6 hours' labour.

Similarly with piece-wages. Let us suppose that in 12 hours our worker makes 12 commodities. Each of these costs a shilling in raw materials and wear-and-tear, and is sold for 2.5 shillings. On our former assumption, the capitalist gives the labourer .25 of a shilling for each piece, which makes a total of 3 shillings for 12 pieces. To earn this, the worker requires 12 hours. The capitalist receives 30 shillings for the 12 pieces; deducting 24 shillings for raw materials and wear-and-tear, there remains 6 shillings, of which he pays 3 shillings in wages and pockets the remaining 3. Just as before! Here also the worker labours 6 hours for himself – i.e., to replace his wages (half-an-hour in each of the 12 hours), and 6 hours for the capitalist.

The rock upon which the best economists were stranded, as long as they started out from the value of labour, vanishes as soon as we make our starting-point the value of labour-power. Labour-power is, in our present-day capitalist society, a commodity like every other commodity, but yet a very peculiar commodity. It has, namely, the peculiarity of being a value-creating force, the source of value, and, moreover, when properly treated, the source of more value than it possesses itself. In the present state of production, human labour-power not only produces in a day a greater value than it itself possesses and costs; but with each new scientific discovery, with each new technical invention, there also rises the surplus of its daily production over its daily cost, while as a consequence there diminishes that part of the working day in which the labourer produces the equivalent of his day's wages, and, on the other hand, lengthens that part of the working day in which he must present labour gratis to the capitalist.

And this is the economic constitution of our entire modern society: the working class alone produces all values. For value is only another expression for labour, that expression, namely, by which is designated, in our capitalist society of today, the amount of socially necessary labour embodied in a particular commodity. But, these values produced by the workers do not belong to the workers. They belong to the owners of the raw materials, machines, tools, and money, which enable them to buy the labour-power of the working class. Hence, the working class gets back only a part of the entire mass of products produced by it. And, as we have just seen, the other portion, which the capitalist class retains, and which it has to share, at most, only with the landlord class, is increasing with every new discovery and invention, while the share which falls to the working class (per capita) rises but little and very slowly, or not at all, and under certain conditions it may even fall.

But these discoveries and inventions which supplant one another with ever-increasing speed, this productiveness of human labour which increases from day to day to unheard-of proportions, at last gives rise to a conflict, in which present capitalistic economy must go to ruin. On the one hand, immeasurable wealth and a superfluidity of products with which the buyers cannot cope. On the other hand, the great mass of society proletarianised, transformed into wage-labourers, and thereby disabled from appropriating to themselves that superfluidity of products. The splitting up of society into a small class, immoderately rich, and a large class of wage-labourers devoid of all property, brings it about that this society smothers in its own superfluidity, while the great majority of its members are scarcely, or not at all, protected from extreme want. This condition becomes every day more absurd and more unnecessary. It must be got rid of; it can be got rid of. A new social order is possible, in which the class differences of today will have disappeared, and in which – perhaps after a short transition period, which, though somewhat deficient in other respects, will in any case be very useful morally – there will be the means of life, of the enjoyment of life, and of the development and activity of all bodily and mental faculties, through the systematic use and further development of the enormous productive powers of society, which exists with us even now, with equal obligation upon all to work. And that the workers are growing ever more determined to achieve this new social order will be proven on both sides of the ocean on this dawning May Day, and on Sunday, May 3.

Friederich Engels
London, April 30, 1891

PRELIMINARY

From various quarters we have been reproached for neglecting to portray the economic conditions which form the material basis of the present struggles between classes and nations. With set purpose we have hitherto touched upon these conditions only when they forced themselves upon the surface of the political conflicts.

It was necessary, beyond everything else, to follow the development of the class struggle in the history of our own day, and to prove empirically, by the actual and daily new-created historical material, that with the subjugation of the working class, accomplished in the days of February and March, the opponents of that class – the bourgeois republicans in France, and the bourgeois and peasant classes who were fighting feudal absolutism throughout the whole continent of Europe – were simultaneously conquered; that the victory of the "moderate republic" in France sounded, at the same time, the fall of the nations which had responded to the February revolution with heroic wars of independence; and finally that, by the victory over the revolutionary workingmen, Europe fell back into its old double slavery, into the English-Russian slavery. The June conflict in Paris, the fall of Vienna, the tragi-comedy in Berlin in November 1848, the desperate efforts of Poland, Italy, and Hungary, the starvation of Ireland into submission – these were the chief events in which the European class struggle between the bourgeoisie and the working class was summed up, and from which we proved that every revolutionary uprising, however remote from the class struggle its object might appear, must of necessity fail until the revolutionary working class will have conquered; – that every social reform must remain a Utopia until the proletarian revolution and the feudalistic counter-revolution will have been pitted against each other in a world-wide war. In our presentation, as in reality, Belgium and Switzerland were tragicomic caricaturish genre pictures in the great historic tableau, the one the model State of the bourgeois monarchy, the other the model State of the bourgeois republic; both of them States that flatter themselves to be just as free from the class struggle as from the European revolution.

But now, after our readers have seen the class struggle of the year 1848 develop into colossal political proportions, it is time to examine more closely the economic conditions themselves upon which is founded the existence of the capitalist class and its class rule, as well as the slavery of the workers.

We shall present the subject in three great divisions:

The relation of wage-labour to capital, the slavery of the worker, the rule of the capitalist.

The inevitable ruin of the middle classes and the so-called commons under the present system.

The commercial subjugation and the exploitation of the borgeois classes of the various European nations by the despot of the world market – England.

We shall seek to portray this as simply and popularly as possible, and shall not presuppose a knowledge of even the most elementary notions of political economy. We wish to be understood by the workers. And, moreover, there prevails in Germany the most remarkable ignorance and confusion of ideas in regard to the simplest economic relations, from the patented defenders of existing conditions, down to the socialist wonder-workers and the unrecognised political geniuses, in which divided Germany is even richer than in duodecimo princelings. We therefore proceed to the consideration of the first problem.

WHAT ARE WAGES? HOW ARE THEY DETERMINED?

If several workmen were to be asked: "How much wages do you get?", one would reply, "I get 1 shilling a day from my employer"; another, "I get two shillings a day", and so on. According to the different branches of industry in which they are employed, they would mention different sums of money that they receive from their respective employers for the completion of a certain task; for example, for weaving a yard of linen, or for setting a page of type. Despite the variety of their statements, they would all agree upon one point: that wages are the amount of money which the capitalist pays for a certain period of work or for a certain amount of work.

Consequently, it appears that the capitalist buys their labour with money, and that for money they sell him their labour. But this is merely an illusion. What they actually sell to the capitalist for money is their labour-power. This labour-power the capitalist buys for a day, a week, a month, etc. And after he has bought it, he uses it up by letting the worker labour during the stipulated time. With the same amount of money with which the capitalist has bought their labour-power (for example, with two shillings) he could have bought a certain amount of sugar or of any other commodity. The two shillings with which he bought 20 pounds of sugar is the price of the 20 pounds of sugar. The two shillings with which he bought 12 hours' use of labour-power, is the price of 12 hours' labour. Labour-power, then, is a commodity, no more, no less so than is the sugar. The first is measured by the clock, the other by the scales.

Their commodity, labour-power, the workers exchange for the commodity of the capitalist, for money, and, moreover, this exchange takes place at a certain ratio. So much money for so long a use of labour-power. For 12 hours' weaving, two shillings. And these two shillings, do they not represent all the other commodities which I can buy for two shillings? Therefore, actually, the worker has exchanged his commodity, labour-power, for commodities of all kinds, and moreover at a certain ratio. By giving him two shillings, the capitalist has given him so much meat, so much clothing, so much wood, light, etc., in exchange for his day's work. The two shillings therefore express the relation in which labour-power is exchanged for other commodities, the exchange-value of labour-power. The exchange value of a commodity estimated in money is called its price. Wages therefore are only a special name for the price of labour-power, and are usually called the price of work; it is the special name for the price of this peculiar commodity, which has no other repository than human flesh and blood.

Let us take any worker; for example, a weaver. The capitalist supplies him with the loom and yarn. The weaver applies himself to work, and the yarn is turned into cloth. The capitalist takes possession of the cloth and sells it for 20 shillings, for example. Now are the wages of the weaver a share of the cloth, of the 20 shillings, of the product of the work? By no means. Long before the cloth is sold, perhaps long before it is fully woven, the weaver has received his wages. The capitalist, then, does not pay his wages out of the money which he will obtain from the cloth, but out of money already on hand. Just as little as loom and yarn are the product of the weaver to whom they are supplied by the employer, just so little are the commodities which he receives in exchange for his commodity – labour-power – his product. It is possible that the employer found no purchasers at all for the cloth. It is possible that he did not get even the amount of the wages by its sale. It is possible that he sells it very profitably in proportion to the weaver's wages. But all that does not concern the weaver. With a part of his existing wealth, of his capital, the capitalist buys the labour-power of the weaver in exactly the same manner as, with another part of his wealth, he has bought the raw material – the yarn – and the instrument of labour – the loom. After he has made these purchases, and among them belongs the labour-power necessary to the production of the cloth he produces only with raw materials and instruments of labour belonging to him. For our good weaver, too, is one of the instruments of labour, and being in this respect on a par with the loom, he has no more share in the product (the cloth), or in the price of the product, than the loom itself has.

Wages, therefore, are not a share of the worker in the commodities produced by himself. Wages are that part of already existing commodities with which the capitalist buys a certain amount of productive labour-power.

Consequently, labour-power is a commodity which its possessor, the wage-worker, sells to the capitalist. Why does he sell it? In order to live.

But the putting of labour-power into action – i.e., the work – is the active expression of the labourer's own life. And this life activity he sells to another person in order to secure the necessary means of life. His life-activity, therefore, is but a means of securing his own existence. He works that he may keep alive. He does not count the labour itself as a part of his life; it is rather a sacrifice of his life. It is a commodity that he has auctioned off to another. The product of his activity, therefore, is not the aim of his activity. What he produces for himself is not the silk that he weaves, not the gold that he draws up the mining shaft, not the palace that he builds. What he produces for himself is the wages, and silk, gold, and the palace are resolved for him into a certain quantity of necessaries of life, perhaps into a cotton jacket, into copper coins, and into a basement dwelling. And the labourer who for 12 hours long, weaves, spins, bores, turns, builds, shovels, breaks stone, carries hods, and so on – is this 12 hours' weaving, spinning, boring, turning, building, shovelling, stone-breaking, regarded by him as a manifestation of his life, as life? Quite the contrary. Life for him begins where this activity ceases, at the table, at the tavern, in bed. The 12 hours' work, on the other hand, has no meaning for him as weaving, spinning, boring, and so on, but only as earnings, which enable him to sit down at a table, to take his seat in the tavern, and to lie down in a bed.

If the silkworm's object in spinning were to prolong its existence as caterpillar, it would be a perfect example of a wage-worker. Labour-power was not always a commodity (merchandise). Labour was not always wage-labour, i.e., free labour. The slave did not sell his labour-power to the slave-owner, any more than the ox sells his labouring force to the farmer. The slave, together with his labour-power, was sold to his owner once for all. He is a commodity that can pass from the hand of one owner to that of another. He himself is a commodity, but his labour-power is not his commodity. The serf sells only a portion of his labour-power. It is not he who receives wages from the owner of the land; it is rather the owner of the land who receives a tribute from him. The serf belongs to the soil, and to the lord of the soil he brings its fruit. The free labourer, on the other hand, sells his very self, and that by fractions. He auctions off eight, 10, 12, 15 hours of his life, one day like the next, to the highest bidder, to the owner of raw materials, tools, and the means of life – i.e., to the capitalist. The labourer belongs neither to an owner nor to the soil, but eight, 10, 12, 15 hours of his daily life belong to whomsoever buys them. The worker leaves the capitalist, to whom he has sold himself, as often as he chooses, and the capitalist discharges him as often as he sees fit, as soon as he no longer gets any use, or not the required use, out of him. But the worker, whose only source of income is the sale of his labour-power, cannot leave the whole class of buyers, i.e., the capitalist class, unless he gives up his own existence. He does not belong to this or that capitalist, but to the capitalist class; and it is for him to find his man – i.e., to find a buyer in this capitalist class.

Before entering more closely upon the relation of capital to wage-labour, we shall present briefly the most general conditions which come into consideration in the determination of wages.

Wages, as we have seen, are the price of a certain commodity, labour-power. Wages, therefore, are determined by the same laws that determine the price of every other commodity. The question then is, How is the price of a commodity determined?

BY WHAT IS THE PRICE OF A COMMODITY DETERMINED?

By what is the price of a commodity determined? By the competition between buyers and sellers, by the relation of the demand to the supply, of the call to the offer. The competition by which the price of a commodity is determined is three-fold.

The same commodity is offered for sale by various sellers. Whoever sells commodities of the same quality most cheaply, is sure to drive the other sellers from the field and to secure the greatest market for himself. The sellers therefore fight among themselves for the sales, for the market. Each one of them wishes to sell, and to sell as much as possible, and if possible to sell alone, to the exclusion of all other sellers. Each one sells cheaper than the other. Thus there takes place a competition among the sellers which forces down the price of the commodities offered by them.

But there is also a competition among the buyers; this upon its side causes the price of the proffered commodities to rise.

Finally, there is competition between the buyers and the sellers: the ones wish to purchase as cheaply as possible, the others to sell as dearly as possible. The result of this competition between buyers and sellers will depend upon the relations between the two above-mentioned camps of competitors – i.e., upon whether the competition in the army of sellers is stronger. Industry leads two great armies into the field against each other, and each of these again is engaged in a battle among its own troops in its own ranks. The army among whose troops there is less fighting, carries off the victory over the opposing host.

Let us suppose that there are 100 bales of cotton in the market and at the same time purchasers for 1,000 bales of cotton. In this case, the demand is 10 times greater than the supply. Competition among the buyers, then, will be very strong; each of them tries to get hold of one bale, if possible, of the whole 100 bales. This example is no arbitrary supposition. In the history of commerce we have experienced periods of scarcity of cotton, when some capitalists united together and sought to buy up not 100 bales, but the whole cotton supply of the world. In the given case, then, one buyer seeks to drive the others from the field by offering a relatively higher price for the bales of cotton. The cotton sellers, who perceive the troops of the enemy in the most violent contention among themselves, and are therefore fully assured of the sale of their whole 100 bales, will beware of falling into one another's hair in order to force down the price of cotton at the very moment in which their opponents race with one another to screw it up high. So, all of a sudden, peace reigns in the army of sellers. They stand opposed to the buyers like one man, fold their arms in philosophic content and their claims would find no limit, did not the offers of even the most importunate of buyers have their very definite limit.

If, then, the supply of a commodity is less than the demand for it, competition among the sellers is very slight, or there may be none at all among them. In the same proportion in which this competition decreases, the competition among the buyers increases. Result: a more or less considerable rise in the prices of commodities.

It is well known that the opposite case, with the opposite result, happens more frequently. Great excess of supply over demand; desperate competition among the sellers, and a lack of buyers; forced sales of commodities at ridiculously low prices.

But what is a rise, and what a fall of prices? What is a high and what is a low price? A grain of sand is high when examined through a microscope, and a tower is low when compared with a mountain. And if the price is determined by the relation of supply and demand, by what is the relation of supply and demand determined?

Let us turn to the first worthy citizen we meet. He will not hesitate one moment, but, like Alexander the Great, will cut this metaphysical knot with his multiplication table. He will say to us: "If the production of the commodities which I sell has cost me 100 pounds, and out of the sale of these goods I make 110 pounds – within the year, you understand – that's an honest, sound, reasonable profit. But if in the exchange I receive 120 or 130 pounds, that's a higher profit; and if I should get as much as 200 pounds, that would be an extraordinary, an enormous profit". What is it, then, that serves this citizen as the standard of his profit? The cost of the production of his commodities. If in exchange for these goods he receives a quantity of other goods whose production has cost less, he has lost. If he receives in exchange for his goods a quantity of other goods whose production has cost more, he has gained. And he reckons the falling or rising of the profit according to the degree at which the exchange value of his goods stands, whether above or below his zero – the cost of production.

We have seen how the changing relation of supply and demand causes now a rise, now a fall of prices; now high, now low prices. If the price of a commodity rises considerably owing to a failing supply or a disproportionately growing demand, then the price of some other commodity must have fallen in proportion; for of course the price of a commodity only expresses in money the proportion in which other commodities will be given in exchange for it. If, for example, the price of a yard of silk rises from two to three shillings, the price of silver has fallen in relation to the silk, and in the same way the prices of all other commodities whose prices have remained stationary have fallen in relation to the price of silk. A large quantity of them must be given in exchange in order to obtain the same amount of silk. Now, what will be the consequence of a rise in the price of a particular commodity? A mass of capital will be thrown into the prosperous branch of industry, and this immigration of capital into the provinces of the favoured industry will continue until it yields no more than the customary profits, or, rather, until the price of its products, owing to overproduction, sinks below the cost of production.

Conversely: if the price of a commodity falls below its cost of production, then capital will be withdrawn from the production of this commodity. Except in the case of a branch of industry which has become obsolete and is therefore doomed to disappear, the production of such a commodity (that is, its supply), will, owing to this flight of capital, continue to decrease until it corresponds to the demand, and the price of the commodity rises again to the level of its cost of production; or, rather, until the supply has fallen below the demand and its price has again risen above its cost of production, for the current price of a commodity is always either above or below its cost of production.

We see how capital continually emigrates out of the province of one industry and immigrates into that of another. The high price produces an excessive immigration, and the low price an excessive emigration.

We could show, from another point of view, how not only the supply, but also the demand, is determined by the cost of production. But this would lead us too far away from our subject.

We have just seen how the fluctuations of supply and demand always bring the price of a commodity back to its cost of production. The actual price of a commodity, indeed, stands always above or below the cost of production; but the rise and fall reciprocally balance each other, so that, within a certain period of time, if the ebbs and flows of the industry are reckoned up together, the commodities will be exchanged for one another in accordance with their cost of production. Their price is thus determined by their cost of production.

The determination of price by the cost of production is not to be understood in the sense of the bourgeois economists. The economists say that the average price of commodities equals the cost of production: that is the law. The anarchic movement, in which the rise is compensated for by a fall and the fall by a rise, they regard as an accident. We might just as well consider the fluctuations as the law, and the determination of the price by cost of production as an accident – as is, in fact, done by certain other economists. But it is precisely these fluctuations which, viewed more closely, carry the most frightful devastation in their train, and, like an earthquake, cause bourgeois society to shake to its very foundations – it is precisely these fluctuations that force the price to conform to the cost of production. In the totality of this disorderly movement is to be found its order. In the total course of this industrial anarchy, in this circular movement, competition balances, as it were, the one extravagance by the other.

We thus see that the price of a commodity is indeed determined by its cost of production, but in such wise that the periods in which the price of these commodities rises above the costs of production are balanced by the periods in which it sinks below the cost of production, and vice versa. Of course this does not hold good for a single given product of an industry, but only for that branch of industry. So also it does not hold good for an individual manufacturer, but only for the whole class of manufacturers.

The determination of price by cost of production is tantamount to the determination of price by the labour time requisite to the production of a commodity, for the cost of production consists, first, of raw materials and wear and tear of tools, etc., i.e., of industrial products whose production has cost a certain number of work-days, which therefore represent a certain amount of labour time, and, secondly, of direct labour, which is also measured by its duration.

BY WHAT ARE WAGES DETERMINED?

Now, the same general laws which regulate the price of commodities in general, naturally regulate wages, or the price of labour-power. Wages will now rise, now fall, according to the relation of supply and demand, according as competition shapes itself between the buyers of labour-power, the capitalists, and the sellers of labour-power, the workers. The fluctuations of wages correspond to the fluctuation in the price of commodities in general. But within the limits of these fluctuations the price of labour-power will be determined by the cost of production, by the labour-time necessary for production of this commodity: labour-power.

What, then, is the cost of production of labour-power?

It is the cost required for the maintenance of the labourer as a labourer, and for his education and training as a labourer.

Therefore, the shorter the time required for training up to a particular sort of work, the smaller is the cost of production of the worker, the lower is the price of his labour-power, his wages. In those branches of industry in which hardly any period of apprenticeship is necessary and the mere bodily existence of the worker, is sufficient, the cost of his production is limited almost exclusively to the commodities necessary for keeping him in working condition. The price of his work will therefore be determined by the price of the necessary means of subsistence.

Here, however, there enters another consideration. The manufacturer who calculates his cost of production and, in accordance with it, the price of the product, takes into account the wear and tear of the instruments of labour. If a machine costs him, for example, 1,000 shillings, and this machine is used up in 10 years, he adds 100 shillings annually to the price of the commodities, in order to be able after 10 years to replace the worn-out machine with a new one. In the same manner, the cost of production of simple labour-power must include the cost of propagation, by means of which the race of workers is enabled to multiply itself, and to replace worn-out workers with new ones. The wear and tear of the worker, therefore, is calculated in the same manner as the wear and tear of the machine.

Thus, the cost of production of simple labour-power amounts to the cost of the existence and propagation of the worker. The price of this cost of existence and propagation constitutes wages. The wages thus determined are called the minimum of wages. This minimum wage, like the determination of the price of commodities in general by cost of production, does not hold good for the single individual, but only for the race. Individual workers, indeed, millions of workers, do not receive enough to be able to exist and to propagate themselves; but the wages of the whole working class adjust themselves, within the limits of their fluctuations, to this minimum.

Now that we have come to an understanding in regard to the most general laws which govern wages, as well as the price of every other commodity, we can examine our subject more particularly.

THE NATURE OF GROWTH AND CAPITAL

Capital consists of raw materials, instruments of labour, and means of subsistence of all kinds, which are employed in producing new raw materials, new instruments, and new means of subsistence. All these components of capital are created by labour, products of labour, accumulated labour. Accumulated labour that serves as a means to new production is capital. So say the economists. What is a negro slave? A man of the black race. The one explanation is worthy of the other.

A negro is a negro. Only under certain conditions does he become a slave. A cotton-spinning machine is a machine for spinning cotton. Only under certain conditions does it become capital. Torn away from these conditions, it is as little capital as gold by itself is money, or sugar is the price of sugar.

In the process of production, human beings work not only upon nature, but also upon one another. They produce only by working together in a specified manner and reciprocally exchanging their activities. In order to produce, they enter into definite connections and relations to one another, and only within these social connections and relations does their influence upon nature operate – i.e., does production take place.

These social relations between the producers, and the conditions under which they exchange their activities and share in the total act of production, will naturally vary according to the character of the means of production. With the discovery of a new instrument of warfare, the firearm, the whole internal organisation of the army was necessarily altered, the relations within which individuals compose an army and can work as an army were transformed, and the relation of different armies to another was likewise changed.

We thus see that the social relations within which individuals produce, the social relations of production, are altered, transformed, with the change and development of the material means of production, of the forces of production. The relations of production in their totality constitute what is called the social relations, society, and, moreover, a society at a definite stage of historical development, a society with peculiar, distinctive characteristics. Ancient society, feudal society, bourgeois (or capitalist) society, are such totalities of relations of production, each of which denotes a particular stage of development in the history of mankind.

Capital also is a social relation of production. It is a bourgeois relation of production, a relation of production of bourgeois society. The means of subsistence, the instruments of labour, the raw materials, of which capital consists – have they not been produced and accumulated under given social conditions, within definite special relations? Are they not employed for new production, under given social conditions, within definite social relations? And does not just the definite social character stamp the products which serve for new production as capital?

Capital consists not only of means of subsistence, instruments of labour, and raw materials, not only as material products; it consists just as much of exchange values. All products of which it consists are commodities. Capital, consequently, is not only a sum of material products, it is a sum of commodities, of exchange values, of social magnitudes. Capital remains the same whether we put cotton in the place of wool, rice in the place of wheat, steamships in the place of railroads, provided only that the cotton, the rice, the steamships – the body of capital – have the same exchange value, the same price, as the wool, the wheat, the railroads, in which it was previously embodied. The bodily form of capital may transform itself continually, while capital does not suffer the least alteration.

But though every capital is a sum of commodities – i.e., of

exchange values – it does not follow that every sum of commodities, of exchange values, is capital.

Every sum of exchange values is an exchange value. Each particular exchange value is a sum of exchange values. For example: a house worth 1,000 pounds is an exchange value of 1,000 pounds: a piece of paper worth one penny is a sum of exchange values of 100 1/100ths of a penny. Products which are exchangeable for others are commodities. The definite proportion in which they are exchangeable forms their exchange value, or, expressed in money, their price. The quantity of these products can have no effect on their character as commodities, as representing an exchange value , as having a certain price. Whether a tree be large or small, it remains a tree. Whether we exchange iron in pennyweights or in hundredweights, for other products, does this alter its character: its being a commodity, or exchange value? According to the quantity, it is a commodity of greater or of lesser value, of higher or of lower price.

How then does a sum of commodities, of exchange values, become capital?

Thereby, that as an independent social power – i.e., as the power of a part of society, it preserves itself and multiplies by exchange with direct, living labour-power.

The existence of a class which possesses nothing but the ability to work is a necessary presupposition of capital.

It is only the dominion of past, accumulated, materialised labour over immediate living labour that stamps the accumulated labour with the character of capital.

Capital does not consist in the fact that accumulated labour serves living labour as a means for new production. It consists in the fact that living labour serves accumulated labour as the means of preserving and multiplying its exchange value.

RELATION OF WAGE-LABOUR TO CAPITAL

What is it that takes place in the exchange between the capitalist and the wage-labourer?

The labourer receives means of subsistence in exchange for his labour-power; the capitalist receives, in exchange for his means of subsistence, labour, the productive activity of the labourer, the creative force by which the worker not only replaces what he consumes, but also gives to the accumulated labour a greater value than it previously possessed. The labourer gets from the capitalist a portion of the existing means of subsistence. For what purpose do these means of subsistence serve him? For immediate consumption. But as soon as I consume means of subsistence, they are irrevocably lost to me, unless I employ the time during which these means sustain my life in producing new means of subsistence, in creating by my labour new values in place of the values lost in consumption. But it is just this noble reproductive power that the labourer surrenders to the capitalist in exchange for means of subsistence received. Consequently, he has lost it for himself.

Let us take an example. For one shilling a labourer works all day long in the fields of a farmer, to whom he thus secures a return of two shillings. The farmer not only receives the replaced value which he has given to the day labourer, he has doubled it. Therefore, he has consumed the one shilling that he gave to the day labourer in a fruitful, productive manner. For the one shilling he has bought the labour-power of the day-labourer, which creates products of the soil of twice the value, and out of one shilling makes two. The day-labourer, on the contrary, receives in the place of his productive force, whose results he has just surrendered to the farmer, one shilling, which he exchanges for means of subsistence, which means of subsistence he consumes more or less quickly. The one shilling has therefore been consumed in a double manner – reproductively for the capitalist, for it has been exchanged for labour-power, which brought forth two shillings; unproductively for the worker, for it has been exchanged for means of subsistence which are lost for ever, and whose value he can obtain again only by repeating the same exchange with the farmer. Capital therefore presupposes wage-labour; wage-labour presupposes capital. They condition each other; each brings the other into existence.

Does a worker in a cotton factory produce only cotton? No. He produces capital. He produces values which serve anew to command his work and to create by means of it new values.

Capital can multiply itself only by exchanging itself for labour-power, by calling wage-labour into life. The labour-power of the wage-labourer can exchange itself for capital only by increasing capital, by strengthening that very power whose slave it is. Increase of capital, therefore, is increase of the proletariat, i.e., of the working class.

And so, the bourgeoisie and its economists maintain that the interest of the capitalist and of the labourer is the same. And in fact, so they are! The worker perishes if capital does not keep him busy. Capital perishes if it does not exploit labour-power, which, in order to exploit, it must buy. The more quickly the capital destined for production – the productive capital – increases, the more prosperous industry is, the more the bourgeoisie enriches itself, the better business gets, so many more workers does the capitalist need, so much the dearer does the worker sell himself.

The fastest possible growth of productive capital is, therefore, the indispensable condition for a tolerable life to the labourer.

But what is growth of productive capital? Growth of the power of accumulated labour over living labour; growth of the rule of the bourgeoisie over the working class. When wage-labour produces the alien wealth dominating it, the power hostile to it, capital, there flow back to it its means of employment, i.e., its means of subsistence, under the condition that it again become a part of capital, that it become again the lever whereby capital is to be forced into an accelerated expansive movement.

To say that the interests of capital and the interests of the workers are identical, signifies only this: that capital and wage-labour are two sides of one and the same relation. The one conditions the other in the same way that the usurer and the borrower condition each other.

As long as the wage-labourer remains a wage-labourer, his lot is dependent upon capital. That is what the boasted community of interests between worker and capitalists amounts to.

If capital grows, the mass of wage-labour grows, the number of wage-workers increases; in a word, the sway of capital extends over a greater mass of individuals.

Let us suppose the most favorable case: if productive capital grows, the demand for labour grows. It therefore increases the price of labour-power, wages.

A house may be large or small; as long as the neighbouring houses are likewise small, it satisfies all social requirement for a residence. But let there arise next to the little house a palace, and the little house shrinks to a hut. The little house now makes it clear that its inmate has no social position at all to maintain, or but a very insignificant one; and however high it may shoot up in the course of civilisation, if the neighboring palace rises in equal or even in greater measure, the occupant of the relatively little house will always find himself more uncomfortable, more dissatisfied, more cramped within his four walls.

An appreciable rise in wages presupposes a rapid growth of productive capital. Rapid growth of productive capital calls forth just as rapid a growth of wealth, of luxury, of social needs and social pleasures. Therefore, although the pleasures of the labourer have increased, the social gratification which they afford has fallen in comparison with the increased pleasures of the capitalist, which are inaccessible to the worker, in comparison with the stage of development of society in general. Our wants and pleasures have their origin in society; we therefore measure them in relation to society; we do not measure them in relation to the objects which serve for their gratification. Since they are of a social nature, they are of a relative nature.

But wages are not at all determined merely by the sum of commodities for which they may be exchanged. Other factors enter into the problem. What the workers directly receive for their labour-power is a certain sum of money. Are wages determined merely by this money price?

In the 16th century, the gold and silver circulation in Europe increased in consequence of the discovery of richer and more easily worked mines in America. The value of gold and silver, therefore, fell in relation to other commodities. The workers received the same amount of coined silver for their labour-power as before. The money price of their work remained the same, and yet their wages had fallen, for in exchange for the same amount of silver they obtained a smaller amount of other commodities. This was one of the circumstances which furthered the growth of capital, the rise of the bourgeoisie, in the 18th century.

Let us take another case. In the winter of 1847, in consequence of bad harvest, the most indispensable means of subsistence – grains, meat, butter, cheese, etc. – rose greatly in price. Let us suppose that the workers still received the same sum of money for their labour-power as before. Did not their wages fall? To be sure. For the same money they received in exchange less bread, meat, etc. Their wages fell, not because the value of silver was less, but because the value of the means of subsistence had increased.

Finally, let us suppose that the money price of labour-power remained the same, while all agricultural and manufactured commodities had fallen in price because of the employment of new machines, of favourable seasons, etc. For the same money the workers could now buy more commodities of all kinds. Their wages have therefore risen, just because their money value has not changed.

The money price of labour-power, the nominal wages, do not therefore coincide with the actual or real wages – i.e., with the amount of commodities which are actually given in exchange for the wages. If then we speak of a rise or fall of wages, we have to keep in mind not only the money price of labour-power, the nominal wages, but also the real wages.

But neither the nominal wages – i.e., the amount of money for which the labourer sells himself to the capitalist – nor the real wages – i.e., the amount of commodities which he can buy for this money – exhausts the relations which are comprehended in the term wages.

Wages are determined above all by their relations to the gain, the profit, of the capitalist. In other words, wages are a proportionate, relative quantity.

Real wages express the price of labour-power in relation to the price of commodities; relative wages, on the other hand, express the share of immediate labour in the value newly created by it, in relation to the share of it which falls to accumulated labour, to capital.

THE GENERAL LAW THAT DETERMINES THE RISE AND FALL OF WAGES AND PROFITS

We have said: "Wages are not a share of the worker in the commodities produced by him. Wages are that part of already existing commodities with which the capitalist buys a certain amount of productive labour-power". But the capitalist must replace these wages out of the price for which he sells the product made by the worker; he must so replace it that, as a rule, there remains to him a surplus above the cost of production expended by him, that is, he must get a profit. The selling price of the commodities produced by the worker is divided, from the point of view of the capitalist, into three parts: First, the replacement of the price of the raw materials advanced by him, in addition to the replacement of the wear and tear of the tools, machines, and other instruments of labour likewise advanced by him; Second, the replacement of the wages advanced; and Third, the surplus leftover – i.e., the profit of the capitalist. While the first part merely replaces previously existing values, it is evident that the replacement of the wages and the surplus (the profit of capital) are as a whole taken out of the new value, which is produced by the labour of the worker and added to the raw materials. And in this sense we can view wages as well as profit, for the purpose of comparing them with each other, as shares in the product of the worker.

Real wages may remain the same, they may even rise, nevertheless the relative wages may fall. Let us suppose, for instance, that all means of subsistence have fallen two-thirds in price, while the day's wages have fallen but one-third; for example, from three to two shillings. Although the worker can now get a greater amount of commodities with these two shillings than he formerly did with three shillings, yet his wages have decreased in proportion to the gain of the capitalist. The profit of the capitalist – the manufacturer's, for instance – has increased one shilling, which means that for a smaller amount of exchange values, which he pays to the worker, the latter must produce a greater amount of exchange values than before. The share of capital in proportion to the share of labour has risen. The distribution of social wealth between capital and labour has become still more unequal. The capitalist commands a greater amount of labour with the same capital. The power of the capitalist class over the working class has grown, the social position of the worker has become worse, has been forced down still another degree below that of the capitalist.

What, then, is the general law that determines the rise and fall of wages and profit in their reciprocal relation?

They stand in inverse proportion to each other. The share of capital (profit) increases in the same proportion in which the share of labour (wages) falls, and vice versa. Profit rises in the same degree in which wages fall; it falls in the same degree in which wages rise.

It might perhaps be argued that the capitalist class can gain by an advantageous exchange of his products with other capitalists, by a rise in the demand for his commodities, whether in consequence of the opening up of new markets, or in consequence of temporarily increased demands in the old markets, and so on; that the profit of the capitalist, therefore, may be multiplied by taking advantage of other capitalists, independently of the rise and fall of wages, of the exchange value of labour-power; or that the profit of the capitalist may also rise through improvements in the instruments of labour, new applications of the forces of nature, and so on.

But in the first place it must be admitted that the result remains the same, although brought about in an opposite manner. Profit, indeed, has not risen because wages have fallen, but wages have fallen because profit has risen. With the same amount of another man's labour the capitalist has bought a larger amount of exchange values without having paid more for the labour on that account – i.e., the work is paid for less in proportion to the net gain which it yields to the capitalist.

In the second place, it must be borne in mind that, despite the fluctuations in the prices of commodities, the average price of every commodity, the proportion in which it exchanges for other commodities, is determined by its cost of production. The acts of overreaching and taking advantage of one another within the capitalist ranks necessarily equalise themselves. The improvements of machinery, the new applications of the forces of nature in the service of production, make it possible to produce in a given period of time, with the same amount of labour and capital, a larger amount of products, but in no wise a larger amount of exchange values. If by the use of the spinning-machine I can furnish twice as much yarn in an hour as before its invention – for instance, 100 pounds instead of 50 pounds – in the long run I receive back, in exchange for this 100 pounds, no more commodities than I did before for 50; because the cost of production has fallen by one-half, or because I can furnish double the product at the same cost.

Finally, in whatsoever proportion the capitalist class, whether of one country or of the entire world-market, distribute the net revenue of production among themselves, the total amount of this net revenue always consists exclusively of the amount by which accumulated labour has been increased from the proceeds of direct labour. This whole amount, therefore, grows in the same proportion in which labour augments capital – i.e., in the same proportion in which profit rises as compared with wages.

THE INTERESTS OF CAPITAL AND WAGE-LABOUR ARE DIAMETRICALLY OPPOSED. EFFECT OF PRODUCTIVE CAPITAL ON PRODUCTIVE CAPITAL ON WAGES

We thus see that, even if we keep ourselves within the relation of capital and wage-labour, the interests of capitals and the interests of wage-labour are diametrically opposed to each other.

A rapid growth of capital is synonymous with a rapid growth of profits. Profits can grow rapidly only when the price of labour – the relative wages – decrease just as rapidly. Relative wages may fall, although real wages rise simultaneously with nominal wages, with the money value of labour, provided only that the real wage does not rise in the same proportion as the profit. If, for instance, in good business years wages rise 5 per cent, while profits rise 30 per cent, the proportional, the relative wage has not increased, but decreased.

If, therefore, the income of the worker increases with the rapid growth of capital, there is at the same time a widening of the social chasm that divides the worker from the capitalist, an increase in the power of capital over labour, a greater dependence of labour upon capital.

To say that "the worker has an interest in the rapid growth of capital", means only this: that the more speedily the worker augments the wealth of the capitalist, the larger will be the crumbs which fall to him, the greater will be the number of workers than can be called into existence, the more can the mass of slaves dependent upon capital be increased.

We have thus seen that even the most favourable situation for the working class, namely, the most rapid growth of capital, however much it may improve the material life of the worker, does not abolish the antagonism between his interests and the interests of the capitalist. Profit and wages remain as before, in inverse proportion.

If capital grows rapidly, wages may rise, but the profit of capital rises disproportionately faster. The material position of the worker has improved, but at the cost of his social position. The social chasm that separates him from the capitalist has widened.

Finally, to say that "the most favourable condition for wage-labour is the fastest possible growth of productive capital", is the same as to say: the quicker the working class multiplies and augments the power inimical to it – the wealth of another which lords over that class – the more favourable will be the conditions under which it will be permitted to toil anew at the multiplication of bourgeois wealth, at the enlargement of the power of capital, content thus to forge for itself the golden chains by which the bourgeoisie drags it in its train.

Growth of productive capital and rise of wages, are they really so indissolubly united as the bourgeois economists maintain? We must not believe their mere words. We dare not believe them even when they claim that the fatter capital is the more will its slave be pampered. The bourgeoisie is too much enlightened, it keeps its accounts much too carefully, to share the prejudices of the feudal lord, who makes an ostentatious display of the magnificence of his retinue. The conditions of existence of the bourgeoisie compel it to attend carefully to its bookkeeping. We must therefore examine more closely into the following question: In what manner does the growth of productive capital affect wages?

If, as a whole, the productive capital of bourgeois society grows, there takes place a more many-sided accumulation of labour. The individual capitals increase in number and in magnitude. The multiplication of individual capitals increases the competition among capitalists. The increasing magnitude of increasing capitals provides the means of leading more powerful armies of workers with more gigantic instruments of war upon the industrial battlefield.

The one capitalist can drive the other from the field and carry off his capital only by selling more cheaply. In order to sell more cheaply without ruining himself, he must produce more cheaply – i.e., increase the productive forces of labour as much as possible. But the productive forces of labour is increased above all by a greater division of labour and by a more general introduction and constant improvement of machinery. The larger the army of workers among whom the labour is subdivided, the more gigantic the scale upon which machinery is introduced, the more in proportion does the cost of production decrease, the more fruitful is the labour. And so there arises among the capitalists a universal rivalry for the increase of the division of labour and of machinery and for their exploitation upon the greatest possible scale. If, now, by a greater division of labour, by the application and improvement of new machines, by a more advantageous exploitation of the forces of nature on a larger scale, a capitalist has found the means of producing with the same amount of labour (whether it be direct or accumulated labour) a larger amount of products of commodities than his competitors – if, for instance, he can produce a whole yard of linen in the same labour-time in which his competitors weave half a yard – how will this capitalist act?

He could keep on selling half a yard of linen at old market price; but this would not have the effect of driving his opponents from the field and enlarging his own market. But his need of a market has increased in the same measure in which his productive power has extended. The more powerful and costly means of production that he has called into existence enable him, it is true, to sell his wares more cheaply, but they compel him at the same time to sell more wares, to get control of a very much greater market for his commodities; consequently, this capitalist will sell his half-yard of linen more cheaply than his competitors.

But the capitalist will not sell the whole yard so cheaply as his competitors sell the half-yard, although the production of the whole yard costs him no more than does that of the half-yard to the others. Otherwise, he would make no extra profit, and would get back in exchange only the cost of production. He might obtain a greater income from having set in motion a larger capital, but not from having made a greater profit on his capital than the others. Moreover, he attains the object he is aiming at if he prices his goods only a small percentage lower than his competitors. He drives them off the field, he wrests from them at least part of their market, by underselling them.

And finally, let us remember that the current price always stands either above or below the cost of production, according as the sale of a commodity takes place in the favourable or unfavorable period of the industry. According as the market price of the yard of linen stands above or below its former cost of production, will the percentage vary at which the capitalist who has made use of the new and more faithful means of production sell above his real cost of production.

But the privilege of our capitalist is not of long duration. Other competing capitalists introduce the same machines, the same division of labour, and introduce them upon the same or even upon a greater scale. And finally this introduction becomes so universal that the price of the linen is lowered not only below its old, but even below its new cost of production.

The capitalists therefore find themselves, in their mutual relations, in the same situation in which they were before the introduction of the new means of production; and if they are by these means enabled to offer double the product at the old price, they are now forced to furnish double the product for less than the old price. Having arrived at the new point, the new cost of production, the battle for supremacy in the market has to be fought out anew. Given more division of labour and more machinery, and there results a greater scale upon which division of labour and machinery are exploited. And competition again brings the same reaction against this result.

EFFECT OF CAPITALIST COMPETITION ON THE CAPITALIST CLASS, THE MIDDLE CLASS AND THE WORKING CLASS

We thus see how the method of production and the means of production are constantly enlarged, revolutionised, how division of labour necessarily draws after it greater division of labour, the employment of machinery, greater employment of machinery, work upon a large scale work upon a still greater scale. This is the law that continually throws capitalist production out of its old ruts and compels capital to strain ever more the productive forces of labour for the very reason that it has already strained them – the law that grants it no respite, and constantly shouts in its ear: March! march!

This is no other law than that which, within the periodical fluctuations of commerce, necessarily adjusts the price of a commodity to its cost of production.

No matter how powerful the means of production which a capitalist may bring into the field, competition will make their adoption general; and from the moment that they have been generally adopted, the sole result of the greater productiveness of his capital will be that he must furnish at the same price, 10, 20, 100 times as much as before. But since he must find a market for, perhaps, 1,000 times as much, in order to outweigh the lower selling price by the greater quantity of the sale; since now a more extensive sale is necessary not only to gain a greater profit, but also in order to replace the cost of production (the instrument of production itself grows always more costly, as we have seen), and since this more extensive sale has become a question of life and death not only for him, but also for his rivals, the old struggle must begin again, and it is all the more violent the more powerful the means of production already invented are. The division of labour and the application of machinery will therefore take a fresh start, and upon an even greater scale.

Whatever be the power of the means of production which are employed, competition seeks to rob capital of the golden fruits of this power by reducing the price of commodities to the cost of production; in the same measure in which production is cheapened - i.e., in the same measure in which more can be produced with the same amount of labour – it compels by a law which is irresistible a still greater cheapening of production, the sale of ever greater masses of product for smaller prices. Thus the capitalist will have gained nothing more by his efforts than the obligation to furnish a greater product in the same labour-time; in a word, more difficult conditions for the profitable employment of his capital. While competition, therefore, constantly pursues him with its law of the cost of production and turns against himself every weapon that he forges against his rivals, the capitalist continually seeks to get the best of competition by restlessly introducing further subdivision of labour and new machines, which, though more expensive, enable him to produce more cheaply, instead of waiting until the new machines shall have been rendered obsolete by competition.

If we now conceive this feverish agitation as it operates in the market of the whole world, we shall be in a position to comprehend how the growth, accumulation, and concentration of capital bring in their train an ever more detailed subdivision of labour, an ever greater improvement of old machines, and a constant application of new machine – a process which goes on uninterruptedly, with feverish haste, and upon an ever more gigantic scale.

But what effect do these conditions, which are inseparable from the growth of productive capital, have upon the determination of wages?

The greater division of labour enables one labourer to accomplish the work of five, 10, or 20 labourers; it therefore increases competition among the labourers fivefold, tenfold, or twentyfold. The labourers compete not only by selling themselves one cheaper than the other, but also by one doing the work of five,

10, or 20; and they are forced to compete in this manner by the division of labour, which is introduced and steadily improved by capital.

Furthermore, to the same degree in which the division of labour increases, is the labour simplified. The special skill of the labourer becomes worthless. He becomes transformed into a simple monotonous force of production, with neither physical nor mental elasticity. His work becomes accessible to all; therefore competitors press upon him from all sides. Moreover, it must be remembered that the more simple, the more easily learned the work is, so much the less is its cost to production, the expense of its acquisition, and so much the lower must the wages sink – for, like the price of any other commodity, they are determined by the cost of production. Therefore, in the same manner in which labour becomes more unsatisfactory, more repulsive, do competition increase and wages decrease. The labourer seeks to maintain the total of his wages for a given time by performing more labour, either by working a greater number of hours, or by accomplishing more in the same number of hours. Thus, urged on by want, he himself multiplies the disastrous effects of division of labour. The result is: the more he works, the less wages he receives. And for this simple reason: the more he works, the more he competes against his fellow workmen, the more he compels them to compete against him, and to offer themselves on the same wretched conditions as he does; so that, in the last analysis, he competes against himself as a member of the working class.

Machinery produces the same effects, but upon a much larger scale. It supplants skilled labourers by unskilled, men by women, adults by children; where newly introduced, it throws workers upon the streets in great masses; and as it becomes more highly developed and more productive it discards them in additional though smaller numbers.

We have hastily sketched in broad outlines the industrial war of capitalists among themselves. This war has the peculiarity that the battles in it are won less by recruiting than by discharging the army of workers. The generals (the capitalists) vie with one another as to who can discharge the greatest number of industrial soldiers.

The economists tell us, to be sure, that those labourers who have been rendered superfluous by machinery find new venues of employment. They dare not assert directly that the same labourers that have been discharged find situations in new branches of labour. Facts cry out too loudly against this lie. Strictly speaking, they only maintain that new means of employment will be found for other sections of the working class; for example, for that portion of the young generation of labourers who were about to enter upon that branch of industry which had just been abolished. Of course, this is a great satisfaction to the disabled labourers. There will be no lack of fresh exploitable blood and muscle for the Messrs. Capitalists – the dead may bury their dead. This consolation seems to be intended more for the comfort of the capitalists themselves than their labourers. If the whole class of the wage-labourer were to be annihilated by machinery, how terrible that would be for capital, which, without wage-labour, ceases to be capital!

But even if we assume that all who are directly forced out of employment by machinery, as well as all of the rising generation who were waiting for a chance of employment in the same branch of industry, do actually find some new employment – are we to believe that this new employment will pay as high wages as did the one they have lost? If it did, it would be in contradiction to the laws of political economy. We have seen how modern industry always tends to the substitution of the simpler and more subordinate employments for the higher and more complex ones. How, then, could a mass of workers thrown out of one branch of industry by machinery find refuge in another branch, unless they were to be paid more poorly?

An exception to the law has been adduced, namely, the workers who are employed in the manufacture of machinery itself. As soon as there is in industry a greater demand for and a greater consumption of machinery, it is said that the number of machines must necessarily increase; consequently, also, the manufacture of machines; consequently, also, the employment of workers in machine manufacture; and the workers employed in this branch of industry are skilled, even educated, workers.

Since the year 1840 this assertion, which even before that date was only half-true, has lost all semblance of truth; for the most diverse machines are now applied to the manufacture of the machines themselves on quite as extensive a scale as in the manufacture of cotton yarn, and the labourers employed in machine factories can but play the role of very stupid machines alongside of the highly ingenious machines.

But in place of the man who has been dismissed by the machine, the factory may employ, perhaps, three children and one woman! And must not the wages of the man have previously sufficed for the three children and one woman? Must not the minimum wages have sufficed for the preservation and propagation of the race? What, then, do these beloved bourgeois phrases prove? Nothing more than that now four times as many workers' lives are used up as there were previously, in order to obtain the livelihood of one working family.

To sum up: the more productive capital grows, the more it

extends the division of labour and the application of machinery; the more the division of labour and the application of machinery extend, the more does competition extend among the workers, the more do their wages shrink together.

In addition, the working class is also recruited from the higher strata of society; a mass of small business men and of people living upon the interest of their capitals is precipitated into the ranks of the working class, and they will have nothing else to do than to stretch out their arms alongside of the arms of the workers. Thus the forest of outstretched arms, begging for work, grows ever thicker, while the arms themselves grow every leaner.

It is evident that the small manufacturer cannot survive in a struggle in which the first condition of success is production upon an ever greater scale. It is evident that the small manufacturers and thereby increasing the number of candidates for the proletariat – all this requires no further elucidation.

Finally, in the same measure in which the capitalists are compelled, by the movement described above, to exploit the already existing gigantic means of production on an ever-increasing scale, and for this purpose to set in motion all the mainsprings of credit, in the same measure do they increase the industrial earthquakes, in the midst of which the commercial world can preserve itself only by sacrificing a portion of its wealth, its products, and even its forces of production, to the gods of the lower world – in short, the crises increase. They become more frequent and more violent, if for no other reason, than for this alone, that in the same measure in which the mass of products grows, and therefore the needs for extensive markets, in the same measure does the world market shrink ever more, and ever fewer markets remain to be exploited, since every previous crisis has subjected to the commerce of the world a hitherto unconquered or but superficially exploited market. But capital not only lives upon labour. Like a master, at once distinguished and barbarous, it drags with it into its grave the corpses of its slaves, whole hecatombs of workers, who perish in the crises. We thus see that if capital grows rapidly, competition among the workers grows with even greater rapidity – i.e., the means of employment and subsistence for the working class decrease in proportion even more rapidly; but, this notwithstanding, the rapid growth of capital is the most favourable condition for wage-labour.

VALUE, PRICE AND PROFIT

Karl Marx

I PRELIMINARY

CITIZENS,

Before entering into the subject-matter, allow me to make a few preliminary remarks.

There reigns now on the Continent a real epidemic of strikes, and a general clamour for a rise of wages. The question will turn up at our Congress. You, as the head of the International Association, ought to have settled convictions upon this paramount question. For my own part, I considered it therefore my duty to enter fully into the matter, even at the peril of putting your patience to a severe test.

Another preliminary remark I have to make in regard to Citizen Weston. He has not only proposed to you, but has publicly defended, in the interest of the working class, as he thinks, opinions he knows to be most unpopular with the working class. Such an exhibition of moral courage all of us must highly honour. I hope that, despite the unvarnished style of my paper, at its conclusion he will find me agreeing with what appears to me the just idea lying at the bottom of his theses, which, however, in their present form, I cannot but consider theoretically false and practically dangerous.

I shall now at once proceed to the business before us.

PRODUCTION AND WAGES

Citizen Weston's argument rested, in fact, upon two premises: firstly, that the *amount of national production* is a *fixed thing*, a *constant* quantity or magnitude, as the mathematicians would say; secondly, that the *amount of real wages*, that is to say, of wages as measured by the quantity of the commodities they can buy, is a *fixed* amount, a *constant* magnitude.

Now, his first assertion is evidently erroneous. Year after year you will find that the value and mass of production increase, that the productive powers of the national labour increase, and that the amount of money necessary to circulate this increasing production continuously changes. What is true at the end of the year, and for different years compared with each other, is true for every average day of the year. The amount or magnitude of national production changes continuously. It is not a *constant* but a *variable* magnitude, and apart from changes in population it must be so, because of the continuous change in the *accumulation of capital* and the *productive powers of labour*. It is perfectly true that if a *rise in the general rate of wages* should take place today, that rise, whatever its ulterior effects might be, would, *by itself*, not *immediately* change the amount of production. It would, in the first instance, proceed from the existing state of things. But if *before* the rise of wages the national production was *variable*, and not *fixed*, it will continue to be variable and not fixed *after* the rise of wages.

But suppose the amount of national production to be *constant* instead of *variable*. Even then, what our friend Weston considers a logical conclusion would still remain a gratuitous assertion. If I have a given number, say eight, the *absolute* limits of this number do not prevent its parts from changing their *relative* limits. If profits were six and wages two, wages might increase to six and profits decrease to two, and still the total amount remain eight. The fixed amount of production would by no means prove the fixed amount of wages. How then does our friend Weston prove this fixity? By asserting it.

But even conceding him his assertion, it would cut both ways, while he presses it only in one direction. If the amount of wages is a constant magnitude, then it can be neither increased nor diminished. If then, in enforcing a temporary rise of wages, the working men act foolishly, the capitalists, in enforcing a temporary fall of wages, would act not less foolishly. Our friend Weston does not deny that, under certain circumstances, the working men *can* enforce a rise of wages, but their amount being naturally fixed, there must follow a reaction. On the other hand, he knows also that the capitalists *can* enforce a fall of wages, and, indeed, continuously try to enforce it. According to the principle of the constancy of wages, a reaction ought to follow in this case not less than in the former. The working men, therefore, reacting against the attempt at, or the act of, lowering wages, would act rightly. They would, therefore, act rightly in enforcing *a rise of wages*, because every *reaction* against the lowering of wages is an *action* for raising wages. According to Citizen Weston's own principle of the *constancy of wages*, the working men ought, therefore, under certain circumstances, to combine and struggle for a rise of wages.

If he denies this conclusion, he must give up the premise from which it flows. He must not say that the amount of wages is a *constant quantity*, but that, although it cannot and must not *rise*, it can and must *fall*, whenever capital pleases to lower it. If the capitalist pleases to feed you upon potatoes instead of upon meat, and upon oats instead of upon wheat, you must accept his will as a law of political economy, and submit to it. If in one country the rate of wages is higher than in another, in the United

States, for example, than in England, you must explain this difference in the rate of wages by a difference between the will of the American capitalist and the will of the English capitalist, a method which would certainly very much simplify, not only the study of economic phenomena, but of all other phenomena.

But even then, we might ask, *why* the will of the American capitalist differs from the will of the English capitalist? And to answer the question you must go beyond the domain of *will*. A *parson* may tell me that God wills one thing in France, and another thing in England. If I summon him to explain this duality of will, he might have the brass to answer me that God wills to have one will in France and another will in England. But our friend Weston is certainly the last man to make an argument of such a complete negation of all reasoning.

The *will* of the capitalist is certainly to take as much as possible. What we have to do is not to talk about his *will*, but to enquire into his *power*, the *limits of that power*, and the *character of those limits*.

II PRODUCTION, WAGES, PROFIT

The address Citizen Weston read to us might have been compressed into a nutshell.

All his reasoning amounted to this: If the working class forces the capitalist class to pay five shillings instead of four shillings in the shape of money wages, the capitalist will return in the shape of commodities four shillings' worth instead of five shillings' worth. The working class would have to pay five shillings for what, before the rise of wages, they bought with four shillings. But why is this the case? Why does the capitalist only return four shillings' worth for five shillings? Because the amount of wages is fixed. By why is it fixed at four shillings' worth of commodities? Why not at three, or two, or any other sum? If the limit of the amount of wages is settled by an economical law, independent alike of the will of the capitalist and the will of the working man, the first thing Citizen Weston had to do was to state that law and prove it. He ought then, moreover, to have proved that the amount of wages actually paid at every given moment always corresponds exactly to the necessary amount of wages, and never deviates from it. If, on the other hand, the given limit of the amount of wages is founded on the *mere will* of the capitalist, or the limits of his avarice, it is an arbitrary limit. There is nothing necessary in it. It may be changed *by* the will of the capitalist, and may, therefore, be changed *against* his will.

Citizen Weston illustrated his theory by telling you that when a bowl contains a certain quantity of soup, to be eaten by a certain number of persons, an increase in the broadness of the spoons would not produce an increase in the amount of soup. He must allow me to find this illustration rather spoony. It reminded me somewhat of the simile employed by Menenius Agrippa. When the Roman plebeians struck against the Roman patricians, the patrician Agrippa told them that the patrician belly fed the plebeian members of the body politic. Agrippa failed to show that you feed the members of one man by filling the belly of another. Citizen Weston, on his part, has forgotten that the bowl from which the workmen eat is filled with the whole produce of national labour, and that what prevents them fetching more out of it is neither the narrowness of the bowl nor the scantiness of its contents, but only the smallness of their spoons.

By what contrivance is the capitalist enabled to return four shillings' worth for five shillings? By raising the price of the commodity he sells. Now, does a rise and more generally a change in the prices of commodities, do the prices of commodities themselves, depend on the mere will of the capitalist? Or are, on the contrary, certain circumstances wanted to give effect to that will? If not, the ups and downs, the incessant fluctuations of market prices, become an insoluble riddle.

As we suppose that no change whatever has taken place either in the productive powers of labour, or in the amount of capital and labour employed, or in the value of the money wherein the values of products are estimated, but *only a change in the rate of wages*, how could that *rise of wages* affect the *prices of commodities*? Only by affecting the actual proportion between the demand for, and the supply of these commodities.

It is perfectly true that, considered as a whole, the working class spends, and must spend, its income upon *necessaries*. A general rise in the rate of wages would, therefore, produce a rise in the demand for, and consequently in the *market prices of, necessaries*. The capitalists who produce these necessaries would be compensated for the risen wages by the rising market prices of their commodities. But how with the other capitalists who do *not* produce necessaries? And you must not fancy them a small body. If you consider that two-thirds of the national produce are consumed by one-fifth of the population – a member of the House of Commons stated it recently to be but one-seventh of the population – you will understand what an immense proportion of the national produce must be produced in the shape of luxuries, or be *exchanged* for luxuries, and what an immense amount of the necessaries themselves must be wasted upon flunkeys, horses, cats, and so forth, a waste we know from experience to become always much limited with the rising prices of necessaries.

Well, what would be the position of those capitalists who do *not* produce necessaries? For the *fall in the rate of profit*, consequent upon the general rise of wages, they could not compensate themselves by a *rise in the price of their commodities*, because the demand for those commodities would not have increased. Their income would have decreased, and from this decreased income they would have to pay more for the same amount of higher-priced necessaries. But this would not be all. As their income had diminished they would have less to spend upon luxuries, and therefore their mutual demand for their respective commodities would diminish. Consequent upon this diminished demand the prices of their commodities would fall. In these branches of industry, therefore, *the rate of profit would fall*, not only in simple proportion to the general rise in the rate of wages, but in the compound ratio of the general rise of wages, the rise in the prices of necessaries, and the fall in the prices of luxuries.

What would be the consequence of *this difference in the rates of profit* for capitals employed in the different branches of industry? Why, the consequence that generally obtains whenever, from whatever reason, the *average rate of profit* comes to differ in the different spheres of production. Capital and labour would be transferred from the less remunerative to the more remunerative branches; and this process of transfer would go on until the supply in the one department of industry would have risen proportionately to the increased demand, and would have sunk in the other departments according to the decreased demand. This change effected, the general rate of profit would again be *equalised* in the different branches. As the whole derangement originally arose from a mere change in the proportion of the demand for, and supply of, different commodities, the cause ceasing, the effect would cease, and *prices* would return to their former level and equilibrium. Instead of being limited to some branches of industry, *the fall in the rate of profit* consequent upon the rise of wages would have become general. According to our supposition, there would have taken place no change in the productive powers of labour, nor in the aggregate amount of production, but *that given amount of production would have changed its form*. A greater part of the produce would exist in the shape of necessaries, a lesser part in the shape of luxuries, or what comes to the same, a lesser part would be exchanged for foreign luxuries, and be consumed in its original form, or, what again comes to the same, a greater part of the native produce would be exchanged for foreign necessaries instead of for luxuries. The general rise in the rate of wages would, therefore, after a temporary disturbance of market prices, only result in a general fall of the rate of profit without any permanent change in the prices of commodities.

If I am told that in the previous argument I assume the whole surplus wages to be spent upon necessaries, I answer that I have made the supposition most advantageous to the opinion of Citizen Weston. If the surplus wages were spent upon articles formerly not entering into the consumption of the working men, the real increase of their purchasing power would need no proof. Being, however, only derived from an advance of wages, that increase of their purchasing power must exactly correspond to the decrease of the purchasing power of the capitalists. The *aggregate demand* for commodities would, therefore, not *increase*, but the constituent parts of that demand would *change*. The increasing demand on the one side would be counterbalanced by the decreasing demand on the other side. Thus the aggregate demand remaining stationary, no change whatever could take place in the market prices of commodities.

You arrive, therefore, at this dilemma: Either the surplus wages are equally spent upon all articles of consumption – then the expansion of demand on the part of the working class must be compensated by the contraction of demand on the part of the capitalist class – or the surplus wages are only spent upon some articles whose market prices will temporarily rise. The consequent rise in the rate of profit in some, and the consequent fall in the rate of profit in other branches of industry will produce a change in the distribution of capital and labour, going on until the supply is brought up to the increased demand in the one department of industry, and brought down to the diminished demand in the other departments of industry. On the one supposition there will occur no change in the prices of commodities. On the other supposition, after some fluctuations of market prices, the exchangeable values of commodities will subside to the former level. On both suppositions the general rise in the rate of wages will ultimately result in nothing else but a general fall in the rate of profit.

To stir up your powers of imagination Citizen Weston requested you to think of the difficulties which a general rise of English agricultural wages from nine shillings to eighteen shillings would produce. Think, he exclaimed, of the immense rise in the demand for necessaries, and the consequent fearful rise in their prices! Now, all of you know that the average wages of the American agricultural labourer amount to more than double that of the English agricultural labourer, although the prices of agricultural produce are lower in the United States than in the United Kingdom, although the general relations of capital and labour obtain in the United States the same as in England, and although the annual amount of production is much smaller in the United States than in England. Why, then, does our friend ring this alarum bell? Simply to shift the real question before us.

A sudden rise of wages from nine shillings to eighteen shillings would be a sudden rise to the amount of 100 per cent. Now, we are not at all discussing the question whether the general rate of wages in England could be suddenly increased by 100 per cent. We have nothing at all to do with the *magnitude* of the rise, which in every practical instance must depend on, and be suited to, given circumstances. We have only to inquire how a general rise in the rate of wages, even if restricted to one per cent, will act.

Dismissing friend Weston's fancy rise of 100 per cent, I propose calling your attention to the real rise of wages that took place in Great Britain from 1849 to 1859.

You are all aware of the Ten Hours' Bill, or rather Ten-and-a-half Hours' Bill, introduced since 1848. This was one of the greatest economic changes we have witnessed. It was a sudden and compulsory rise of wages, not in some local trades, but in the leading industrial branches by which England sways the markets of the world. It was a rise of wages under circumstances singularly unpropitious. Dr. Ure, Professor Senior, and all the other official economical mouthpieces of the middle class, *proved*, and I must say upon much stronger grounds than those of our friend Weston, that it would sound the death-knell of English industry. They proved that it not only amounted to a simple rise of wages, but to a rise of wages initiated by, and based upon, a diminution of the quantity of labour employed. They asserted that the twelfth hour you wanted to take from the capitalist was exactly the only hour from which he derived his profit. They threatened a decrease of accumulation, rise of prices, loss of markets, stinting of production, consequent reaction upon wages, ultimate ruin. In fact, they declared Maximilien Robespierre's Maximum Laws to be a small affair compared to it; and they were right in a certain sense. Well, what was the result? A rise in the money wages of the factory operatives, despite the curtailing of the working day, a great increase in the number of factory hands employed, a continuous fall in the prices of their products, a marvellous development in the productive powers of their labour, an unheard-of progressive expansion of the markets for their commodities. In Manchester, at the meeting, in 1860, of the Society for the Advancement of Science, I myself heard Mr. Newman confess that he, Dr. Ure, Senior, and all other official propounders of economical science had been wrong, while the instinct of the people had been right. I mention Mr. W. Newman, not Professor Francis Newman, because he occupies an eminent position in economical science, as the contributor to, and editor of, Mr. Thomas Tooke's *History Of Prices*, that magnificent work which traces the history of prices from 1793 to 1856. If our friend Weston's fixed idea of a fixed amount of wages, a fixed amount of production, a fixed degree of the productive power of labour, a fixed and permanent will of the capitalist, and all his other fixedness and finality were correct, Professor Senior's woeful forebodings would been right, and Robert Owen, *who already in 1815 proclaimed a general limitation of the* working day the first preparatory step to the emancipation of *the working class, and actually in the teeth of the general prejudice* inaugurated it on his own hook in his cotton factory at New Lanark, would have been wrong.

In the very same period during which the introduction of the Ten Hours' Bill, and the rise of wages consequent upon it, occurred, there took place in Great Britain, for reasons which it would be out of place to enumerate here, *a general rise in agricultural wages.*

Although it is not required for my immediate purpose, in order not to mislead you, I shall make some preliminary remarks.

If a man got two shillings weekly wages, and if his wages rose to four shillings, the *rate of wages* would have risen by 100 per cent. This would seem a very magnificent thing if expressed as a rise in the *rate of wages, although the actual amount of wages*, four shillings weekly, would still remain a wretchedly small, a starvation pittance. You must not, therefore, allow yourselves to be carried away by the high-sounding per cents in *rate* of wages. You must always ask: What was the *original* amount?

Moreover, you will understand, that if there were ten men receiving each 2*s*. per week, five men receiving each 5*s*., and five men receiving 11*s*. weekly, the twenty men together would receive 100*s*., or £5, weekly. If then a rise, say by 20 per cent, upon the *aggregate* sum of their weekly wages took place, there would be an advance from £5 to £6. Taking the average, we might say that the *general rate of wages* had risen by 20 per cent, although, in fact, the wages of the ten men had remained stationary, the wages of the one lot of five men had risen from 5*s*. to 6*s*. only, and the wages of the other lot of five from 55*s*. to 70*s*. One half of the men would not have improved at all their position, one quarter would have improved it in an imperceptible degree, and only one quarter would have bettered it really. Still, reckoning by the *average*, the total amount of the wages of those twenty men would have increased by 20 per cent, and as far as the aggregate capital that employs them, and the prices of the commodities they produce, are concerned, it would be exactly the same as if all of them had equally shared in the average rise of wages. In the case of agricultural labour, the standard wages being very different in the different counties of England and Scotland, the rise affected them very unequally.

Lastly, during the period when that rise of wages took place counteracting influences were at work such as the new taxes consequent upon the Russian war, the extensive demolition of the dwelling-houses of the agricultural labourers, and so forth.

Having premised so much, I proceed to state that from 1849 to 1859 there took place a *rise of about 40 per cent* in the average rate of the agricultural wages of Great Britain. I could give you ample details in proof of my assertion, but for the present purpose think it sufficient to refer you to the conscientious and critical paper read in 1860 by the late Mr. John C. Morton at the London Society of Arts on *The Forces used in Agriculture*. Mr. Morton gives the returns, from bills and other authentic documents, which he had collected from about one hundred farmers, residing in twelve Scotch and thirty-five English counties.

According to our friend Weston's opinion, and taken together with the simultaneous rise in the wages of the factory operatives, there ought to have occurred a tremendous rise in the prices of agricultural produce during the period 1849 to 1859. But what is the fact? Despite the Russian war, and the consecutive unfavourable harvests from 1854 to 1856, the average price of wheat, which is the leading agricultural produce of England, fell from about £3 per quarter for the years 1838 to 1848 to about £2 10*s*. per quarter for the years 1849 to 1859. This constitutes a fall in the price of wheat of more than 16 per cent simultaneously with an average rise of agricultural wages of 40 per cent. During the same period, if we compare its end with its beginning, 1859 with 1849, there was a decrease of official pauperism from 934,419 to 860,470, the difference being 73,949; a very small decrease, I grant, and which in the following years was again lost, but still a decrease.

It might be said that, consequent upon the abolition of the Corn Laws, the import of foreign corn was more than doubled during the period from 1849 to 1859, as compared with the period from 1838 to 1848. And what of that? From Citizen Weston's standpoint one would have expected that this sudden, immense, and continuously increasing demand upon foreign markets must have sent up the prices of agricultural produce there to a frightful height, the effect of increased demand remaining the same, whether it comes from without or from within. What was the fact? Apart from some years of failing harvests, during all that period the ruinous fall in the price of corn formed a standing theme of declamation in France; the Americans were again and again compelled to burn their surplus produce; and Russia, if we are to believe Mr. Urquhart, prompted the Civil War in the United States because her agricultural exports were crippled by the Yankee competition in the markets of Europe.

Reduced to its abstract form, Citizen Weston's argument would come to this: Every rise in demand occurs always on the basis of a given amount of production. It can, therefore, *never increase the supply of the articles demanded*, but can *only enhance their money prices*. Now the most common observation shows than an increased demand will, in some instances, leave the market prices of commodities altogether unchanged, and will, in other instances, cause a temporary rise of market prices followed by an increased supply, followed by a reduction of the prices to their original level, and in many cases *below* their original level. Whether the rise of demand springs from surplus wages, or from any other cause, does not at all change the conditions of the problem. From Citizen Weston's standpoint the general phenomenon was as difficult to explain as the phenomenon occurring under the exceptional circumstances of a rise of wages. His argument had, therefore, no peculiar bearing whatever upon the subject we treat. It only expressed his perplexity at accounting for the laws by which an increase of demand produces an increase of supply, instead of an ultimate rise of market prices.

III WAGES AND CURRENCY

On the second day of the debate our friend Weston clothed his old assertions in new forms. He said: Consequent upon a general rise in money wages, more currency will be wanted to pay the same wages. The currency being *fixed*, how can you pay with this fixed currency increased money wages? First the difficulty arose from the fixed amount of commodities accruing to the working man, despite his increase of money wages; now it arises from the increased money wages, despite the fixed amount of commodities. Of course, if you reject his original dogma, his secondary grievance will disappear.

However, I shall show that this currency question has nothing at all to do with the subject before us.

In your country the mechanism of payments is much more perfected than in any other country of Europe. Thanks to the extent and concentration of the banking system, much less currency is wanted to circulate the same amount of values, and to transact the same or a greater amount of business. For example, as far as wages are concerned, the English factory operative pays his wages weekly to the shopkeeper, who sends them weekly to the banker, who returns them weekly to the manufacturer, who again pays them away to his working men, and so forth. By this contrivance the yearly wages of an operative, say of £52, may be paid by one single sovereign turning round every week in the same circle. Even in England the mechanism is less perfect than in Scotland, and is not everywhere equally perfect; and therefore we find, for example, that in some agricultural districts, much more currency is wanted to circulate a much smaller amount of values.

If you cross the Channel you will find that the *money wages* are much lower than in England, but that they are circulated in Germany, Italy, Switzerland, and France by a *much larger amount of currency*. The same sovereign will not be so quickly intercepted by the banker or returned to the industrial capitalist; and, therefore, instead of one sovereign circulating £52 yearly, you want, perhaps, three sovereigns to circulate yearly wages to the amount of £25. Thus, by comparing continental countries with England, you will see at once that low money wages may require a much larger currency for their circulation than high money wages, and that this is, in fact, a merely technical point, quite foreign to our subject.

According to the best calculations I know, the yearly income of the working class of this country may be estimated at £250,000,000. This immense sum is circulated by about £3,000,000. Suppose a rise of wages of 50 per cent to take place. Then, instead of £3,000,000 of currency, £4,500,000 would be wanted. As a very considerable part of the workingman's daily expenses is laid out in silver and copper, that is to say, in mere tokens, whose relative value to gold is arbitrarily fixed by law, like that of inconvertible money paper, a rise of money wages by 50 per cent would, in the extreme case, require an additional circulation of sovereigns, say to the amount of one million. One million, now dormant, in the shape of bullion or coin, in the cellars of the Bank of England, or of private bankers, would circulate. But even the trifling expense resulting from the additional minting or the additional wear and tear of that million might be spared, and would actually be spared, if any friction should arise from the want of the additional currency. All of you know that the currency of this country is divided into two great departments. One sort, supplied by bank-notes of different descriptions, is used in the transactions between dealers and dealers, and the larger payments from consumers to dealers, while another sort of currency, metallic coin, circulates in the retail trade. Although distinct, these two sorts of currency interwork with each other. Thus gold coin, to a very great extent, circulates even in larger payments for all the odd sums under £5. If tomorrow £4 notes, or £3 notes, or £2 notes were issued, the gold filling these channels of circulation would at once be driven out of them, and flow into those channels where they would be needed from the increase of money wages. Thus the additional million required by an advance of wages by 50 per cent would be supplied without the addition of one single sovereign. The same effect might be produced, without one additional bank-note, by an additional bill circulation, as was the case in Lancashire for a very considerable time.

If a general rise in the rate of wages, for example, of 100 per cent, as Citizen Weston supposed it to take place in agricultural wages, would produce a great rise in the prices of necessaries, and, according to his views, require an additional amount of currency not to be procured, *a general fall in wages* must produce the same effect, on the same scale, in the opposite direction. Well! All of you know that the years 1858 to 1860 were the most prosperous years for the cotton industry, and that peculiarly the year 1860 stands in that respect unrivalled in the annals of commerce, while at the same time all other branches of industry were most flourishing. The wages of the cotton operatives and of all the other working men connected with their trade stood, in 1860, higher than ever before. The American crisis came, and those aggregate wages were suddenly reduced to about one-fourth of their former amount. This would have been in the opposite direction a rise of 300 per cent. If wages rise from five to twenty, we say that they rise by 300 per cent; if they fall from twenty to five, we say that they fall by 75 per cent; but the amount of rise in the one and the amount of fall in the other case would be the same, namely, fifteen shillings. This, then, was a sudden change in the rate of wages unprecedented, and at the same time extending over a number of operatives which, if we count all the operatives not only directly engaged in but indirectly dependent upon the cotton trade, was larger by one-half than the number of agricultural labourers. Did the price of wheat fall? It *rose* from the annual average of 47*s*. 8*d*. per quarter during the three years of 1858–1860 to the annual average of 55*s*. 10*d*. per quarter during the three years 1861–1863. As to the currency, there were coined in the mint in 1861 £8,673,323, against £3,378,792 in 1860. That is to say, there were coined £5,294,440 more in 1861 than in 1860. It is true the bank-note circulation was in 1861 less by £1,319,000 than in 1860. Take this off. There remains still a surplus of currency for the year 1861, as compared with the prosperity year, 1860, to the amount of £3,975,440, or about £4,000,000; but the bullion reserve in the Bank of England had simultaneously decreased, not quite to the same, but in an approximating proportion.

Compare the year 1862 with 1842. Apart from the immense increase in the value and amount of commodities circulated, in 1862 the capital paid in regular transactions for shares, loans, etc., for the railways in England and Wales amounted alone to £320,000,000, a sum that would have appeared fabulous in 1842.

Still, the aggregate amounts in currency in 1862 and 1842 were pretty nearly equal, and generally you will find a tendency to a progressive diminution of currency in the face of enormously increasing value, not only of commodities, but of monetary transactions generally. From our friend Weston's standpoint this is an unsolvable riddle.

Looking somewhat deeper into this matter, he would have found that, quite apart from wages, and supposing them to be fixed, the value and mass of the commodities to be circulated, and generally the amount of monetary transactions to be settled, vary daily; that the amount of bank-notes issued varies daily; that the amount of payments realised without the intervention of any money, by the instrumentality of bills, cheques, book-credits, clearing houses, varies daily; that, as far as actual metallic currency is required, the proportion between the coin in circulation and the coin and bullion in reserve or sleeping in the cellars of banks varies daily; that the amount of bullion absorbed by the national circulation and the amount being sent abroad for international circulation vary daily. He would have found that this dogma of a fixed currency is a monstrous error, incompatible with our everyday movement. He would have inquired into the laws which enable a currency to adapt itself to circumstances so continually changing, instead of turning his misconception of the laws of currency into an argument against a rise of wages.

IV SUPPLY AND DEMAND

Our friend Weston accepts the Latin proverb that *repetitio est mater studiorum*, that is to say, that repetition is the mother of study, and consequently he repeated his original dogma again under the new form, that the contraction of currency, resulting from an enhancement of wages, would produce a diminution of capital, and so forth. Having already dealt with his currency crotchet, I consider it quite useless to enter upon the imaginary consequences he fancies to flow from his imaginary currency mishap. I shall proceed to at once reduce his *one and the same dogma*, repeated in so many different shapes, to its simplest theoretical form.

The uncritical way in which he has treated his subject will become evident from one single remark. He pleads against a rise of wages or against high wages as the result of such a rise. Now, I ask him: What are high wages and what are low wages? Why constitute, for example, five shillings weekly low, and twenty shillings weekly high wages? If five is low as compared with twenty, twenty is still lower as compared with two hundred. If a man was to lecture on the thermometer, and commenced by declaiming on high and low degrees, he would impart no knowledge whatever. He must first tell me how the freezing-point is found out, and how the boiling-point, and how these standard points are settled by natural laws, not by the fancy of the sellers or makers of thermometers. Now, in regard to wages and profits, Citizen Weston has not only failed to deduce such standard points from economical laws, but he has not even felt the necessity to look after them. He satisfied himself with the acceptance of the popular slang terms of low and high as something having a fixed meaning, although it is self-evident that wages can only be said to be high or low as compared with a standard by which to measure their magnitudes.

He will be unable to tell me why a certain amount of money is given for a certain amount of labour. If he should answer me, "This was settled by the law of supply and demand", I should ask him, in the first instance, by what law supply and demand are themselves regulated. And such an answer would at once put him out of court. The relations between the supply and demand of labour undergo perpetual change, and with them the market prices of labour. If the demand overshoots the supply wages rise; if the supply overshoots the demand wages sink, although it might in such circumstances be necessary to *test* the real state of demand and supply by a strike, for example, or any other method. But if you accept supply and demand as the law regulating wages, it would be as childish as useless to declaim against a rise of wages, because, according to the supreme law you appeal to, a periodical rise of wages is quite as necessary and legitimate as a periodical fall of wages. If you do *not* accept supply and demand as the law regulating wages, I again repeat the question, why a certain amount of money is given for a certain amount of labour?

But to consider matters more broadly: You would be altogether mistaken in fancying that the value of labour or any other commodity whatever is ultimately fixed by supply and demand. Supply and demand regulate nothing but the temporary *fluctuations* of market prices. They will explain to you why the market price of a commodity rises above or sinks below its *value*, but they can never account for the value itself. Suppose supply and demand to equilibrate, or, as the economists call it, to cover each other. Why, the very moment these opposite forces become equal they paralyse each other, and cease to work in the one or other direction. At the moment when supply and demand equilibrate each other, and therefore cease to act, the *market* price of a commodity coincides with its *real value*, with the standard price round which its market prices oscillate. In inquiring into the nature of that *value*, we have, therefore, nothing at all to do with the temporary effects on market prices of supply and demand. The same holds true of wages and of the prices of all other commodities.

V WAGES AND PRICES

Reduced to their simplest theoretical expression, all our friend's arguments resolve themselves into this one dogma: "*The prices of commodities are determined or regulated by wages*".

I might appeal to practical observation to bear witness against this antiquated and exploded fallacy. I might tell you that the English factory operatives, miners, shipbuilders, and so forth, whose labour is relatively high-priced, undersell by the cheapness of their produce all other nations; while the English agricultural labourer, for example, whose labour is relatively low-priced, is undersold by almost every other nation because of the dearness of his produce. By comparing article with article in the same country, and the commodities of different countries, I might show, apart from some exceptions more apparent than real, that on an average the high-priced labour produces the low-priced, and low priced labour produces the high-priced commodities. This, of course, would not prove that the high price of labour in the one, and its low price in the other instance, are the respective causes of those diametrically opposed effects, but at all events it would prove that the prices of commodities are not ruled by the prices of labour. However, it is quite superfluous for us to employ this empirical method.

It might, perhaps, be denied that Citizen Weston has put forward the dogma: "*The prices of commodities are determined or regulated by wages*". In point of fact, he has never formulated it.

He said, on the contrary, that profit and rent also form constituent parts of the prices of commodities, because it is out of the prices of commodities that not only the working man's wages, but also the capitalist's profits and the landlord's rents must be paid. But how in his idea are prices formed? First by wages. Then an additional percentage is joined to the price on behalf of the capitalist, and another additional percentage on behalf of the landlord. Suppose the wages of the labour employed in the production of a commodity to be ten. If the rate of profit was 100 per cent, to the wages advanced the capitalist would add ten, and if the rate of rent was also 100 per cent upon the wages, there would be added ten more, and the aggregate price of the commodity would amount to thirty. But such a determination of prices would be simply their determination by wages. If wages in the above case rose to twenty, the price of the commodity would rise to sixty, and so forth. Consequently all the superannuated writers on political economy who propounded the dogma that wages regulate prices, have tried to prove it by treating profit and rent *as mere additional percentages upon wages*. None of them were, of course, able to reduce the limits of those percentages to any economic law. They seem, on the contrary, to think profits settled by tradition, custom, the will of the capitalist, or by some other equally arbitrary and inexplicable method. If they assert that they are settled by the competition between the capitalists, they say nothing. That competition is sure to equalise the different rates of profit in different trades, or reduce them to one average level, but it can never determine the level itself, or the general rate of profit.

What do we mean by saying that the prices of the commodities are determined by wages? Wages being but a name for the price of labour, we mean that the prices of commodities are regulated by the price of labour. As "*price*" is exchangeable value – and in speaking of value I speak always of exchangeable value – is exchangeable *value expressed in money*, the proposition comes to this, that "the *value of commodities* is determined by the value of labour", or that "the *value of labour is the general measure of value*".

But how, then, is the "*value of labour*" itself determined? Here we come to a standstill. Of course, we come to a standstill if we try reasoning logically, yet the propounders of that doctrine make short work of logical scruples. Take our friend Weston, for example. First he told us that wages regulate the price of commodities and that consequently when wages rise prices must rise. Then he turned round to show us that a rise of wages will be no good because the prices of commodities had risen, and because wages were indeed measured by the prices of the commodities upon which they are spent. Thus we begin by saying that the value of labour determines the value of commodities, and we wind up by saying that the value of commodities determines the value of labour. Thus we move to and fro in the most vicious circle, and arrive at no conclusion at all.

On the whole it is evident that by making the value of one commodity, say labour, corn, or any other commodity, the general measure and regulator of value, we only shift the difficulty, since we determine one value by another, which on its side wants to be determined.

The dogma that "wages determine the price of commodities", expressed in its most abstract terms, comes to this, that "value is determined by value", and this tautology means that, in fact, we know nothing at all about value. Accepting this premise, all reasoning about the general laws of political economy turns into mere twaddle. It was, therefore, the great merit of Ricardo that in his work on *The Principles of Political Economy*, published in 1817, he fundamentally destroyed the old, popular, and worn-out fallacy that "wages determine prices", a fallacy which Adam Smith and his French predecessors had spurned in the really scientific parts of their researches, but which they reproduced in their more exoterical and vulgarising chapters.

VI VALUE AND LABOUR

Citizens, I have now arrived at a point where I must enter upon the real development of the question. I cannot promise to do this in a very satisfactory way, because to do so I should be obliged to go over the whole field of political economy. I can, as the French would say, but "*effleurer la question*", touch upon the main points.

The first question we have to put is: What is the *value* of a commodity? How is it determined?

At first sight it would seem that the value of a commodity is a thing quite *relative*, and not to be settled without considering one commodity in its relations to all other commodities. In fact, in speaking of the value, the value in exchange of a commodity, we mean the proportional quantities in which it exchanges with all other commodities. But then arises the question: How are the proportions in which commodities exchange with each other regulated?

We know from experience that these proportions vary infinitely. Taking one single commodity, wheat, for instance, we shall find that a quarter of wheat exchanges in almost countless variations of proportion with different commodities. Yet, *its value remaining always the same*, whether expressed in silk, gold, or any other commodity, it must be something distinct from, and independent of, these *different rates of exchange* with different articles. It must be possible to express, in a very different form, these various equations with various commodities.

Besides, if I say a quarter of wheat exchanges with iron in a certain proportion, or the value of a quarter of wheat is expressed in a certain amount of iron, I say that the value of wheat and its equivalent in iron are equal *to some third thing*, which is neither wheat nor iron, because I suppose them to express the same magnitude in two different shapes. Either of them, the wheat or the iron, must, therefore, independently of the other, be reducible to this third thing which is their common measure.

To elucidate this point I shall recur to a very simple geometrical illustration. In comparing the areas of triangles of all possible forms and magnitudes, or comparing triangles with rectangles, or any other rectilinear figure, how do we proceed? We reduce the area of any triangle whatever to an expression quite different from its visible form. Having found from the nature of the triangle that its area is equal to half the product of its base by its height, we can then compare the different values of all sorts of triangles, and of all rectilinear figures whatever, because all of them may be resolved into a certain number of triangles.

The same mode of procedure must obtain with the values of commodities. We must be able to reduce all of them to an expression common to all, and distinguishing them only by the proportions in which they contain that identical measure.

As the *exchangeable values* of commodities are only *social functions* of those things, and have nothing at all to do with the *natural* qualities, we must first ask: What is the common *social substance* of all commodities? It is *Labour*. To produce a commodity a certain amount of labour must be bestowed upon it, or worked up in it. And I say not only *Labour*, but *social Labour*. A man who produces an article for his own immediate use, to consume it himself, creates a *product*, but not a commodity. As a self-sustaining producer he has nothing to do with society. But to produce a *commodity*, a man must not only produce an article satisfying some *social* want, but his labour itself must form part and parcel of the total sum of labour expended by society. It must be subordinate to the *Division of Labour within Society*. It is nothing without the other divisions of labour, and on its part is required to integrate them.

If we consider *commodities as values*, we consider them exclusively under the single aspect of *realised, fixed*, or, if you like, *crystallised social labour*. In this respect they can *differ* only by representing greater or smaller quantities of labour, as, for example, a greater amount of labour may be worked up in a silken handkerchief than in a brick. But how does one measure *quantities of labour*? By the *time the labour lasts*, in measuring the labour by the hour, the day, etc. Of course, to apply this measure, all sorts of labour are reduced to average or simple labour as their unit.

We arrive, therefore, at this conclusion. A commodity has a *value*, because it is a *crystallisation of social labour*. The *greatness* of its value, or its *relative* value, depends upon the greater or less amount of that social substance contained in it; that is to say, on the relative mass of labour necessary for its production. The *relative values of commodities* are, therefore, determined by the *respective quantities or amounts of labour, worked up, realised, fixed in them*. The *correlative* quantities of commodities which can be produced in the *same time of labour* are *equal*. Or the value of one commodity is to the value of another commodity as the quantity of labour fixed in the one is to the quantity of labour fixed in the other.

I suspect that many of you will ask: Does then, indeed, there exist such a vast or any difference whatever, between determining the values of commodities by *wages*, and determining them by the *relative quantities of labour* necessary for their production? You must, however, be aware that the *reward* for labour, and *quantity* of labour, are quite disparate things. Suppose, for example, *equal quantities of labour* to be fixed in one quarter of wheat and one ounce of gold. I resort to the example because it was used by Benjamin Franklin in his first Essay published in 1721, and entitled *A Modest Enquiry into the Nature and Necessity of a Paper Currency*, where he, one of the first, hit upon the true nature of value. Well. We suppose, then, that one quarter of wheat and one ounce of gold are *equal values or equivalents*, because they are *crystallisations of equal amounts of average labour*, of so many days' or so many weeks' labour respectively fixed in them. In thus determining the relative values of gold and corn, do we refer in any way whatever to the *wages* of the agricultural labourer and the miner? Not a bit. We leave it quite *indeterminate how* their day's or their week's labour was paid, or even whether wage labour was employed at all. If it was, wages may have been very unequal. The labourer whose labour is realised in the quarter of wheat may receive two bushels only, and the labourer employed in mining may receive one-half of the ounce of gold. Or, supposing their wages to be equal, they may deviate in all possible proportions from the values of the commodities produced by them. They may amount to one-half, one-third, one-fourth, one-fifth, or any other proportional part of the one quarter of corn or the one ounce of gold. Their *wages* can, of course, not *exceed*, not be *more* than the values of the commodities they produced, but they can be *less* in every possible degree. Their *wages* will be *limited* by the *values* of the products, but the *values of their products* will not be limited by the wages. And above all, the values, the relative values of corn and gold, for example, will have been settled without any regard whatever to the value of the labour employed, that is to say, to *wages*. To determine the values of commodities by the *relative quantities of labour fixed in them*, is, therefore, a thing quite different from the tautological method of determining the values of commodities by the value of labour, or by *wages*. This point, however, will be further elucidated in the progress of our inquiry.

In calculating the exchangeable value of a commodity we must add to the quantity of labour *last* employed, the quantity of labour *previously* worked up in the raw material of the commodity, and the labour bestowed on the implements, tools, machinery, and buildings, with which such labour is assisted. For example, the value of a certain amount of cotton yarn is the crystallisation of the quantity of labour added to the cotton during the spinning process, the quantity of labour previously realised in the cotton itself, the quantity of labour realised in the coal, oil, and other auxiliary substances used, the quantity of labour fixed in the steam-engine, the spindles, the factory building, and so forth. Instruments of production properly so-called, such as tools, machinery, buildings, serve again and again for longer or shorter period during repeated processes of production. If they were used up at once, like the raw material, their whole value would at once be transferred to the commodities they assist in producing. But as a spindle, for example, is but gradually used up, an average calculation is made, based upon the average time it lasts, and its average waste or wear and tear during a certain period, say a day. In this way we calculate how much of the value of the spindle is transferred to the yarn daily spin, and how much, therefore, of the total amount of labour realised in a pound of yarn, for example, is due to the quantity of labour previously realised in the spindle. For our present purpose it is not necessary to dwell any longer upon this point.

It might seem that if the value of a commodity is determined by the *quantity of labour bestowed upon its production*, the lazier a man, or the clumsier a man, the more valuable his commodity, because the greater the time of labour required for finishing the commodity. This, however, would be a sad mistake. You will recollect that I used the word "*social* labour", and many points are involved in this qualification of "*social*". In saying that the value of a commodity is determined by the *quantity of labour* worked up or crystallised in it, we mean the *quantity of labour necessary* for its production in a given state of society, under certain social average conditions of production, with a given social average intensity, and average skill of the labour employed. When, in England, the power-loom came to compete with the hand-loom, only half the former time of labour was wanted to convert a given amount of yarn into a yard of cotton or cloth. The poor hand-loom weaver now worked seventeen or eighteen hours daily, instead of the nine or ten hours he had worked before. Still the product of twenty hours of his labour represented now only ten social hours of labour, or ten hours of labour socially necessary for the conversion of a certain amount of yarn into textile stuffs. His product of twenty hours had, therefore, no more value than his former product of ten hours.

If then the quantity of socially necessary labour realised in commodities regulates their exchangeable values, every increase in the quantity of labour wanted for the production of a commodity must augment its value, as every diminution must lower it.

If the respective quantities of labour necessary for the production of the respective commodities remained constant, their relative values also would be constant. But such is not the case. The quantity of labour necessary for the production of a commodity changes continuously with the changes in the productive powers of the labour employed. The greater the productive powers of labour, the more produce is finished in a given time of labour; and the smaller the productive powers of labour, the less produce is finished in the same time. If, for example, in the progress of population it should become necessary to cultivate less fertile soils, the same amount of produce would be only attainable by a greater amount of labour spent, and the value of agricultural produce would consequently rise. On the other hand, if, with the modern means of production, a single spinner converts into yarn, during one working day, many thousand times the amount of cotton which he could have spun during the same time with the spinning wheel, it is evident that every single pound of cotton will absorb many thousand times less of spinning labour than it did before, and consequently, the value added by spinning to every single pound of cotton will be a thousand times less than before. The value of yarn will sink accordingly.

Apart from the different natural energies and acquired working abilities of different peoples, the productive powers of labour must principally depend:

Firstly. Upon the *natural* conditions of labour, such as fertility of soil, mines, and so forth.

Secondly. Upon the progressive improvement of the *Social Powers of Labour*, such as are derived from production on a grand scale, concentration of capital and combination of labour, subdivision of labour, machinery, improved methods, appliance of chemical and other natural agencies, shortening of time and space by means of communication and transport, and every other contrivance by which science presses natural agencies into the service of labour, and by which the social or co-operative character of labour is developed. The greater the productive powers of labour, the less labour is bestowed upon a given amount of produce; hence the smaller the value of the produce. The smaller the productive powers of labour, the more labour is bestowed upon the same amount of produce; hence the greater its value. As a general law we may, therefore, set it down that:

The values of commodities are directly as the times of labour employed in their production, and are inversely as the productive powers of the labour employed.

Having till now only spoken of *Value*, I shall add a few words about *Price*, which is a peculiar form assumed by value.

Price, taken by itself, is nothing but the *monetary expression of value*. The values of all commodities of the country, for example, are expressed in gold prices, while on the Continent they are mainly expressed in silver prices. The value of gold or silver, like that of all other commodities, is regulated by the quantity of labour necessary for getting them. You exchange a certain amount of your national products, in which a certain amount of your national labour is crystallised, for the produce of the gold and silver producing countries, in which a certain quantity of *their* labour is crystallised. It is in this way, in fact by barter, that you learn to express in gold and silver the values of all commodities, that is the respective quantities of labour bestowed upon them. Looking somewhat closer into the *monetary expression of value*, or what comes to the same, the conversion of value into price, you will find that it is a process by which you give to the *values* of all commodities an *independent* and *homogeneous form*, or by which you express them as quantities of equal social labour. So far as it is but the monetary expression of value, price has been called *natural price* by Adam Smith, "*prix nécessaire*" by the French physiocrats.

What then is the relation between *value* and *market prices*, or between *natural prices* and *market prices*? You all know that the *market price* is the *same* for all commodities of the same kind, however the conditions of production may differ for the individual producers. The market price expresses only the *average amount of social labour* necessary, under the average conditions of production, to supply the market with a certain mass of a certain article. It is calculated upon the whole lot of a commodity of a certain description.

So far the *market price* of a commodity coincides with its *value*. On the other hand, the oscillations of market prices, rising now over, sinking now under the value or natural price, depend upon the fluctuations of supply and demand. The deviations of market prices from values are continual, but as Adam Smith says:

> "The natural price . . . is the central price, to which the prices of all commodities are continually gravitating. Different accidents may sometimes keep them suspended a good deal above it, and sometimes force them down even somewhat below it. But whatever may be the obstacles which hinder them from settling in this centre of repose and continuance, they are constantly tending towards it".

I cannot now sift this matter. It suffices to say that *if* supply and demand equilibrate each other, the market prices of commodities will correspond with their natural prices, that is to say with their values, as determined by the respective quantities of labour required for their production. But supply and demand *must* constantly tend to equilibrate each other, although they do so only by compensating one fluctuation by another, a rise by a fall, and vice versa. If instead of considering only the daily fluctuations you analyse the movement of market prices for longer periods, as Mr. Tooke, for example, has done in his *History of Prices*, you will find that the fluctuations of market prices, their deviations from values, their ups and downs, paralyse and compensate each other; so that apart from the effect of monopolies and some other modifications I must now pass by, all descriptions of commodities are, on average, sold at their respective *values* or natural prices. The average periods during which the fluctuations of market prices compensate each other are different for different kinds of commodities, because with one kind it is easier to adapt supply to demand than with the other.

If then, speaking broadly, and embracing somewhat longer periods, all descriptions of commodities sell at their respective values, it is nonsense to suppose that profit, not in individual cases; but that the constant and usual profits of different trades spring from *surcharging* the prices of commodities, or selling them at a price over and above their *value*. The absurdity of this notion becomes evident if it is generalised. What a man would constantly win as a seller he would constantly lose as a purchaser. It would not do to say that there are men who are buyers without being sellers, or consumers without being producers. What these people pay to the producers, they must first get from them for nothing. If a man first takes your money and afterwards returns that money in buying your commodities, you will never enrich yourselves by selling your commodities too dear to that same man. This sort of transaction might diminish a loss, but would never help in realising a profit.

To explain, therefore, the *general nature of profits*, you must start from the theorem that, on an average, commodities are *sold at their real value*, and *that profits are derived from selling them at their values*, that is, in proportion to the quantity of labour realised in them. If you cannot explain profit upon this supposition, you cannot explain it at all. This seems paradox and contrary to everyday observation. It is also paradox that the earth moves round the sun, and that water consists of two highly inflammable gases. Scientific truth is always paradox, if judged by everyday experience, which catches only the delusive appearance of things.

VII LABOURING POWER

Having now, as far as it could be done in such a cursory manner, analysed the nature of *Value*, of the *Value of any commodity whatever*, we must turn our attention to the specific *Value of Labour*. And here, again, I must startle you by a seeming paradox. All of you feel sure that what they daily sell is their Labour; that, therefore, Labour has a Price, and that, the price of a commodity being only the monetary expression of its value, there must certainly exist such a thing as the *Value of Labour*. However, there exists no such thing as the *Value of Labour* in the common acceptance of the word. We have seen that the amount of necessary labour crystallised in a commodity constitutes its value. Now, applying this notion of value, how could we define, say, the value of a ten hours' working day? How much labour is contained in that day? Ten hours' labour. To say that the value of a ten hours' working day is equal to ten hours' labour, or the quantity of labour contained in it, would be a tautological and, moreover, a nonsensical expression. Of course, having once found out the true but hidden sense of the expression "*Value of Labour*", we shall be able to interpret this irrational, and seemingly impossible application of value, in the same way that, having once made sure of the real movement of the celestial bodies, we shall be able to explain their apparent or merely phenomenal movements.

What the working man sells is not directly his *Labour*, but his *Labouring Power*, the temporary disposal of which he makes over to the capitalist. This is so much the case that I do not know whether by the English Laws, but certainly by some Continental Laws, the *maximum time* is fixed for which a man is allowed to sell his labouring power. If allowed to do so for any indefinite period whatever, slavery would be immediately restored. Such a sale, if it comprised his lifetime, for example, would make him at once the lifelong slave of his employer.

One of the oldest economists and most original philosophers of England – Thomas Hobbes – has already, in his *Leviathan*, instinctively hit upon this point overlooked by all his successors. He says: "*The value or worth of a man* is, as in all other things, his *price*: that is so much as would be given for the *Use of his Power*". Proceeding from this basis, we shall be able to determine the *Value of Labour* as that of all other commodities.

But before doing so, we might ask, how does this strange phenomenon arise, that we find on the market a set of buyers, possessed of land, machinery, raw material, and the means of subsistence, all of them, save land in its crude state, the *products of labour*, and on the other hand, a set of sellers who have nothing to sell except their labouring power, their working arms and brains? That the one set buys continually in order to make a profit and enrich themselves, while the other set continually sells in order to earn their livelihood? The inquiry into this question would be an inquiry into what the economists call "*Previous or Original Accumulation*", but which ought to be called *Original Expropriation*. We should find that this so-called *Original Accumulation* means nothing but a series of historical processes, resulting in a *Decomposition of the Original Union* existing *between the Labouring Man and his Instruments of Labour.* Such an inquiry, however, lies beyond the pale of my present subject. The *Separation* between the Man of Labour and the Instruments of Labour once established, such a state of things will maintain itself and reproduce itself upon a constantly increasing scale, until a new and fundamental revolution in the mode of production should again overturn it, and restore the original union in a new historical form.

What, then, is the *Value of Labouring Power*?

Like that of every other commodity, its value is determined by the quantity of labour necessary to produce it. The labouring power of a man exists only in his living individuality. A certain mass of necessaries must be consumed by a man to grow up and maintain his life. But the man, like the machine, will wear out, and must be replaced by another man. Beside the mass of necessaries required for *his own* maintenance, he wants another amount of necessaries to bring up a certain quota of children that are to replace him on the labour market and to perpetuate the race of labourers. Moreover, to develop his labouring power, and acquire a given skill, another amount of values must be spent. For our purpose it suffices to consider only *average* labour, the costs of whose education and development are vanishing magnitudes. Still I must seize upon this occasion to state that, as the costs of producing labouring powers of different quality differ, so must differ the values of the labouring powers employed in different trades. The cry for an *equality of wages* rests, therefore, upon a mistake, is an *insane* wish never to be fulfilled. It is an offspring of that false and superficial radicalism that accepts premises and tries to evade conclusions. Upon the basis of the wages system the value of labouring power is settled like that of every other commodity; and as different kinds of labouring power have different values, or require different quantities of labour for their production, they *must* fetch different prices in the labour market. To clamour for *equal or even equitable retribution* on the basis of the wages system is the same as to clamour for *freedom* on the basis of the slavery system. What you think just or equitable is out of the question. The question is: What is necessary and unavoidable with a given system of production?

After what has been said, it will be seen that the *value of labouring power* is determined by the *value of the necessaries* required to produce, develop, maintain, and perpetuate the labouring power.

VIII PRODUCTION OF SURPLUS VALUE

Now suppose that the average amount of the daily necessaries of a labouring man require *six hours of average labour* for their production. Suppose, moreover, six hours of average labour to be also realised in a quantity of gold equal to 3*s*. Then 3*s*. would be the *Price*, or the monetary expression of the *Daily Value* of that man's *Labouring Power*. If he worked daily six hours he would daily produce a value sufficient to buy the average amount of his daily necessaries, or to maintain himself as a labouring man.

But our man is a wages labourer. He must, therefore, sell his labouring power to a capitalist. If he sells it at 3*s*. daily, or 18*s*. weekly, he sells it at its value. Suppose him to be a spinner. If he works six hours daily he will add to the cotton a value of 3*s*. daily. This value, daily added by him, would be an exact equivalent for the wages, or the price of his labouring power, received daily. But in that case *no surplus value* or *surplus produce* whatever would go to the capitalist. Here, then, we come to the rub.

In buying the labouring power of the workman, and paying its value, the capitalist, like every other purchaser, has acquired the right to consume or use the commodity bought. You consume or use the labouring power of a man by making him work, as you consume or use a machine by making it run. By paying the daily or weekly value of the labouring power of the workman, the capitalist has, therefore, acquired the right to use or make that labouring power during the *whole day or week*. The working day or the working week has, of course, certain limits, but those we shall afterwards look more closely at.

For the present I want to turn your attention to one decisive point.

The *value* of the labouring power is determined by the quantity of labour necessary to maintain or reproduce it, but the *use* of that labouring power is only limited by the active energies and physical strength of the labourer. The daily or weekly *value* of the labouring power is quite distinct from the daily or weekly exercise of that power, the same as the food a horse wants and the time it can carry the horseman are quite distinct. The quantity of labour by which the *value* of the workman's labouring power is limited forms by no means a limit to the quantity of labour which his labouring power is apt to perform. Take the example of our spinner. We have seen that, to daily reproduce his labouring power, he must daily reproduce a value of three shillings, which he will do by working six hours daily. But this does not disable him from working ten or twelve or more hours a day. But by paying the daily or weekly *value* of the spinner's labouring power the capitalist has acquired the right of using that labouring power during *the whole day or week*. He will, therefore, make him work say, daily, *twelve* hours. *Over and above* the six hours required to replace his wages, or the value of his labouring power, he will, therefore, have to work *six other hours*, which I shall call hours of *surplus labour*, which surplus labour will realise itself in a *surplus value* and a *surplus produce*. If our spinner, for example, by his daily labour of six hours, added three shillings' value to the cotton, a value forming an exact equivalent to his wages, he will, in twelve hours, add six shillings' worth to the cotton, and produce a *proportional surplus of yarn*. As he has sold his labouring power to the capitalist, the whole value of produce created by him belongs to the capitalist, the owner *pro tem*. of his labouring power. By advancing three shillings, the capitalist will, therefore, realise a value of six shillings, because, advancing a value in which six hours of labour are crystallised, he will receive in return a value in which twelve hours of labour are crystallised. By repeating this same process daily, the capitalist will daily advance three shillings and daily pocket six shillings, one half of which will go to pay wages anew, and the other half of which will form *surplus value*, for which the capitalist pays no equivalent. It is this *sort of exchange between capital and labour* upon which capitalistic production, or the wages system, is founded, and which must constantly result in reproducing the working man as a working man, and the capitalist as a capitalist.

The rate of surplus value, all other circumstances remaining the same, will depend on the proportion between that part of the working day necessary to reproduce the value of the labouring power and the *surplus time* or *surplus labour* performed for the capitalist. It will, therefore, depend on the *ratio in which the working day is prolonged over and above that extent*, by working which the working man would only reproduce the value of his labouring power, or replace his wages.

IX VALUE OF LABOUR

We must now return to the expression, "*Value, or Price of Labour*". We have seen that, in fact, it is only the value of the labouring power, measured by the values of commodities necessary for its maintenance. But since the workman receives his wages *after* his labour is perıformed, and knows, moreover, that what he actually gives to the capitalist is his labour, the value or price of his labouring power necessarily appears to him as the *price* or *value of his labour itself*. If the price of his labouring power is three shillings, in which six hours of labour are realised, and if he works twelve hours, he necessarily considers these three shillings as the value or price of twelve hours of labour, although these twelve hours of labour realise themselves in a value of six shillings. A double consequence flows from this.

Firstly. *The value or price of the labouring power* takes the semblance of the *price or value of labour itself*, although, strictly speaking, value and price of labour are senseless terms.

Secondly. Although one part only of the workman's daily labour is *paid*, while the other part is *unpaid*, and while that unpaid or surplus labour constitutes exactly the fund out of which *surplus value* or *profit* is formed, it seems as if the aggregate labour was paid labour.

This false appearance distinguishes wages labour from other *historical* forms of labour. On the basis of the wages system even the *unpaid* labour seems to be *paid* labour. With the *slave*, on the contrary, even that part of his labour which is paid appears to be unpaid. Of course, in order to work the slave must live, and one part of his working day goes to replace the value of his own maintenance. But since no bargain is struck between him and his master, and no acts of selling and buying are going on between the two parties, all his labour seems to be given away for nothing.

Take, on the other hand, the peasant serf, such as he, I might say, until yesterday existed in the whole of East of Europe. This peasant worked, for example, three days for himself on his own field or the field allotted to him, and the three subsequent days he performed compulsory and gratuitous labour on the estate of his lord. Here, then, the paid and unpaid parts of labour were sensibly separated, separated in time and space; and our Liberals overflowed with moral indignation at the preposterous notion of making a man work for nothing.

In point of fact, however, whether a man works three days of the week for himself on his own field and three days for nothing on the estate of his lord, or whether he works in the factory or the workshop six hours daily for himself and six for his employer, comes to the same, although in the latter case the paid and unpaid portions of labour are inseparably mixed up with each other, and the nature of the whole transaction is completely masked by the *intervention of a contract* and the *pay* received at the end of the week. The gratuitous labour appears to be voluntarily given in the one instance, and to be compulsory in the other. That makes all the difference.

In using the word "*value of labour*", I shall only use it as a popular slang term for "*value of labouring power*".

X PROFIT IS MADE BY SELLING A COMMODITY AT ITS VALUE

Suppose an average hour of labour to be realised in a value equal to sixpence, or twelve average hours of labour to be realised in six shillings. Suppose, further, the value of labour to be three shillings or the produce of six hours' labour. If, then, in the raw material, machinery, and so forth, used up in a commodity, twenty-four hours of average labour were realised, its value would amount to twelve shillings. If, moreover, the workman employed by the capitalist added twelve hours of labour to those means of production, these twelve hours would be realised in an additional value of six shillings. The *total value of the product* would, therefore, amount to thirty-six hours of realised labour, and be equal to eighteen shillings. But as the value of labour, or the wages paid to the workman, would be three shillings only, no equivalent would have been paid by the capitalist for the six hours of surplus labour worked by the workman, and realised in the value of the commodity. By selling this commodity at its value for eighteen shillings, the capitalist would, therefore, realise a value of three shillings, for which had paid no equivalent. These three shillings would constitute the surplus value or profit pocketed by him. The capitalist would consequently realise the profit of three shillings, not by selling his commodity at a price *over and above* its value, but by selling it *at its real value.*

The value of a commodity is determined by the *total quantity of labour* contained in it. But part of that quantity of labour is realised in a value for which and equivalent has been paid in the form of wages; part of it is realised in a value for which *no* equivalent has been paid. Part of the labour contained in the commodity is *paid* labour; part is *unpaid* labour. By selling, therefore, the commodity *at its value*, that is, as the crystallisation of the *total quantity of labour* bestowed upon it, the capitalist must necessarily sell it at a profit. He sells not only what has cost him an equivalent, but he sells also what has cost him nothing, although it has cost his workman labour. The cost of the commodity to the capitalist and its real cost are different things. I repeat, therefore, that normal and average profits are made by selling commodities not *above*, but *at their real values*.

XI THE DIFFERENT PARTS INTO WHICH SURPLUS VALUE IS DECOMPOSED

The *surplus value*, or that part of the total value of the commodity in which the *surplus labour* or *unpaid labour* of the working man is realised, I call *Profit*. The whole of that profit is not pocketed by the employing capitalist. The monopoly of land enables the landlord to take one part of that *surplus value*, under the name of *rent*, whether the land is used for agriculture, buildings or railways, or for any other productive purpose. On the other hand, the very fact that the possession of the *instruments of labour* enables the employing capitalist to produce a *surplus value*, or, what comes to the same, *to appropriate to himself a certain amount of unpaid labour*, enables the owner of the means of labour, which he lends wholly or partly to the employing capitalist – enables, in one word, the money-lending capitalist to claim for himself under the name of *interest* another part of that surplus value, so that there remains to the employing capitalist *as such* only what is called *industrial* or *commercial profit*.

By what laws this division of the total amount of surplus value amongst the three categories of people is regulated is a question quite foreign to our subject. This much, however, results from what has been stated.

Rent, Interest, and Industrial Profit are only *different names for different parts* of the *surplus value* of the commodity, or the *unpaid labour enclosed in it*, and they are *equally derived from this source and from this source alone*. They are not derived from *land* as such or from *capital* as such, but land and capital enable their owners to get their respective shares out of the surplus value extracted by the employing capitalist from the labourer. For the labourer himself it is a matter of subordinate importance whether that surplus value, the result of his surplus labour, or unpaid labour, is altogether pocketed by the employing capitalist, or whether the latter is obliged to pay portions of it, under the name of rent and interest, away to third parties. Suppose the employing capitalist to use only his own capital and to be his own landlord, then the whole surplus value would go into his pocket.

It is the employing capitalist who immediately extracts from the labourer this surplus value, whatever part of it he may ultimately be able to keep for himself. Upon this relation, therefore between the employing capitalist and the wages labourer the whole wages system and the whole present system of production hinge. Some of the citizens who took part in our debate were, there, wrong in trying to mince matters, and to treat this fundamental relation between the employing capitalist and the working man as a secondary question, although they were right in stating that, under given circumstances, a rise of prices might affect in very unequal degrees the employing capitalist, the landlord, the moneyed capitalist, and, if you please, the tax-gatherer.

Another consequence follows from what has been stated.

That part of the value of the commodity which represents only the value of the raw materials, the machinery, in one word, the value of the means of production used up, forms *no revenue* at all, but replaces *only capital*. But, apart from this, it is false that the other part of the value of the commodity *which forms revenue*, or may be spent in the form of wages, profits, rent, interest, is *constituted* by the value of wages, the value of rent, the value of profits, and so forth. We shall, in the first instance, discard wages, and only treat industrial profits, interest, and rent. We have just seen that the *surplus value* contained in the commodity, or that part of its value in which *unpaid labour* is realised, resolves itself into different fractions, bearing three different names. But it would be quite the reverse of the truth to say that its value is *composed* of, or *formed* by, the *addition* of the *independent values of these three constituents*.

If one hour of labour realises itself in a value of sixpence, if the working day of the labourer comprises twelve hours, if half of this time is unpaid labour, that surplus labour will add to the commodity a *surplus value* of three shillings, that is of value for which no equivalent has been paid. This surplus value of three shillings constitutes the *whole fund* which the employing capitalist may divide, in whatever proportions, with the landlord and the money-lender. The value of these three shillings constitutes the limit of the value they have to divide amongst them. But it is not the employing capitalist who adds to the value of the commodity an arbitrary value for his profit, to which another value is added for the landlord, and so forth, so that the addition of these arbitrarily fixed values would constitute the total value. You see, therefore, the fallacy of the popular notion, which confounds the *decomposition of a given value* into three parts, with the *formation* of that value by the addition of three *independent* values, thus converting the aggregate value, from which rent, profit, and interest are derived, into an arbitrary magnitude.

If the total profit realised by a capitalist is equal to £100, we call this sum, considered as *absolute* magnitude, the *amount of profit*. But if we calculate the ratio which those £100 bear to the capital advanced, we call this *relative* magnitude, the *rate of profit*. It is evident that this rate of profit may be expressed in a double way.

Suppose £100 to be the capital *advanced in wages*. If the surplus value created is also £100 – and this would show us that half the working day of the labourer consists of *unpaid* labour – and if we measured this profit by the value of the capital advanced in wages, we should say that the *rate of profit* amounted to one hundred per cent, because the value advanced would be one hundred and the value realised would be two hundred.

If, on the other hand, we should not only consider the *capital advanced in wages*, but the *total capital* advanced, say, for example, £500, of which £400 represented the value of raw materials, machinery, and so forth, we should say that the *rate of profit* amounted only to twenty per cent, because the profit of one hundred would be but the fifth part of the *total* capital advanced.

The first mode of expressing the rate of profit is the only one which shows you the real ratio between paid and unpaid labour, the real degree of the *exploitation* (you must allow me this French word) *of labour*. The other mode of expression is that in common use, and is, indeed, appropriate for certain purposes. At all events, it is very useful for concealing the degree in which the capitalist extracts gratuitous labour from the workman.

In the remarks I have still to make I shall use the word *Profit* for the whole amount of the surplus value extracted by the capitalist without any regard to the division of that surplus value between different parties, and in using the words *Rate of Profit*, I shall always measure profits by the value of the capital advanced in wages.

XII GENERAL RELATION OF PROFITS, WAGES AND PRICES

Deduct from the value of a commodity the value replacing the value of the raw materials and other means of production used upon it, that is to say, deduct the value representing the *past* labour contained in it, and the remainder of its value will resolve into the quantity of labour added by the working man *last* employed. If that working man works twelve hours daily, if twelve hours of average labour crystallise themselves in an amount of gold equal to six shillings, this additional value of six shillings is the *only* value his labour will have created. This given value, determined by the time of his labour, is the only fund from which both he and the capitalist have to draw their respective shares or dividends, the only value to be divided into wages and profits. It is evident that this value itself will not be altered by the variable proportions in which it may be divided amongst the two parties. There will also be nothing changed if in the place of one working man you put the whole working population, twelve million working days, for example, instead of one.

Since the capitalist and workman have only to divide this limited value, that is, the value measured by the total labour of the working man, the more the one gets the less will the other get, and *vice versa*. Whenever a quantity is given, one part of it will increase inversely as the other decreases. If the wages change, profits will change in an opposite direction. If wages fall, profits will rise; and if wages rise, profits will fall. If the working man, on our former supposition, gets three shillings, equal to one half of the value he has created, or if his whole working day consists half of paid, half of unpaid labour, the *rate of profit* will be 100 per cent, because the capitalist would also get three shillings. If the working man receives only two shillings, or works only one-third of the whole day for himself, the capitalist will get four shillings, and the rate of profit will be 200 per cent. If the working man receives four shillings, the capitalist will only receive two, and the rate of profit would sink to 50 percent, but all these variations will not affect the value of the commodity. A general rise of wages would, therefore, result in a fall of the general rate of profit, but not affect values.

But although the values of commodities, which must ultimately regulate their market prices, are exclusively determined by the total quantities of labour fixed in them, and not by the division of that quantity into paid and unpaid labour, it by no means follows that the values of the single commodities, *or* lots of commodities, produced during twelve hours, for example, will remain constant. The *number* or mass of commodities produced in a given time of labour, or by a given quantity of labour, depends upon the *productive power* of the labour employed, and not upon its *extent* or length. With one degree of the productive power of spinning labour, for example, a working day of twelve hours may produce twelve pounds of yarn, with a lesser degree of productive power only two pounds. If then twelve hours' average labour were realised in the value of six shillings in the one case, the twelve pounds of yarn would cost six shillings, in the other case the two pounds of yarn would also cost six shillings.

One pound of yarn would, therefore, cost sixpence in the one case, and three shillings in the other. The difference of price would result from the difference in the productive powers of labour employed. One hour of labour would be realised in one pound of yarn with the greater productive power, while with the smaller productive power, six hours of labour would be realised in one pound of yarn. The price of a pound of yarn would, in the one instance, be only sixpence, although wages were relatively high and the rate of profit low; it would be three shillings in the other instance, although wages were low and the rate of profit high. This would be so because the price of the pound of yarn is regulated by the *total amount of labour worked up in it*, and not by the *proportional division of that total amount into paid and unpaid labour*. The fact I have mentioned before that high-priced labour may produce cheap, and low-priced labour may produce dear commodities, loses, therefore, its paradoxical appearance. It is only the expression of the general law that the value of a commodity is regulated by the quantity of labour worked up in it, and the quantity of labour worked up in it depends altogether upon the productive powers of labour employed, and will therefore, vary with every variation in the productivity of labour.

XIII MAIN CASES OF ATTEMPTS AT RAISING WAGES OR RESISTING THEIR FALL

Let us now seriously consider the main cases in which a rise of wages is attempted or a reduction of wages resisted.

1. We have seen that the *value of the labouring power*, or in more popular parlance, the *value of labour*, is determined by the value

of necessaries, or the quantity of labour required to produce them. If, then, in a given country the value of the daily average necessaries of the labourer represented six hours of labour expressed in three shillings, the labourer would have to work six hours daily to produce an equivalent for this daily maintenance. If the whole working day was twelve hours, the capitalist would pay him the value of his labour by paying him three shillings. Half the working day would be unpaid labour, and the rate of profit would amount to 100 per cent. But now suppose that, consequent upon a decrease of productivity, more labour should be wanted to produce, say, the same amount of agricultural produce, so that the price of the average daily necessaries should rise from three to four shillings. In that case the *value of labour* would rise by one third, or 33 1/3 per cent. Eight hours of the working day would be required to produce an equivalent for the daily maintenance of the labourer, according to his old standard of living. The surplus labour would therefore sink from six hours to four, and the rate of profit from 100 to 50 per cent. But in insisting upon a rise of wages, the labourer would only insist upon getting the *increased value of his labour*, like every other seller of a commodity, who, the costs of his commodities having increased, tries to get its increased value paid. If wages did not rise, or not sufficiently rise, to compensate for the increased values of necessaries, the *price* of labour would sink below the *value of labour*, and the labourer's standard of life would deteriorate.

But a change might also take place in an opposite direction. By virtue of the increased productivity of labour, the same amount of the average daily necessaries might sink from three to two shillings, or only four hours out of the working day, instead of six, be wanted to reproduce an equivalent for the value of the daily necessaries. The working man would now be able to buy with two shillings as many necessaries as he did before with three shillings. Indeed, the *value of labour* would have sunk, but diminished value would command the same amount of commodities as before. Then profits would rise from three to four shillings, and the rate of profit from 100 to 200 per cent. Although the labourer's absolute standard of life would have remained the same, his *relative* wages, and therewith his *relative social position*, as compared with that of the capitalist, would have been lowered. If the working man should resist that reduction of relative wages, he would only try to get some share in the increased productive powers of his own labour, and to maintain his former relative position in the social scale. Thus, after the abolition of the Corn Laws, and in flagrant violation of the most solemn pledges given during the anti-corn law agitation, the English factory lords generally reduced wages ten per cent. The resistance of the workmen was at first baffled, but, consequent upon circumstances I cannot now enter upon, the ten per cent lost were afterwards regained.

2. The *values* of necessaries, and consequently the *value of labour*, might remain the same, but a change might occur in their *money prices*, consequent upon a previous change in the *value of money*.

By the discovery of more fertile mines and so forth, two ounces of gold might, for example, cost no more labour to produce than one ounce did before. The *value* of gold would then be depreciated by one half, or fifty per cent. As the *values* of all other commodities would then be expressed in twice their former *money prices*, so also the same with the *value of labour*. Twelve hours of labour, formerly expressed in six shillings, would now be expressed in twelve shillings. If the working man's wages should remain three shillings, instead of rising to six shillings, the *money price of his labour* would only be equal to *half the value of his labour*, and his standard of life would fearfully deteriorate. This would also happen in a greater or lesser degree if his wages should rise, but not proportionately to the fall in the value of gold. In such a case nothing would have been changed, either in the productive powers of labour, or in supply and demand, or in values. Nothing would have changed except the money *names* of those values. To say that in such a case the workman ought not to insist upon a proportionate rise of wages, is to say that he must be content to be paid with names, instead of with things. All past history proves that whenever such a depreciation of money occurs, the capitalists are on the alert to seize this opportunity for defrauding the workman. A very large school of political economists assert that, consequent upon the new discoveries of gold lands, the better working of silver mines, and the cheaper supply of quicksilver, the value of precious metals has again depreciated. This would explain the general and simultaneous attempts on the Continent at a rise of wages.

3. We have till now supposed that the *working day* has given limits. The working day, however, has, by itself, no constant limits. It is the constant tendency of capital to stretch it to its utmost physically possible length, because in the same degree surplus labour, and consequently the profit resulting therefrom, will be increased. The more capital succeeds in prolonging the working day, the greater the amount of other peoples' labour it will appropriate. During the seventeenth and even the first two-thirds of the eighteenth century a ten hours' working day was the normal working day all over England. During the anti-Jacobin

war, which was in fact a war waged by the British barons against the British working masses, capital celebrated its bacchanalia, and prolonged the working day from ten to twelve, fourteen, eighteen hours. Malthus, by no means a man whom you would suspect of a maudlin sentimentalism declared in a pamphlet, published about 1815, that if this sort of thing was to go on the life of the nation would be attacked at its very source. A few years before the general introduction of newly-invented machinery, about 1765, a pamphlet appeared in England under the title, *An Essay On Trade*. The anonymous author, an avowed enemy of the working classes, declaims on the necessity of expanding the limits of the working day. Amongst other means to this end, he proposes *working houses*, which, he says, ought to be "Houses of Terror". And what is the length of the working he prescribes for these "Houses of Terror"? *Twelve hours*, the very same time which in 1832 was declared by capitalists, political economists, and ministers to be not only the existing but the necessary time of labour for a child under twelve years.

By selling his labouring power, and he must do so under the present system, the working man makes over to the capitalist the consumption of that power, but within certain rational limits. He sells his labouring power in order to maintain it, apart from its natural wear and tear, but not to destroy it. In selling his labouring power at its daily or weekly value, it is understood that in one day or one week that labouring power shall not be submitted to two days' or two weeks' waste or wear and tear. Take a machine worth £1000. If it is used up in ten years it will add to the value of the commodities in whose production it assists £100 yearly. If it is used up in five years it will add £200 yearly, or the value of its annual wear and tear is in inverse ratio to the quickness with which it is consumed. But this distinguishes the working man from the machine. Machinery does not wear out exactly in the same ratio in which it is used. Man, on the contrary, decays in a greater ratio than would be visible from the mere numerical addition of work.

In their attempts at reducing the working day to its former rational dimensions, or, where they cannot enforce a legal fixation of a normal working day, at checking overwork by a rise of wages, a rise not only in proportion to the surplus time exacted, but in a greater proportion, working men fulfill only a duty to themselves and their race. They only set limits to the tyrannical usurpations of capital. Time is the room of human development. A man who has no free time to dispose of, whose whole lifetime, apart from the mere physical interruptions by sleep, meals, and so forth, is absorbed by his labour for the capitalist, is less than a beast of burden. He is a mere machine for producing Foreign Wealth, broken in body and brutalised in mind. Yet the whole history of modern industry shows that capital, if not checked, will recklessly and ruthlessly work to cast down the whole working class to this utmost state of degradation.

In prolonging the working day the capitalist may pay *higher wages* and still lower the *value of labour*, if the rise of wages does not correspond to the greater amount of labour extracted, and the quicker decay of the labouring power thus caused. This may be done in another way. Your middle-class statisticians will tell you, for instance, that the average wages of factory families in Lancashire has risen. They forget that instead of the labour of the man, the head of the family, his wife and perhaps three or four children are now thrown under the Juggernaut wheels of capital, and that the rise of the aggregate wages does not correspond to the aggregate surplus labour extracted from the family.

Even with given limits of the working day, such as they now exist in all branches of industry subjected to the factory laws, a rise of wages may become necessary, if only to keep up the old standard *value of labour*. By increasing the *intensity* of labour, a man may be made to expend as much vital force in one hour as he formerly did in two. This has, to a certain degree, been effected in the trades, placed under the Factory Acts, by the acceleration of machinery, and the greater number of working machines which a single individual has now to superintend. If the increase in the intensity of labour or the mass of labour spent in an hour keeps some fair proportion to the decrease in the extent of the working day, the working man will still be the winner. If this limit is overshot, he loses in one form what he has gained in another, and ten hours of labour may then become as ruinous as twelve hours were before. In checking this tendency of capital, by struggling for a rise of wages corresponding to the rising intensity of labour, the working man only resists the depreciation of his labour and the deterioration of his race.

4. All of you know that, from reasons I have not now to explain, capitalistic production moves through certain periodical cycles. It moves through a state of quiescence, growing animation, prosperity, overtrade, crisis, and stagnation. The market prices of commodities, and the market rates of profit, follow these phases, now sinking below their averages, now rising above them. Considering the whole cycle, you will find that one deviation of the market price is being compensated by the other, and that, taking the average of the cycle, the market prices of commodities are regulated by their values. Well! During the phases of sinking market prices and the phases of crisis and stagnation, the working man, if not thrown out of employment altogether,

is sure to have his wages lowered. Not to be defrauded, he must, even with such a fall of market prices, debate with the capitalist in what proportional degree a fall of wages has become necessary. If, during the phases of prosperity, when extra profits are made, he did not battle for a rise of wages, he would, taking the average of one industrial cycle, not even receive his *average wages*, or the *value* of his labour. It is the utmost height of folly to demand, that while his wages are necessarily affected by the adverse phases of the cycle, he should exclude himself from compensation during the prosperous phases of the cycle. Generally, the *values* of all commodities are only realised by the compensation of the continuously changing market prices, springing from the continuous fluctuations of demand and supply. On the basis of the present system labour is only a commodity like others. It must, therefore, pass through the same fluctuations to fetch an average price corresponding to its value. It would be absurd to treat it on the one hand as a commodity, and to want on the other hand to exempt it from the laws which regulate the prices of commodities. The slave receives a permanent and fixed amount of maintenance; the wage-labourer does not. He must try to get a rise of wages in the one instance, if only to compensate for a fall of wages in the other. If he resigned himself to accept the will, the dictates of the capitalist as a permanent economical law, he would share in all the miseries of the slave, without the security of the slave.

5. In all the cases I have considered, and they form ninety-nine out of a hundred, you have seen that a struggle for a rise of wages follows only in the track of *previous* changes, and is the necessary offspring of previous changes in the amount of production, the productive powers of labour, the value of labour, the value of

money, the extent or the intensity of labour extracted, the fluctuations of market prices, dependent upon the fluctuations of demand and supply, and consistent with the different phases of the industrial cycle; in one word, as reactions of labour against the previous action of capital. By treating the struggle for a rise of wages independently of all these circumstances, by looking only upon the change of wages, and overlooking all the other changes from which they emanate, you proceed from a false premise in order to arrive at false conclusions.

XIV THE STRUGGLE BETWEEN CAPITAL AND LABOUR AND ITS RESULTS

1. Having shown that the periodical resistance on the part of the working men against a reduction of wages, and their periodical attempts at getting a rise of wages, are inseparable from the wages system, and dictated by the very fact of labour being assimilated to commodities, and therefore subject to the laws, regulating the general movement of prices; having furthermore, shown that a general rise of wages would result in a fall in the general rate of profit, but not affect the average prices of commodities, or their values, the question now ultimately arises, how far, in this incessant struggle between capital and labour, the latter is likely to prove successful.

I might answer by a generalisation, and say that, as with all other commodities, so with labour, its *market price* will, in the long run, adapt itself to its *value*; that, therefore, despite all the ups and downs, and do what he may, the working man will, on an average, only receive the value of his labour, which resolves into the value of his labouring power, which is determined by the value of the necessaries required for its maintenance and reproduction, which value of necessaries finally is regulated by the quantity of labour wanted to produce them.

But there are some peculiar features which distinguish the *value of the labouring power, or the value of labour*, from the values of all other commodities. The value of the labouring power is formed by two elements – the one merely physical, the other historical or social. Its *ultimate limit* is determined by the *physical* element, that is to say, to maintain and reproduce itself, to perpetuate its physical existence, the working class must receive the necessaries absolutely indispensable for living and multiplying. The *value* of those indispensable necessaries forms, therefore, the ultimate limit of the *value of labour*. On the other hand, the length of the working day is also limited by ultimate, although very elastic boundaries. Its ultimate limit is given by the physical force of the labouring man. If the daily exhaustion of his vital forces exceeds a certain degree, it cannot be exerted anew, day by day. However, as I said, this limit is very elastic. A quick succession of unhealthy and short-lived generations will keep the labour market as well supplied as a series of vigorous and long-lived generations.

Besides this mere physical element, the value of labour is in every country determined by a *traditional standard of life*. It is not mere physical life, but it is the satisfaction of certain wants springing from the social conditions in which people are placed and reared up. The English standard of life may be reduced to the Irish standard; the standard of life of a German peasant to that of a Livonian peasant. The important part which historical tradition and social habitude play in this respect, you may learn from Mr Thornton's work on *Over-population*, where he shows that the average wages in different agricultural districts of

England still nowadays differ more or less according to the more or less favourable circumstances under which the districts have emerged from the state of serfdom.

This historical or social element, entering into the value of labour, may be expanded, or contracted, or altogether extinguished, so that nothing remains but the *physical limit*. During the time of the anti-Jacobin war, undertaken, as the incorrigible tax-eater and sinecurist, old George Rose, used to say, to save the comforts of our holy religion from the inroads of the French infidels, the honest English farmers, so tenderly handled in a former chapter of ours, depressed the wages of the agricultural labourers even beneath that *mere physical minimum*, but made up by Poor Laws the remainder necessary for the physical perpetuation of the race. This was a glorious way to convert the wages labourer into a slave, and Shakespeare's proud yeoman into a pauper.

By comparing the standard wages or values of labour in different countries, and by comparing them in different historical epochs of the same country, you will find that the *value of labour* itself is not a fixed but a variable magnitude, even supposing the values of all other commodities to remain constant.

A similar comparison would prove that not only the *market rates* of profit change, but its *average* rates.

But as to *profits*, there exists no law which determines their *minimum*. We cannot say what is the ultimate limit of their decrease. And why cannot we fix that limit? Because, although we can fix the *minimum* of wages, we cannot fix their *maximum*. We can only say that, the limits of the working day being given, the *maximum* of profit corresponds to the *physical minimum* of wages; and that wages being given, the *maximum of profit* corresponds to such a prolongation of the working day as is compatible with the physical forces of the labourer. The maximum of profit is, therefore, limited by the physical minimum of wages and the physical maximum of the working day. It is evident that between the two limits of the *maximum rate of profit* an immense scale of variations is possible. The fixation of its actual degree is only settled by the continuous struggle between capital and labour, the capitalist constantly tending to reduce wages to their physical minimum, and to extend the working day to its physical maximum, while the working man constantly presses in the opposite direction.

The matter resolves itself into a question of the respective powers of the combatants.

2. As to the *limitation of the working day* in England, as in all other countries, it has never been settled except by *legislative interference*. Without the working men's continuous pressure from without that interference would never have taken place. But at all events, the result was not to be attained by private settlement between the working men and the capitalists. This very necessity of *general political action* affords the proof that in its merely economical action capital is the stronger side.

As to the *limits* of the *value of labour*, its actual settlement always depends upon supply and demand, I mean the demand for labour on the part of capital, and the supply of labour by the working men. In colonial countries the law of supply and demand favours the working man. Hence the relatively high standard of wages in the United States. Capital may there try its utmost. It cannot prevent the labour market from being continuously emptied by the continuous conversion of wages labourers into independent, self-sustaining peasants. The position of wages labourer is for a very large part of the American people but a probational state, which they are sure to leave within a longer or shorter term. To mend this colonial state of things the paternal British Government accepted for some time what is called the modern colonisation theory, which consists in putting an artificial high price upon colonial land, in order to prevent the too quick conversion of the wages labourer into the independent peasant.

But let us now come to old civilised countries, in which capital domineers over the whole process of production. Take, for example, the rise in England of agricultural wages from 1849 to 1859. What was its consequence? The farmers could not, as our friend Weston would have advised them, raise the value of wheat, nor even its market prices. They had, on the contrary, to submit to their fall. But during these eleven years they introduced machinery of all sorts, adopted more scientific methods, converted part of arable land into pasture, increased the size of farms, and with this the scale of production, and by these and other processes diminishing the demand for labour by increasing its productive power, made the agricultural population again relatively redundant. This is the general method in which a reaction, quicker or slower, of capital against a rise of wages takes place in old, settled countries. Ricardo has justly remarked that machinery is in constant competition with labour, and can often be only introduced when the price of labour has reached a certain height, but the appliance of machinery is but one of the many methods for increasing the productive powers of labour. The very same development which makes common labour relatively redundant simplifies, on the other hand, skilled labour, and thus depreciates it.

The same law obtains in another form. With the development of the productive powers of labour the accumulation of capital will be accelerated, even despite a relatively high rate of wages. Hence, one might infer, as Adam Smith, in whose days modern industry was still in its infancy, did infer, that the accelerated accumulation of capital must turn the balance in favour of the working man, by securing a growing demand for his labour. From this same standpoint many contemporary writers have wondered that English capital having grown in that last twenty years so much quicker than English population, wages should not have been more enhanced. But simultaneously with the progress of accumulation there takes place a *progressive change* in the *composition of capital.* That part of the aggregate capital which consists of fixed capital, machinery, raw materials, means of production in all possible forms, progressively increases as compared with the other part of capital, which is laid out in wages or in the purchase of labour. This law has been stated in a more or less accurate manner by Mr. Barton, Ricardo, Sismondi, Professor Richard Jones, Professor Ramsay, Cherbuliez, and others.

If the proportion of these two elements of capital was originally one to one, it will, in the progress of industry, become five to one, and so forth. If of a total capital of 600, 300 is laid out in instruments, raw materials, and so forth, and 300 in wages, the total capital wants only to be doubled to create a demand for 600 working men instead of for 300. But if of a capital of 600, 500 is laid out in machinery, materials, and so forth, and 100 only in wages, the same capital must increase from 600 to 3,600 in order to create a demand for 600 workmen instead of 300. In the progress of industry the demand for labour keeps, therefore, no pace with the accumulation of capital. It will still increase, but increase in a constantly diminishing ratio as compared with the increase of capital.

These few hints will suffice to show that the very development of modern industry must progressively turn the scale in favour of the capitalist against the working man, and that consequently the general tendency of capitalistic production is not to raise, but to sink the average standard of wages, or to push the *value of labour* more or less to its *minimum limit*. Such being the tendency of *things* in this system, is this saying that the working class ought to renounce their resistance against the encroachments of capital, and abandon their attempts at making the best of the occasional chances for their temporary improvement? If they did, they would be degraded to one level mass of broken wretches past salvation. I think I have shown that their struggles for the standard of wages are incidents inseparable from the whole wages system, that in 99 cases out of 100 their efforts at raising wages are only efforts at maintaining the given value of labour, and that the necessity of debating their price with the capitalist is inherent to their condition of having to sell themselves as commodities. By cowardly giving way in their everyday conflict with capital, they would certainly disqualify themselves for the initiating of any larger movement.

At the same time, and quite apart from the general servitude involved in the wages system, the working class ought not to exaggerate to themselves the ultimate working of these everyday struggles. They ought not to forget that they are fighting with effects, but not with the causes of those effects; that they are retarding the downward movement, but not changing its direction; that they are applying palliatives, not curing the malady. They ought, therefore, not to be exclusively absorbed in these unavoidable guerilla fights incessantly springing up from the never ceasing encroachments of capital or changes of the market. They ought to understand that, with all the miseries it imposes upon them, the present system simultaneously engenders the *material conditions* and the *social forms* necessary for an economical reconstruction of society. Instead of the *conservative* motto: "*A fair day's wage for a fair day's work!*" they ought to inscribe on their banner the *revolutionary* watchword: "*Abolition of the wages system!*"

After this very long and, I fear, tedious exposition, which I was obliged to enter into to do some justice to the subject matter, I shall conclude by proposing the following resolutions:

Firstly. A general rise in the rate of wages would result in a fall of the general rate of profit, but, broadly speaking, not affect the prices of commodities.

Secondly. The general tendency of capitalist production is not to raise, but to sink the average standard of wages.

Thirdly. Trades Unions work well as centres of resistance against the encroachments of capital. They fail partially from an injudicious use of their power. They fail generally from limiting themselves to a guerilla war against the effects of the existing system, instead of simultaneously trying to change it, instead of using their organised forces as a lever for the final emancipation of the working class that is to say the ultimate abolition of the wages system.

SOCIALISM: UTOPIAN AND SCIENTIFIC

Friedrich Engels

I THE DEVELOPMENT OF UTOPIAN SOCIALISM

Modern socialism is, in its essence, the direct product of the recognition, on the one hand, of the class antagonisms existing in the society of today between proprietors and non-proprietors, between capitalists and wage-workers; on the other hand, of the anarchy existing in production. But, in its theoretical form, modern socialism originally appears ostensibly as a more logical extension of the principles laid down by the great French philosophers of the eighteenth century. Like every new theory, modern socialism had, at first, to connect itself with the intellectual stock-in-trade ready to its hand, however deeply its roots lay in material economic facts.

The great men, who in France prepared men's minds for the coming revolution, were themselves extreme revolutionists. They recognised no external authority of any kind whatever. Religion, natural science, society, political institutions – everything was subjected to the most unsparing criticism: everything must justify its existence before the judgment-seat of reason or give up existence. Reason became the sole measure of everything. It was the time when, as Hegel says, the world stood upon its head; first in the sense that the human head, and the principles arrived at by its thought, claimed to be the basis of all human action and association; but by and by, also, in the wider sense that the reality which was in contradiction to these principles had, in fact, to be turned upside down. Every form of society and government then existing, every old traditional notion, was flung into the lumber-room as irrational; the world had hitherto allowed itself to be led solely by prejudices; everything in the past deserved only pity and contempt. Now, for the first time, appeared the light of day, the kingdom of reason; henceforth superstition, injustice, privilege, oppression, were to be superseded by eternal truth, eternal Right, equality based on Nature and the inalienable rights of man.

We know today that this kingdom of reason was nothing more than the idealised kingdom of the bourgeoisie; that this eternal Right found its realisation in bourgeois justice; that this equality reduced itself to bourgeois equality before the law; that bourgeois property was proclaimed as one of the essential rights of man; and that the government of reason, the *Contrat Social* of Rousseau, came into being, and only could come into being, as a democratic bourgeois republic. The great thinkers of the eighteenth century could, no more than their predecessors, go beyond the limits imposed upon them by their epoch.

But, side by side with the antagonisms of the feudal nobility and the burghers, who claimed to represent all the rest of society, was the general antagonism of exploiters and exploited, of rich idlers and poor workers. It was this very circumstance that made it possible for the representatives of the bourgeoisie to put themselves forward as representing not one special class, but the whole of suffering humanity. Still further. From its origin the bourgeoisie was saddled with its antithesis: capitalists cannot exist without wage-workers, and, in the same proportion as the mediaeval burgher of the guild developed into the modern bourgeois, the guild journeyman and the day-labourer, outside the guilds, developed into the proletarian. And although, upon the whole, the bourgeoisie, in their struggle with the nobility, could claim to represent at the same time the interests of the different working-classes of that period, yet in every great *bourgeois movement there were independent outbursts of that class which was the forerunner, more or less developed, of the modern proletariat. For example, at the time of the German Reformation and the Peasants' War, the Anabaptists and Thomas Münzer;* in the great English Revolution, the Levellers; in the great French Revolution, Babeuf.

These were theoretical enunciations, corresponding with these revolutionary uprisings of a class not yet developed; in the sixteenth and seventeenth centuries, Utopian pictures of ideal social conditions; in the eighteenth century, actual communistic theories (Morelly and Mably). The demand for equality was no longer limited to political rights; it was extended also to the social conditions of individuals. It was not simply class privileges that were to be abolished, but class distinctions themselves. A communism, ascetic, denouncing all the pleasures of life, Spartan, was the first form of the new teaching. Then came the three great Utopians: Saint-Simon, to whom the middle-class movement, side by side with the proletarian, still had a certain significance; Fourier; and Owen, who in the country where capitalist production was most developed, and under the influence of the antagonisms begotten of this, worked out his proposals for the removal of class distinction systematically and in direct relation to French materialism.

One thing is common to all three. Not one of them appears as a representative of the interests of that proletariat which historical development had, in the meantime, produced. Like the French philosophers, they do not claim to emancipate a particular class to begin with, but all humanity at once. Like them, they wish to bring in the kingdom of reason and eternal justice, but this kingdom, as they see it, is as far as Heaven from Earth, from that of the French philosophers.

For, to our three social reformers, the bourgeois world, based upon the principles of these philosophers, is quite as irrational and unjust, and, therefore, finds its way to the dust-hole quite as readily as feudalism and all the earlier stages of society. If pure reason and justice have not, hitherto, ruled the world, this has been the case only because men have not rightly understood them. What was wanted was the individual man of genius, who has now arisen and who understands the truth. That he has now arisen, that the truth has now been clearly understood, is not an inevitable event, following of necessity in the chain of historical development, but a mere happy accident. He might just as well have been born 500 years earlier, and might then have spared humanity 500 years of error, strife, and suffering.

We saw how the French philosophers of the eighteenth century, the forerunners of the Revolution, appealed to reason as the sole judge of all that is. A rational government, rational society, were to be founded; everything that ran counter to eternal reason was to be remorselessly done away with. We saw also that this eternal reason was in reality nothing but the idealised understanding of the eighteenth-century citizen, just then evolving into the bourgeois. The French Revolution had realised this rational society and government.

But the new order of things, rational enough as compared with earlier conditions, turned out to be by no means absolutely rational. The state based upon reason completely collapsed. Rousseau's *Contrat Social* had found its realisation in the Reign of Terror, from which the bourgeoisie, who had lost confidence in their own political capacity, had taken refuge first in the corruption of the Directorate, and, finally, under the wing of the Napoleonic despotism. The promised eternal peace was turned into an endless war of conquest. The society based upon reason had fared no better. The antagonism between rich and poor, instead of dissolving into general prosperity, had become intensified by the removal of the guild and other privileges, which had to some extent bridged it over, and by the removal of the charitable institutions of the Church. The "freedom of property" from feudal fetters, now veritably accomplished, turned out to be, for the small capitalists and small proprietors, the freedom to sell their small property, crushed under the overmastering competition of the large capitalists and landlords, to these great lords, and thus, as far as the small capitalists and peasant proprietors were concerned, became "freedom *from* property". The development of industry upon a capitalistic basis made poverty and misery of the working masses conditions of existence of society. Cash payment became more and more, in Carlyle's phrase, the sole nexus between man and man. The number of crimes increased from year to year. Formerly, the feudal vices had openly stalked about in broad daylight; though not eradicated, they were now at any rate thrust into the background. In their stead, the bourgeois vices, hitherto practised in secret, began to blossom all the more luxuriantly. Trade became to a greater and greater extent cheating. The "fraternity" of the revolutionary motto was realised in the chicanery and rivalries of the battle of competition. Oppression by force was replaced by corruption; the sword, as the first social lever, by gold. The right of the first night was transferred from the feudal lords to the bourgeois manufacturers. Prostitution increased to an extent never heard of. Marriage itself remained, as before, the legally recognised form, the official cloak of prostitution, and, moreover, was supplemented by rich crops of adultery.

In a word, compared with the splendid promises of the philosophers, the social and political institutions born of the "triumph of reason" were bitterly disappointing caricatures. All that was wanting was the men to formulate this disappointment, and they came with the turn of the century. In 1802, Saint-Simon's Geneva letters appeared; in 1808 appeared Fourier's first work, although the groundwork of his theory dated from 1799; on January 1, 1800, Robert Owen undertook the direction of New Lanark.

At this time, however, the capitalist mode of production, and with it the antagonism between the bourgeoisie and the proletariat, was still very incompletely developed. Modern industry, which had just arisen in England, was still unknown in France. But modern industry develops, on the one hand, the conflicts which make absolutely necessary a revolution in the mode of production, and the doing away with its capitalistic character – conflicts not only between the classes begotten of it, but also between the very productive forces and the forms of exchange created by it. And, on the other hand, it develops, in these very gigantic productive forces, the means of ending these conflicts. If, therefore, about the year 1800, the conflicts arising from the new social order were only just beginning to take shape, this holds still more fully as to the means of ending them. The "have-nothing" masses of Paris, during the Reign of Terror, were able for a moment to gain the mastery, and thus to lead the bourgeois revolution to victory in spite of the bourgeoisie themselves. But, in doing so, they only proved how impossible it was for their domination to last under the conditions then obtaining. The proletariat, which then for the first time evolved itself from these "have-nothing" masses as the nucleus of a new class, as yet quite incapable of independent political action, appeared as an oppressed, suffering order, to whom, in its incapacity to help itself, help could, at best, be brought in from without or down from above.

This historical situation also dominated the founders of socialism. To the crude conditions of capitalistic production and the crude class conditions corresponded crude theories. The solution of the social problems, which as yet lay hidden in undeveloped economic conditions, the Utopians attempted to evolve out of the human brain. Society presented nothing but wrongs; to remove these was the task of reason. It was necessary, then, to discover a new and more perfect system of social order and to impose this upon society from without by propaganda, and, wherever it was possible, by the example of model experiments. These new social systems were foredoomed as Utopian; the more completely they were worked out in detail, the more they could not avoid drifting off into pure phantasies.

These facts once established, we need not dwell a moment longer upon this side of the question, now wholly belonging to the past. We can leave it to the literary small fry to solemnly quibble over these phantasies, which today only make us smile, and to crow over the superiority of their own bald reasoning, as compared with such "insanity". For ourselves, we delight in the stupendously grand thoughts and germs of thought that everywhere break out through their phantastic covering, and to which these Philistines are blind.

Saint-Simon was a son of the great French Revolution, at the outbreak of which he was not yet thirty. The Revolution was the victory of the third estate – i.e., of the great masses of the nation, *working* in production and in trade, over the privileged *idle* classes, the nobles and the priests. But the victory of the third estate soon revealed itself as exclusively the victory of a smaller part of this "estate", as the conquest of political power by the socially privileged section of it – i.e., the propertied bourgeoisie. And the bourgeoisie had certainly developed rapidly during the Revolution, partly by speculation in the lands of the nobility and of the Church, confiscated and afterwards put up for sale, and partly by frauds upon the nation by means of army contracts. It was the domination of these swindlers that, under the Directorate, brought France to the verge of ruin, and thus gave Napoleon the pretext for his *coup d'ëtat*.

Hence, to Saint-Simon the antagonism between the third estate and the privileged classes took the form of an antagonism between "workers" and "idlers". The idlers were not merely the old privileged classes, but also all who, without taking any part in production or distribution, lived on their incomes. And the workers were not only the wage-workers, but also the manufacturers, the merchants, the bankers. That the idlers had lost the capacity for intellectual leadership and political supremacy had been proved, and was by the Revolution finally settled. That the non-possessing classes had not this capacity seemed to Saint-Simon proved by the experiences of the Reign of Terror. Then, who was to lead and command? According to Saint-Simon, science and industry, both united by a new religious bond, destined to restore that unity of religious ideas which had been lost since the time of the Reformation – a necessarily mystic and rigidly hierarchic "new Christianity". But science, that was the scholars; and industry, that was, in the first place, the working bourgeois, manufacturers, merchants, bankers. These bourgeois were, certainly, intended by Saint-Simon to transform themselves into a kind of public officials, of social trustees; but they were still to hold, *vis-à-vis* of the workers, a commanding and economically privileged position. The bankers especially were to be called upon to direct the whole of social production by the regulation of credit. This conception was in exact keeping with a time in which Modern Industry in France and, with it, the chasm between bourgeoisie and proletariat was only just coming into existence. But what Saint-Simon especially lays stress upon is this: what interests him first, and above all other things, is the lot of the class that is the most numerous and the most poor ("*la classe la plus nombreuse et la plus pauvre*").

Already in his Geneva letters, Saint-Simon lays down the proposition that "all men ought to work". In the same work he recognises also that the Reign of Terror was the reign of the non-possessing masses. "See", says he to them, "what happened in France at the time when your comrades held sway there; they brought about a famine".

But to recognise the French Revolution as a class war, and not simply one between nobility and bourgeoisie, but between nobility, bourgeoisie, and the non-possessors, was, in the year 1802, a most pregnant discovery. In 1816, he declares that politics is the science of production, and foretells the complete absorption of politics by economics. The knowledge that economic conditions are the basis of political institutions appears here only in embryo. Yet what is here already very plainly expressed is the idea of the future conversion of political rule over men into an administration of things and a direction of processes of production – that is to say, the "abolition of the state", about which recently there has been so much noise.

Saint-Simon shows the same superiority over his contemporaries, when in 1814, immediately after the entry of the allies into Paris, and again in 1815, during the Hundred Days' War, he proclaims the alliance of France and England, and then of both of these countries, with Germany, as the only guarantee for the prosperous development and peace of Europe. To preach to the French in 1815 an alliance with the victors of Waterloo required as much courage as historical foresight.

If in Saint-Simon we find a comprehensive breadth of view, by virtue of which almost all the ideas of later Socialists that are not strictly economic are found in him in embryo, we find in Fourier a criticism of the existing conditions of society, genuinely French and witty, but not upon that account any the less thorough. Fourier takes the bourgeoisie, their inspired prophets before the Revolution, and their interested eulogists after it, at their own word. He lays bare remorselessly the material and moral misery of the bourgeois world. He confronts it with the earlier philosophers' dazzling promises of a society in which reason alone should reign, of a civilisation in which happiness should be universal, of an illimitable human perfectibility, and with the rose-coloured phraseology of the bourgeois ideologists of his time. He points out how everywhere the most pitiful reality corresponds with the most high-sounding phrases, and he overwhelms this hopeless fiasco of phrases with his mordant sarcasm.

Fourier is not only a critic; his imperturbably serene nature makes him a satirist, and assuredly one of the greatest satirists of all time. He depicts, with equal power and charm, the swindling speculations that blossomed out upon the downfall of the Revolution, and the shopkeeping spirit prevalent in, and characteristic of, French commerce at that time. Still more masterly is his criticism of the bourgeois form of the relations between sexes, and the position of woman in bourgeois society.

He was the first to declare that in any given society the degree of woman's emancipation is the natural measure of the general emancipation.

But Fourier is at his greatest in his conception of the history of society. He divides its whole course, thus far, into four stages of evolution – savagery, barbarism, the patriarchate, civilisation. This last is identical with the so-called civil, or bourgeois, society of today – i.e., with the social order that came in with the sixteenth century. He proves "that the civilised stage raises every vice practised by barbarism in a simple fashion into a form of existence, complex, ambiguous, equivocal, hypocritical" – that civilisation moves "in a vicious circle", in contradictions which it constantly reproduces without being able to solve them; hence it constantly arrives at the very opposite to that which it wants to attain, or pretends to want to attain, so that, e.g., "under civilisation poverty is born of super-abundance itself".

Fourier, as we see, uses the dialectic method in the same masterly way as his contemporary, Hegel. Using these same dialectics, he argues against talk about illimitable human perfectibility, that every historical phase has its period of ascent and also its period of descent, and he applies this observation to the future of the whole human race. As Kant introduced into natural science the idea of the ultimate destruction of the Earth, Fourier introduced into historical science that of the ultimate destruction of the human race.

Whilst in France the hurricane of the Revolution swept over the land, in England a quieter, but not on that account less tremendous, revolution was going on. Steam and the new tool-making machinery were transforming manufacture into modern industry, and thus revolutionising the whole foundation of bourgeois society. The sluggish march of development of the manufacturing period changed into a veritable storm and stress period of production. With constantly increasing swiftness the splitting-up into large capitalists and non-possessing proletarians went on. Between these, instead of the former stable middle-class, an unstable mass of artisans and small shopkeepers, the most fluctuating portion of the population, now led a precarious existence.

The new mode of production was, as yet, only at the beginning of its period of ascent; as yet it was the normal, regular method of production – the only one possible under existing conditions. Nevertheless, even then it was producing crying social abuses – the herding together of a homeless population in the worst quarters of the large towns; the loosening of all traditional moral bonds, of patriarchal subordination, of family relations; overwork, especially of women and children, to a frightful extent; complete demoralisation of the working-class, suddenly flung into altogether new conditions, from the country into the town, from agriculture into modern industry, from stable conditions of existence into insecure ones that changed from day to day.

At this juncture, there came forward as a reformer a manufacturer twenty-nine years old – a man of almost sublime, childlike simplicity of character, and at the same time one of the few born leaders of men. Robert Owen had adopted the teaching of the materialistic philosophers: that man's character is the product, on the one hand, of heredity; on the other, of the environment of the individual during his lifetime, and especially during his period of development. In the industrial revolution most of his class saw only chaos and confusion, and the opportunity of fishing in these troubled waters and making large fortunes quickly. He saw in it the opportunity of putting into practice his favourite theory, and so of bringing order out of chaos. He had already tried it with success, as superintendent of more than 500 men in a Manchester factory. From 1800 to 1829, he directed the great cotton mill at New Lanark, in Scotland, as managing partner, along the same lines, but with greater freedom of action and with a success that made him a European reputation. A population, originally consisting of the most diverse and, for the most part, very demoralised elements, a population that gradually grew to 2,500, he turned into a model colony, in which drunkenness, police, magistrates, lawsuits, poor laws, charity, were unknown. And all this simply by placing the people in conditions worthy of human beings, and especially by carefully bringing up the rising generation. He was the founder of infant schools, and introduced them first at New Lanark. At the age of two, the children came to school, where they enjoyed themselves so much that they could scarely be got home again. Whilst his competitors worked their people thirteen or fourteen hours a day, in New Lanark the working-day was only ten and a half hours. When a crisis in cotton stopped work for four months, his workers received their full wages all the time. And with all this the business more than doubled in value, and to the last yielded large profits to its proprietors.

In spite of all this, Owen was not content. The existence which he secured for his workers was, in his eyes, still far from being worthy of human beings. "The people were slaves at my mercy". The relatively favourable conditions in which he had placed them were still far from allowing a rational development of the character and of the intellect in all directions, much less of the free exercise of all their faculties.

> And yet, the working part of this population of 2,500 persons was daily producing as much real wealth for

> society as less than half a century before, it would have required the working part of a population of 600,000 to create. I asked myself, what became of the difference between the wealth consumed by 2,500 persons and that which would have been consumed by 600,000?

The answer was clear. It had been used to pay the proprietors of the establishment 5 per cent on the capital they had laid out, in addition to over £300,000 clear profit. And that which held for New Lanark held to a still greater extent for all the factories in England.

> If this new wealth had not been created by machinery, imperfectly as it has been applied, the wars of Europe, in opposition to Napoleon, and to support the aristocratic principles of society, could not have been maintained. And yet this new power was the creation of the working class.

To them, therefore, the fruits of this new power belonged. The newly-created gigantic productive forces, hitherto used only to enrich individuals and to enslave the masses, offered to Owen the foundations for a reconstruction of society; they were destined, as the common property of all, to be worked for the common good of all.

Owen's communism was based upon this purely business foundation, the outcome, so to say, of commercial calculation. Throughout, it maintained this practical character. Thus, in 1823, Owen proposed the relief of the distress in Ireland by Communist colonies, and drew up complete estimates of costs of founding them, yearly expenditure, and probable revenue. And in his definite plan for the future, the technical working out of details is managed with such practical knowledge – ground plan, front and side and bird's-eye views all included – that the Owen method of social reform once accepted, there is from the practical point of view little to be said against the actual arrangement of details.

His advance in the direction of Communism was the turning-point in Owen's life. As long as he was simply a philanthropist, he was rewarded with nothing but wealth, applause, honour, and glory. He was the most popular man in Europe. Not only men of his own class, but statesmen and princes listened to him approvingly. But when he came out with his Communist theories that was quite another thing. Three great obstacles seemed to him especially to block the path to social reform: private property, religion, the present form of marriage. He knew what confronted him if he attacked these – outlawry, excommunication from official society, the loss of his whole social position. But nothing of this prevented him from attacking them without fear of consequences, and what he had foreseen happened. Banished from official society, with a conspiracy of silence against him in the press, ruined by his unsuccessful Communist experiments in America, in which he sacrificed all his fortune, he turned directly to the working class and continued working in their midst for thirty years. Every social movement, every real advance in England on behalf of the workers links itself on to the name of Robert Owen. He forced through in 1819, after five years' fighting, the first law limiting the hours of labour of women and children in factories. He was president of the first Congress at which all the Trade Unions of England united in a single great trade association. He introduced as transition measures to the complete communistic organisation of society, on the one hand, cooperative societies for retail trade and production. These have since that time, at least, given practical proof that the merchant and the manufacturer are socially quite unnecessary. On the other hand, he introduced labour bazaars for the exchange of the products of labour through the medium of labour notes, whose unit was a single hour of work; institutions necessarily doomed to failure, but completely anticipating Proudhon's bank of exchange of a much later period, and differing entirely from this in that it did not claim to be the panacea for all social ills, but only a first step towards a much more radical revolution of society.

The Utopians' mode of thought has for a long time governed the socialist ideas of the nineteenth century, and still governs some of them. Until very recently, all French and English Socialists did homage to it. The earlier German communism, including that of Weitling, was of the same school. To all these, socialism is the expression of absolute truth, reason and justice, and has only to be discovered to conquer all the world by virtue of its own power. And as an absolute truth is independent of time, space, and of the historical development of man, it is a mere accident when and where it is discovered. With all this, absolute truth, reason, and justice are different with the founder of each different school. And as each one's special kind of absolute truth, reason, and justice is again conditioned by his subjective understanding, his conditions of existence, the measure of his knowledge and his intellectual training, there is no other ending possible in this conflict of absolute truths than that they shall be mutually exclusive of one another. Hence, from this nothing could come but a kind of eclectic, average socialism, which, as a matter of fact, has up to the present time dominated the minds of most of the socialist workers in France and England. Hence, a mish-mash allowing of the most manifold shades of opinion; a mish-mash of such critical statements, economic theories, pictures of future society by the founders of different sects, as excite a minimum of opposition; a mish-mash which is the more easily brewed the more definite sharp edges of the individual constituents are rubbed down in the stream of debate, like rounded pebbles in a brook.

To make a science of socialism, it had first to be placed upon a real basis.

II DIALETICS

In the meantime, along with and after the French philosophy of the eighteenth century had arisen the new German philosophy, culminating in Hegel. Its greatest merit was the taking up again of dialectics as the highest form of reasoning. The old Greek philosophers were all born natural dialecticians, and Aristotle, the most encyclopaedic of them, had already analysed the most essential forms of dialectic thought. The newer philosophy, on the other hand, although in it also dialectics had brilliant exponents (e.g. Descartes and Spinoza), had, especially through English influence, become more and more rigidly fixed in the so-called metaphysical mode of reasoning, by which also the French of the eighteenth century were almost wholly dominated, at all events in their special philosophical work. Outside philosophy in the restricted sense, the French nevertheless produced masterpieces of dialectic. We need only call to mind Diderot's *Le Neveu de Rameau*, and Rousseau's *Discours sur l'origine et les fondements de inégalité parmi les hommes*. We give here, in brief, the essential character of these two modes of thought.

When we consider and reflect upon Nature at large, or the

history of mankind, or our own intellectual activity, at first we see the picture of an endless entanglement of relations and reactions, permutations and combinations, in which nothing remains what, where and as it was, but everything moves, changes, comes into being and passes away. We see, therefore, at first the picture as a whole, with its individual parts still more or less kept in the background; we observe the movements, transitions, connections, rather than the things that move, combine, and are connected. This primitive, naive but intrinsically correct conception of the world is that of ancient Greek philosophy, and was first clearly formulated by Heraclitus: everything is and is not, for everything is fluid, is constantly changing, constantly coming into being and passing away.

But this conception, correctly as it expresses the general character of the picture of appearances as a whole, does not suffice to explain the details of which this picture is made up, and so long as we do not understand these, we have not a clear idea of the whole picture. In order to understand these details, we must detach them from their natural or historical connection and examine each one separately, its nature, special causes, effects, etc. This is, primarily, the task of natural science and historical research: branches of science which the Greeks of classical times, on very good grounds, relegated to a subordinate position, because they had first of all to collect materials for these sciences to work upon. A certain amount of natural and historical material must be collected before there can be any critical analysis, comparison, and arrangement in classes, orders, and species. The foundations of the exact natural sciences were, therefore, first worked out by the Greeks of the Alexandrian period, and later on, in the Middle Ages, by the Arabs. Real natural science dates from the second half of the fifteenth century, and thence onward it had advanced with constantly increasing rapidity. The analysis of Nature into its individual parts, the grouping of the different natural processes and objects in definite classes, the study of the internal anatomy of organised bodies in their manifold forms – these were the fundamental conditions of the gigantic strides in our knowledge of Nature that have been made during the last 400 years. But this method of work has also left us as legacy the habit of observing natural objects and processes in isolation, apart from their connection with the vast whole; of observing them in repose, not in motion; as constraints, not as essentially variables; in their death, not in their life. And when this way of looking at things was transferred by Bacon and Locke from natural science to philosophy, it begot the narrow, metaphysical mode of thought peculiar to the last century.

To the metaphysician, things and their mental reflexes, ideas, are isolated, are to be considered one after the other and apart from each other, are objects of investigation fixed, rigid, given once for all. He thinks in absolutely irreconcilable antitheses. "His communication is 'yea, yea; nay, nay'; for whatsoever is more than these cometh of evil". For him, a thing either exists or does not exist; a thing cannot at the same time be itself and something else. Positive and negative absolutely exclude one another; cause and effect stand in a rigid antithesis, one to the other.

At first sight, this mode of thinking seems to us very luminous, because it is that of so-called sound common sense. Only sound common sense, respectable fellow that he is, in the homely realm of his own four walls, has very wonderful adventures directly he ventures out into the wide world of research. And the metaphysical mode of thought, justifiable and necessary as it is in a number of domains whose extent varies according to the nature of the particular object of investigation, sooner or later reaches a limit, beyond which it becomes one-sided, restricted, abstract, lost in insoluble contradictions. In the contemplation of individual things, it forgets the connection between them; in the contemplation of their existence, it forgets the beginning and end of that existence; of their repose, it forgets their motion. It cannot see the woods for the trees.

For everyday purposes, we know and can say, e.g., whether an animal is alive or not. But, upon closer inquiry, we find that this is, in many cases, a very complex question, as the jurists know very well. They have cudgelled their brains in vain to discover a rational limit beyond which the killing of the child in its mother's womb is murder. It is just as impossible to determine absolutely the moment of death, for physiology proves that death is not an instantaneous, momentary phenomenon, but a very protracted process.

In like manner, every organic being is every moment the same and not the same; every moment it assimilates matter supplied from without, and gets rid of other matter; every moment, some cells of its body die and others build themselves anew; in a longer or shorter time, the matter of its body is completely renewed, and is replaced by other molecules of matter, so that every organic being is always itself, and yet something other than itself.

Further, we find upon closer investigation that the two poles of an antithesis, positive and negative, e.g., are as inseparable as they are opposed, and that despite all their opposition, they mutually interpenetrate. And we find, in like manner, that cause and effect are conceptions which only hold good in their application to individual cases; but as soon as we consider the individual cases in their general connection with the universe as a whole, they run into each other, and they become confounded when we contemplate that universal action and reaction in which causes and effects are eternally changing places, so that what is effect here and now will be cause there and then, and vice versa.

None of these processes and modes of thought enters into the framework of metaphysical reasoning. Dialectics, on the other hand, comprehends things and their representations, ideas, in their essential connection, concatenation, motion, origin and ending. Such processes as those mentioned above are, therefore, so many corroborations of its own method of procedure.

Nature is the proof of dialectics, and it must be said for modern science that it has furnished this proof with very rich materials increasing daily, and thus has shown that, in the last resort, Nature works dialectically and not metaphysically; that she does not move in the eternal oneness of a perpetually recurring circle, but goes through a real historical evolution. In this connection, Darwin must be named before all others. He dealt the metaphysical conception of Nature the heaviest blow by his proof that all organic beings, plants, animals, and man himself, are the products of a process of evolution going on through millions of years. But the naturalists who have learned to think dialectically are few and far between, and this conflict of the results of discovery with preconceived modes of thinking, explains the endless confusion now reigning in theoretical natural science, the despair of teachers as well as learners, of authors and readers alike.

An exact representation of the universe, of its evolution, of the development of mankind, and of the reflection of this evolution in the minds of men, can therefore only be obtained by the methods of dialectics with its constant regard to the innumerable actions and reactions of life and death, of progressive or retrogressive changes. And in this spirit, the new German philosophy has worked. Kant began his career by resolving the stable solar system of Newton and its eternal duration, after the famous initial impulse had once been given, into the result of a historical process, the formation of the sun and all the planets out of a rotating, nebulous mass. From this, he at the same time drew the conclusion that, given this origin of the solar system, its future death followed of necessity. His theory, half a century later, was established mathematically by Laplace, and half a century after that, the spectroscope proved the existence in space of such incandescent masses of gas in various stages of condensation.

This new German philosophy culminated in the Hegelian system. In this system – and herein is its great merit – for the first time the whole world, natural, historical, intellectual, is represented as a process – i.e., in constant motion, change, transformation, development; and the attempt is made to trace out the internal connection that makes a continuous whole of all this movement and development. From this point of view, the history of mankind no longer appeared as a wild whirl of senseless deeds of violence, all equally condemnable at the judgment seat of mature philosophic reason and which are best forgotten as quickly as possible, but as the process of evolution of man himself. It was now the task of the intellect to follow the gradual march of this process through all its devious ways, and to trace out the inner law running through all its apparently accidental phenomena.

That the Hegelian system did not solve the problem it propounded is here immaterial. Its epoch-making merit was that it propounded the problem. This problem is one that no single individual will ever be able to solve. Although Hegel was – with

Saint-Simon – the most encyclopaedic mind of his time, yet he was limited, first, by the necessary limited extent of his own knowledge and, second, by the limited extent and depth of the knowledge and conceptions of his age. To these limits, a third must be added; Hegel was an idealist. To him, the thoughts within his brain were not the more or less abstract pictures of actual things and processes, but, conversely, things and their evolution were only the realised pictures of the "Idea", existing somewhere from eternity before the world was. This way of thinking turned everything upside down, and completely reversed the actual connection of things in the world. Correctly and ingeniously as many individual groups of facts were grasped by Hegel, yet, for the reasons just given, there is much that is botched, artificial, laboured, in a word, wrong in point of detail. The Hegelian system, in itself, was a colossal miscarriage – but it was also the last of its kind. It was suffering, in fact, from an internal and incurable contradiction. Upon the one hand, its essential proposition was the conception that human history is a process of evolution, which, by its very nature, cannot find its intellectual final term in the discovery of any so-called absolute truth. But, on the other hand, it laid claim to being the very essence of this absolute truth. A system of natural and historical knowledge, embracing everything, and final for all time, is a contradiction to the fundamental law of dialectic reasoning. This law, indeed, by no means excludes, but, on the contrary, includes the idea that the systematic knowledge of the external universe can make giant strides from age to age.

The perception of the fundamental contradiction in German idealism led necessarily back to materialism, but – *nota bene* – not to the simply metaphysical, exclusively mechanical materialism of the eighteenth century. Old materialism looked upon all previous history as a crude heap of irrationality and violence; modern materialism sees in it the process of evolution of humanity, and aims at discovering the laws thereof. With the French of the eighteenth century, and even with Hegel, the conception obtained of Nature as a whole – moving in narrow circles, and forever immutable, with its eternal celestial bodies, as Newton, and unalterable organic species, as Linnaeus, taught. Modern materialism embraces the more recent discoveries of natural science, according to which Nature also has its history in time, the celestial bodies, like the organic species that, under favorable conditions, people them, being born and perishing. And even if Nature, as a whole, must still be said to move in recurrent cycles, these cycles assume infinitely larger dimensions. In both aspects, modern materialism is essentially dialectic, and no longer requires the assistance of that sort of philosophy which, queen-like, pretended to rule the remaining mob of sciences. As soon as each special science is bound to make clear its position in the great totality of things and of our knowledge of things, a special science dealing with this totality is superfluous or unnecessary. That which still survives of all earlier philosophy is the science of thought and its law – formal logic and dialectics. Everything else is subsumed in the positive science of Nature and history.

Whilst, however, the revolution in the conception of Nature could only be made in proportion to the corresponding positive materials furnished by research, already much earlier certain historical facts had occurred which led to a decisive change in the conception of history. In 1831, the first working-class rising took place in Lyons; between 1838 and 1842, the first national working-class movement, that of the English Chartists, reached its height. The class struggle between proletariat and bourgeoisie came to the front in the history of the most advanced countries in Europe, in proportion to the development, upon the one hand, of modern industry, upon the other, of the newly-acquired political supremacy of the bourgeoisie. Facts more and more strenuously gave the lie to the teachings of bourgeois economy as to the identity of the interests of capital and labour, as to the universal harmony and universal prosperity that would be the consequence of unbridled competition. All these things could no longer be ignored, any more than the French and English socialism, which was their theoretical, though very imperfect, expression. But the old idealist conception of history, which was not yet dislodged, knew nothing of class struggles based upon economic interests, knew nothing of economic interests; production and all economic relations appeared in it only as incidental, subordinate elements in the "history of civilisation".

The new facts made imperative a new examination of all past history. Then it was seen that *all* past history, with the exception of its primitive stages, was the history of class struggles; that these warring classes of society are always the products of the modes of production and of exchange – in a word, of the *economic* conditions of their time; that the economic structure of society always furnishes the real basis, starting from which we can alone work out the ultimate explanation of the whole superstructure of juridical and political institutions as well as of the religious, philosophical, and other ideas of a given historical period. Hegel has freed history from metaphysics – he made it dialectic; but his conception of history was essentially idealistic. But now idealism was driven from its last refuge, the philosophy of history; now a materialistic treatment of history was propounded, and a method found of explaining man's "knowing" by his "being", instead of, as heretofore, his "being" by his "knowing".

From that time forward socialism was no longer an accidental discovery of this or that ingenious brain, but the necessary outcome of the struggle between two historically developed classes – the proletariat and the bourgeoisie. Its task was no longer to manufacture a system of society as perfect as possible, but to examine the historico-economic succession of events from which these classes and their antagonism had of necessity sprung, and to discover in the economic conditions thus created the means of ending the conflict. But the Socialism of earlier days was as incompatible with this materialist conception as the conception of Nature of the French materialists was with dialectics and modern natural science. The socialism of earlier days certainly criticised the existing capitalistic mode of production and its consequences. But it could not explain them, and, therefore, could not get the mastery of them. It could only simply reject them as bad. The more strongly this earlier socialism denounced the exploitation of the working class, inevitable under capitalism, the less able was it clearly to show in what this exploitation consisted and how it arose. But for this it was necessary – (1) to present the capitalistic mode of production in its historical connection and its inevitableness during a particular historical period, and therefore, also, to present its inevitable downfall; and (2) to lay bare its essential character, which was still a secret. This was done by the discovery of *surplus value*. It was shown that the appropriation of unpaid labour is the basis of the capitalist mode of production and of the exploitation of the worker that occurs under it; that even if the capitalist buys the labour power of his labourer at its full value as a commodity on the market, he yet extracts more value from it than he paid for; and that in the ultimate analysis, this surplus value forms those sums of value from which are heaped up the constantly increasing masses of capital in the hands of the possessing classes. The genesis of capitalist production and the production of capital were both explained.

These two great discoveries, the materialistic conception of history and the revelation of the secret of capitalistic production through surplus value, we owe to Marx. With these discoveries, socialism became a science. The next thing was to work out all its details and relations.

III

The materialist conception of history starts from the proposition that the production of the means to support human life and, next to production, the exchange of things produced, is the basis of all social structure; that in every society that has appeared in history, the manner in which wealth is distributed and society divided into classes or orders is dependent upon what is produced, how it is produced, and how the products are exchanged. From this point of view, the final causes of all social changes and political revolutions are to be sought, not in men's brains, not in men's better insights into eternal truth and justice, but in changes in the modes of production and exchange. They are to be sought, not in the *philosophy*, but in the *economics* of each particular epoch. The growing perception that existing social institutions are unreasonable and unjust, that reason has become unreason, and right wrong, is only proof that in the modes of production and exchange changes have silently taken place with which the social order, adapted to earlier economic conditions, is no longer in keeping. From this it also follows that the means of getting rid of the incongruities that have been brought to light must also be present, in a more or less developed condition, within the changed modes of production themselves. These means are not to be invented by deduction from fundamental principles, but are to be discovered in the stubborn facts of the existing system of production.

What is, then, the position of modern socialism in this connection?

The present structure of society – this is now pretty generally conceded – is the creation of the ruling class of today, of the bourgeoisie. The mode of production peculiar to the bourgeoisie, known, since Marx, as the capitalist mode of production, was incompatible with the feudal system, with the privileges it conferred upon individuals, entire social ranks and local corporations, as well as with the hereditary ties of subordination which constituted the framework of its social organisation. The bourgeoisie broke up the feudal system and built upon its ruins the capitalist order of society, the kingdom of free competition, of personal liberty, of the equality, before the law, of all commodity owners, of all the rest of the capitalist blessings. Thenceforward, the capitalist mode of production could develop in freedom. Since steam, machinery, and the making of machines by machinery transformed the older manufacture into modern industry, the productive forces, evolved under the guidance of the bourgeoisie, developed with a rapidity and in a degree unheard of before. But just as the older manufacture, in its time, and handicraft, becoming more developed under its influence, had come into collision with the feudal trammels of the guilds, so now modern industry, in its complete development, comes into collision with the bounds within which the capitalist mode of production holds it confined. The new productive forces have already outgrown the capitalistic mode of using them. And this conflict between productive forces and modes of production is not a conflict engendered in the mind of man, like that between original sin and divine justice. It exists, in fact, objectively, outside us, independently of the will and actions even of the men that have brought it on. Modern socialism is nothing but the reflex, in thought, of this conflict in fact; its ideal reflection in the minds, first, of the class directly suffering under it, the working class.

Now, in what does this conflict consist?

Before capitalist production – i.e., in the Middle Ages, the system of petty industry obtained generally, based upon the private property of the labourers in their means of production; in the country, the agriculture of the small peasant, freeman, or serf; in the towns, the handicrafts organised in guilds. The instruments of labour – land, agricultural implements, the workshop, the tool – were the instruments of labour of single individuals, adapted for the use of one worker, and, therefore, of necessity, small, dwarfish, circumscribed. But, for this very reason, they belonged as a rule to the producer himself. To concentrate these scattered, limited means of production, to enlarge them, to turn them into the powerful levers of production of the present day – this was precisely the historic role of capitalist production and of its upholder, the bourgeoisie. In the fourth section of *Capital*, Marx has explained in detail how since the fifteenth century this has been historically worked out through the three phases of simple co-operation, manufacture and modern industry. But the bourgeoisie, as is shown there, could not transform these puny means of production into mighty productive forces without transforming them, at the same time, from means of production of the individual into *social* means of production only workable by a collectivity of men. The spinning wheel, the handloom, the blacksmith's hammer, were replaced by the spinning-machine, the power-loom, the steam-hammer; the individual workshop, by the factory implying the co-operation of hundreds and thousands of workmen. In like manner, production itself changed from a series of individual into a series of social acts, and the production from individual to social products. The yarn, the cloth, the metal articles that now come out of the factory were the joint product of many workers, through whose hands they had successively to pass before they were ready. No one person could say of them: "I made that; this is *my* product".

But where, in a given society, the fundamental form of production is that spontaneous division of labour which creeps in gradually and not upon any preconceived plan, there the products take on the form of *commodities*, whose mutual exchange, buying and selling, enable the individual producers to satisfy their manifold wants. And this was the case in the Middle Ages. The peasant, e.g., sold to the artisan agricultural products and bought from him the products of handicraft. Into this society of individual producers, of commodity producers, the new mode of production thrust itself. In the midst of the old division of labour, grown up spontaneously and upon *no definite plan*, which had governed the whole of society, now arose division of labour upon a *definite plan*, as organised in the factory; side by side with *individual* production appeared *social* production. The products of both were sold in the same market, and, therefore, at prices at least approximately equal. But organisation upon a definite plan was stronger than spontaneous division of labour. The factories working with the combined social forces of a collectivity of individuals produced their commodities far more cheaply than the individual small producers. Individual production succumbed in one department after another. Socialised production revolutionised all the old methods of production. But its revolutionary character was, at the same time, so little recognised that it was, on the contrary, introduced as a means of increasing and developing the production of commodities. When it arose, it found ready-made, and made liberal use of, certain machinery for the production and exchange of commodities: merchants' capital, handicraft, wage-labour. Socialised production thus introducing itself as a new form of the production of commodities, it was a matter of course that under it the old forms of appropriation remained in full swing, and were applied to its products as well.

In the medieval stage of evolution of the production of commodities, the question as to the owner of the product of labour could not arise. The individual producer, as a rule, had, from raw material belonging to himself, and generally his own handiwork, produced it with his own tools, by the labour of his own hands or of his family. There was no need for him to appropriate the new product. It belonged wholly to him, as a matter of course. His property in the product was, therefore, based *upon his own labour*. Even where external help was used, this was, as a rule, of little importance, and very generally was compensated by something other than wages. The apprentices and journeymen of the guilds worked less for board and wages than for education, in order that they might become master craftsmen themselves.

Then came the concentration of the means of production and of the producers in large workshops and manufactories, their transformation into actual socialised means of production and socialised producers. But the socialised producers and means of production and their products were still treated, after this change, just as they had been before, i.e., as the means of production and the products of individuals. Hitherto, the owner of the instruments of labour had himself appropriated the product, because, as a rule, it was his own product and the assistance of others was the exception. Now, the owner of the instruments of labour always appropriated to himself the product, although it was no longer *his* product but exclusively the product of the *labour of others*. Thus, the products now produced socially were not appropriated by those who had actually set in motion the means of production and actually produced the commodities, but by the *capitalists*. The means of production, and production itself, had become in essence socialised. But they were subjected to a form of appropriation which presupposes the private production of individuals, under which, therefore, everyone owns his own product and brings it to market. The mode of production is subjected to this form of appropriation, although it abolishes the conditions upon which the latter rests.

This contradiction, which gives to the new mode of production its capitalistic character, *contains the germ of the whole of the social antagonisms of today*. The greater the mastery obtained by the new mode of production over all important fields of production and in all manufacturing countries, the more it reduced individual production to an insignificant residuum, *the more clearly was brought out the incompatibility of socialised production with capitalistic appropriation*.

The first capitalists found, as we have said, alongside of other forms of labour, wage-labour ready-made for them on the market. But it was exceptional, complementary, accessory, transitory wage-labour. The agricultural labourer, though, upon occasion, he hired himself out by the day, had a few acres of his own land on which he could at all events live at a pinch. The guilds were so organised that the journeyman of today became the master of tomorrow. But all this changed, as soon as the means of production became socialised and concentrated in the hands of capitalists. The means of production, as well as the product, of the individual producer became more and more worthless; there was nothing left for him but to turn wage-worker under the capitalist. Wage-labour, aforetime the exception and accessory, now became the rule and basis of all production; aforetime complementary, it now became the sole remaining function of the worker. The wage-worker for a time became a wage-worker for life. The number of these permanent wage-workers was further enormously increased by the breaking-up of the feudal system that occurred at the same time, by the disbanding of the retainers of the feudal lords, the eviction of the peasants from their homesteads, etc. The separation was made complete between the means of production concentrated in the hands of the capitalists, on the one side, and the producers, possessing nothing but their labour-power, on the other. *The contradiction between socialised production and capitalistic appropriation manifested itself as the antagonism of proletariat and bourgeoisie.*

We have seen that the capitalistic mode of production thrust its way into a society of commodity-producers, of individual producers, whose social bond was the exchange of their products. But every society based upon the production of commodities has this peculiarity: that the producers have lost control over their own social inter relations. Each man produces for himself with such means of production as he may happen to have, and for such exchange as he may require to satisfy his remaining wants. No one knows how much of his particular article is coming on the market, nor how much of it will be wanted. No one knows whether his individual product will meet an actual demand, whether he will be able to make good his costs of production or even to sell his commodity at all. Anarchy reigns in socialised production.

But the production of commodities, like every other form of production, has its peculiar, inherent laws inseparable from it; and these laws work, despite anarchy, in and through anarchy. They reveal themselves in the only persistent form of social inter relation, i.e., in exchange, and here they affect the individual producers as compulsory laws of competition. They are, at first, unknown to these producers themselves, and have to be discovered by them gradually and as the result of experience. They work themselves out, therefore, independently of the producers, and in antagonism to them, as inexorable natural laws of their particular form of production. The product governs the producers.

In mediaeval society, especially in the earlier centuries, production was essentially directed towards satisfying the wants of the individual. It satisfied, in the main, only the wants of the producer and his family. Where relations of personal dependence existed, as in the country, it also helped to satisfy the wants of the feudal lord. In all this there was, therefore, no exchange; the products, consequently, did not assume the character of commodities. The family of the peasant produced almost everything they wanted: clothes and furniture, as well as means of subsistence. Only when it began to produce more than was sufficient to supply its own wants and the payments in kind to the feudal lord, only then did it also produce commodities. This surplus, thrown into socialised exchange and offered for sale, became commodities.

The artisans of the towns, it is true, had from the first to produce for exchange. But they, also, themselves supplied the greatest part of their individual wants. They had gardens and plots of land. They turned their cattle out into the communal forest, which, also, yielded them timber and firing. The women spun flax, wool, and so forth. Production for the purpose of exchange, production of commodities, was only in its infancy. Hence, exchange was restricted, the market narrow, the methods of production stable; there was local exclusiveness without, local unity within; the mark in the country; in the town, the guild.

But with the extension of the production of commodities, and especially with the introduction of the capitalist mode of production, the laws of commodity-production, hitherto latent, came into action more openly and with greater force. The old bonds were loosened, the old exclusive limits broken through, the producers were more and more turned into independent, isolated producers of commodities. It became apparent that the production of society at large was ruled by absence of plan, by accident, by anarchy; and this anarchy grew to greater and greater height. But the chief means by aid of which the capitalist mode of production intensified this anarchy of socialised production was the exact opposite of anarchy. It was the increasing organisation of production, upon a social basis, in every individual productive establishment. By this, the old, peaceful, stable condition of things was ended. Wherever this organisation of production was introduced into a branch of industry, it brooked no other method of production by its side. The field of labour became a battle-ground. The great geographical discoveries, and the colonisation following upon them, multiplied markets and quickened the transformation of handicraft into manufacture. The war did not simply break out between the individual producers of particular localities. The local struggles begot in their turn national conflicts, the commercial wars of the seventeenth and eighteenth centuries.

Finally, modern industry and the opening of the world market made the struggle universal, and at the same time gave it an unheard-of virulence. Advantages in natural or artificial conditions of production now decide the existence or non-existence of individual capitalists, as well as of whole industries and countries. He that falls is remorselessly cast aside. It is the Darwinian struggle of the individual for existence transferred from Nature to society with intensified violence. The conditions of existence natural to the animal appear as the final term of human development. The contradiction between socialised production and capitalistic appropriation now presents itself as an antagonism between the organisation of production in the individual workshop and the anarchy of production in society generally.

The capitalistic mode of production moves in these two forms of the antagonism immanent to it from its very origin. It is never able to get out of that "vicious circle" which Fourier had already discovered. What Fourier could not, indeed, see in his time is that this circle is gradually narrowing; that the movement becomes more and more a spiral, and must come to an end, like the movement of the planets, by collision with the centre. It is the compelling force of anarchy in the production of society at large that more and more completely turns the great majority of men into proletarians; and it is the masses of the proletariat again who will finally put an end to anarchy in production. It is the compelling force of anarchy in social production that turns the limitless perfectibility of machinery under modern industry into a compulsory law by which every individual industrial capitalist must perfect his machinery more and more, under penalty of ruin.

But the perfecting of machinery is making human labour superfluous. If the introduction and increase of machinery means the displacement of millions of manual by a few machine-workers, improvement in machinery means the displacement of more and more of the machine-workers themselves. It means, in the last instance, the production of a number of available wage-workers in excess of the average needs of capital, the formation of a complete industrial reserve army, as I called it in 1845, available at the times when industry is working at high pressure, to be cast out upon the street when the inevitable crash comes, a constant dead weight upon the limbs of the working class in its struggle for existence with capital, a regulator for the keeping of wages down to the low level that suits the interests of capital. Thus it comes about, to quote Marx, that machinery becomes the most powerful weapon in the war of capital against the working class; that the instruments of labour constantly tear the means of subsistence out of the hands of the labourer that the very product of the worker is turned into an instrument for his subjugation. Thus it comes about that the economising of the instruments of labour becomes at the same time, from the outset, the most reckless waste of labour-power, and robbery based upon the normal conditions under which labour functions; that machinery, the most powerful instrument for shortening labour time, becomes the most unfailing means for placing every moment of the labourer's time and that of his family at the disposal of the capitalist for the purpose of expanding the value of his capital. Thus it comes about that the overwork of some becomes the preliminary condition for the idleness of others, and that modern industry, which hunts after new consumers over the whole world, forces the consumption of the masses at home down to a starvation minimum, and in doing thus destroys its own home market. "The law that always equilibrates the relative surplus population, or industrial reserve army, to the extent and energy of accumulation, this law rivets the labourer to capital more firmly than the wedges of Vulcan did Prometheus to the rock. It establishes an accumulation of misery, corresponding with the accumulation of capital. Accumulation of wealth at one pole is, therefore, at the same time accumulation of misery, agony of toil, slavery, ignorance, brutality, mental degradation, at the opposite pole, i.e., on the side of the class that produces its own product in the form of capital (Marx's *Capital*, p. 661) And to expect any other division of the products from the capitalistic mode of production is the same as expecting the electrodes of a battery not to decompose acidulated water, not to liberate oxygen at the positive, hydrogen at the negative pole, so long as they are connected with the battery.

We have seen that the ever-increasing perfectibility of modern machinery is, by the anarchy of social production, turned into a compulsory law that forces the individual industrial capitalist always to improve his machinery, always to increase its productive force. The bare possibility of extending the field of production is transformed for him into a similar compulsory law. The enormous expansive force of modern industry, compared with which that of gases is mere child's play, appears to us now as a *necessity* for expansion, both qualitative and quantative, that laughs at all resistance. Such resistance is offered by consumption, by sales, by the markets for the products of modern industry. But the capacity for extension, extensive and intensive, of the markets is primarily governed by quite different laws that work much less energetically. The extension of the markets cannot keep pace with the extension of production. The collision becomes inevitable, and as this cannot produce any real solution so long as it does not break in pieces the capitalist mode of production, the collisions become periodic. Capitalist production has begotten another "vicious circle".

As a matter of fact, since 1825, when the first general crisis broke out, the whole industrial and commercial world, production and exchange among all civilised peoples and their more or less barbaric hangers-on, are thrown out of joint about once every ten years. Commerce is at a stand still, the markets are glutted, products accumulate, as multitudinous as they are unsaleable, hard cash disappears, credit vanishes, factories are closed, the mass of the workers are in want of the means of subsistence, because they have produced too much of the means of subsistence; bankruptcy follows upon bankruptcy, execution upon execution. The stagnation lasts for years; productive forces and products are wasted and destroyed wholesale, until the accumulated mass of commodities finally filter off, more or less depreciated in value, until production and exchange gradually begin to move again. Little by little, the pace quickens. It becomes a trot. The industrial trot breaks into a canter, the canter in turn grows into the headlong gallop of a perfect steeplechase of industry, commercial credit, and speculation, which finally, after breakneck leaps, ends where it began – in the ditch of a crisis. And so over and over again. We have now, since the year 1825, gone through this five times, and at the present moment (1877) we are going through it for the sixth time. And the character of these crises is so clearly defined that Fourier hit all of them off when he described the first "*crise pléthorique*", a crisis from plethora.

In these crises, the contradiction between socialised production and capitalist appropriation ends in a violent explosion.

The circulation of commodities is, for the time being, stopped. Money, the means of circulation, becomes a hindrance to circulation. All the laws of production and circulation of commodities are turned upside down. The economic collision has reached its apogee. *The mode of production is in rebellion against the mode of exchange.*

The fact that the socialised organisation of production within the factory has developed so far that it has become incompatible with the anarchy of production in society, which exists side by side with and dominates it, is brought home to the capitalist themselves by the violent concentration of capital that occurs during crises, through the ruin of many large, and a still greater number of small, capitalists. The whole mechanism of the capitalist mode of production breaks down under the pressure of the productive forces, its own creations. It is no longer able to turn all this mass of means of production into capital. They lie fallow, and for that very reason the industrial reserve army must also lie fallow. Means of production, means of subsistence, available labourers, all the elements of production and of general wealth, are present in abundance. But "abundance becomes the source of distress and want" (Fourier), because it is the very thing that prevents the transformation of the means of production and subsistence into capital. For in capitalistic society, the means of production can only function when they have undergone a preliminary transformation into capital, into the means of exploiting human labour power. The necessity of this transformation into capital of the means of production and subsistence stands like a ghost between these and the workers. It alone prevents the coming together of the material and personal levers of production; it alone forbids the means of production to function, the workers to work and live. On the one hand, therefore, the capitalistic mode of production stands convicted of its own incapacity to further direct these productive forces. On the other, these productive forces themselves, with increasing energy, press forward to the removal of the existing contradiction, to the abolition of their quality as capital, to the *practical recognition of their character as social productive forces.*

This rebellion of the productive forces, as they grow more and more powerful, against their quality as capital, this stronger and stronger command that their social character shall be recognised, forces the capital class itself to treat them more and more as social productive forces, so far as this is possible under capitalist conditions. The period of industrial high pressure, with its unbounded inflation of credit, not less than the crash itself, by the collapse of great capitalist establishments, tends to bring about that form of the socialisation of great masses of the means of production which we meet with in the different kinds of joint-stock companies. Many of these means of production and of distribution are, from the outset, so colossal that, like the railways, they exclude all other forms of capitalistic exploitation. At a further stage of evolution, this form also becomes insufficient. The producers on a large scale in a particular branch of an industry in a particular country unite in a trust, a union for the purpose of regulating production. They determine the total amount to be produced, parcel it out among themselves, and thus enforce the selling price fixed beforehand. But trusts of this kind, as soon as business becomes bad, are generally liable to break up, and on this very account compel a yet greater concentration of association. The whole of a particular industry is turned into one gigantic joint-stock company; internal competition gives place to the internal monopoly of this one company. This has happened in 1890 with the English alkali production, which is now, after the fusion of 48 large works, in the hands of one company, conducted upon a single plan, and with a capital of £6,000,000.

In the trusts, freedom of competition changes into its very opposite – into monopoly; and the production without any definite plan of capitalistic society capitulates to the production upon a definite plan of the invading socialistic society. Certainly, this is so far still to the benefit and advantage of the capitalists. But, in this case, the exploitation is so palpable that it must break down. No nation will put up with production conducted by trusts, with so barefaced an exploitation of the community by a small band of dividend-mongers.

In any case, with trusts or without, the official representative of capitalist society – the state – will ultimately have to undertake the direction of production. This necessity for conversion into state property is felt first in the great institutions for intercourse and communication – the post office, the telegraphs, the railways.

If the crises demonstrate the incapacity of the bourgeoisie for managing any longer modern productive forces, the transformation of the great establishments for production and distribution into joint-stock companies, trusts, and state property, show how unnecessary the bourgeoisie are for that purpose. All the social functions of the capitalist has no further social function than that of pocketing dividends, tearing off coupons, and gambling on the Stock Exchange, where the different capitalists despoil one another of their capital. At first, the capitalistic mode of production forces out the workers. Now, it forces out the capitalists, and reduces them, just as it reduced the workers, to the ranks of the surplus population, although not immediately into those of the industrial reserve army.

But the transformation, either into joint-stock companies and trusts, or into state ownership, does not do away with the capitalistic nature of the productive forces. In the joint-stock companies and trusts, this is obvious. And the modern state, again, is only the organisation that bourgeois society takes on in order to support the external conditions of the capitalist mode of production against the encroachments as well of the workers as of individual capitalists. The modern state, no matter what its form, is essentially a capitalist machine, the state of the capitalists, the ideal personification of the total national capital. The more it proceeds to the taking over of productive forces, the more does it actually become the national capitalist, the more citizens does it exploit. The workers remain wage-workers – proletarians. The capitalist relation is not done away with. It is, rather, brought to a head. But, brought to a head, it topples over. State ownership of the productive forces is not the solution of the conflict, but concealed within it are the technical conditions that form the elements of that solution.

This solution can only consist in the practical recognition of the social nature of the modern forces of production, and therefore in the harmonising of the modes of production, appropriation, and exchange with the socialised character of the means of production. And this can only come about by society openly and directly taking possession of the productive forces which have outgrown all control except that of society as a whole. The social character of the means of production and of the products today reacts against the producers, periodically disrupts all production and exchange, acts only like a law of Nature working blindly, forcibly, destructively. But with the taking over by society of the productive forces, the social character of the means of production and of the products will be utilised by the producers with a perfect understanding of its nature, and instead of being a source of disturbance and periodical collapse, will become the most powerful lever of production itself.

Active social forces work exactly like natural forces: blindly, forcibly, destructively, so long as we do not understand, and reckon with, them. But when once we understand them, when once we grasp their action, their direction, their effects, it depends only upon ourselves to subject them more and more to our own will, and, by means of them, to reach our own ends. And this holds quite especially of the mighty productive forces of today. As long as we obstinately refuse to understand the nature and the character of these social means of action – and this understanding goes against the grain of the capitalist mode of production, and its defenders – so long these forces are at work in spite of us, in opposition to us, so long they master us, as we have shown above in detail.

But when once their nature is understood, they can, in the hands of the producers working together, be transformed from master demons into willing servants. The difference is as that between the destructive force of electricity in the lightning in the storm, and electricity under command in the telegraph and the voltaic arc; the difference between a conflagration, and fire working in the service of man. With this recognition, at last, of the real nature of the productive forces of today, the social anarchy of production gives place to a social regulation of production upon a definite plan, according to the needs of the community and of each individual. Then the capitalist mode of appropriation, in which the product enslaves first the producer, and then the appropriator, is replaced by the mode of appropriation of the products that is based upon the nature of the modern means of production; upon the one hand, direct social appropriation, as means to the maintenance and extension of production – on the other, direct individual appropriation, as means of subsistence and of enjoyment.

Whilst the capitalist mode of production more and more completely transforms the great majority of the population into proletarians, it creates the power which, under penalty of its own destruction, is forced to accomplish this revolution. Whilst it forces on more and more of the transformation of the vast means of production, already socialised, into state property, it shows itself the way to accomplishing this revolution. *The proletariat seizes political power and turns the means of production into state property.*

But, in doing this, it abolishes itself as proletariat, abolishes all class distinction and class antagonisms, abolishes also the state as state. Society thus far, based upon class antagonisms, had need of the state. That is, of an organisation of the particular class which was *pro tempore* the exploiting class, an organisation for the purpose of preventing any interference from without with the existing conditions of production, and, therefore, especially, for the purpose of forcibly keeping the exploited classes in the condition of oppression corresponding with the given mode of production (slavery, serfdom, wage-labour). The state was the official representative of society as a whole; the gathering of it together into a visible embodiment. But it was this only in so far as it was the state of that class which itself represented, for the time being, society as a whole: in ancient times, the state of slave-owning citizens; in the Middle Ages, the feudal lords; in our own times, the bourgeoisie. When at last it becomes the real representative of the whole of society, it renders itself unnecessary. As soon as there is no longer any social class to be held in subjection; as soon as class rule, and the individual struggle for existence based upon our present anarchy in production, with the collisions and excesses arising from these, are removed, nothing more remains to be repressed, and a special repressive force, a state, is no longer necessary. The first act by virtue of which the state really constitutes itself the representative of the whole of society – the taking possession of the means of production in the name of society – this is, at the same time, its last independent act as a state. State interference in social relations becomes, in one domain after another, superfluous, and then dies out of itself; the government of persons is replaced by the administration of things, and by the conduct of processes of production. The state is not "abolished". *It dies out*. This gives the measure of the value of the phrase: "*a free state*", both as to its justifiable use at times by agitators, and as to its ultimate scientific insufficiency; and also of the demands of the so-called anarchists for the abolition of the state out of hand.

Since the historical appearance of the capitalist mode of production, the appropriation by society of all the means of production has often been dreamed of, more or less vaguely, by individuals, as well as by sects, as the ideal of the future. But it could become possible, could become a historical necessity, only when the actual conditions for its realisation were there. Like every other social advance, it becomes practicable, not by men understanding that the existence of classes is in contradiction to justice, equality, etc., not by the mere willingness to abolish these classes, but by virtue of certain new economic conditions. The separation of society into an exploiting and an exploited class, a ruling and an oppressed class, was the necessary consequences of the deficient and restricted development of production in former times. So long as the total social labour only yields a produce which but slightly exceeds that barely necessary for the existence of all; so long, therefore, as labour engages all or almost all the time of the great majority of the members of society – so long, of necessity, this society is divided into classes. Side by side with the great majority, exclusively bond slaves to labour, arises a class freed from directly productive labour, which looks after the general affairs of society: the direction of labour, state business, law, science, art, etc. It is, therefore, the law of division of labour that lies at the basis of the division into classes. But this does not prevent this division into classes from being carried out by means of violence and robbery, trickery and fraud. it does not prevent the ruling class, once having the upper hand, from consolidating its power at the expense of the working class, from turning its social leadership into an intensified exploitation of the masses.

But if, upon this showing, division into classes has a certain historical justification, it has this only for a given period, only under given social conditions. It was based upon the insufficiency of production. It will be swept away by the complete development of modern productive forces. And, in fact, the abolition of classes in society presupposes a degree of historical evolution at which the existence, not simply of this or that particular ruling class, but of any ruling class at all, and, therefore, the existence of class distinction itself, has become an obsolete anachronism. It presupposes, therefore, the development of production carried out to a degree at which appropriation of the means of production and of the products, and, with this, of political domination, of the monopoly of culture, and of intellectual leadership by a particular class of society, has become not only superfluous but economically, politically, intellectually, a hindrance to development.

This point is now reached. Their political and intellectual bankruptcy is scarcely any longer a secret to the bourgeoisie themselves. Their economic bankruptcy recurs regularly every 10 years. In every crisis, society is suffocated beneath the weight of its own productive forces and products, which it cannot use, and stands helpless, face-to-face with the absurd contradiction that the producers have nothing to consume, because consumers are wanting. The expansive force of the means of production bursts the bonds that the capitalist mode of production had imposed upon them. Their deliverance from these bonds is the one pre-condition for an unbroken, constantly accelerated development of the productive forces, and therewith for a practically unlimited increase of production itself. Nor is this all. The socialised appropriation of the means of production does away, not only with the present artificial restrictions upon production, but also with the positive waste and devastation of productive forces and products that are at the present time the inevitable concomitants of production, and that reach their height in the crises. Further, it sets free for the community at large a mass of means of production and of products, by doing away with the senseless extravagance of the ruling classes of today, and their political representatives. The possibility of securing for every member of society, by means of socialised production, an existence not only fully sufficient materially, and becoming day by day more full, but an existence guaranteeing to all the free development and exercise of their physical and mental faculties – this possibility is now for the first time here, but *it is here*.

With the seizing of the means of production by society, production of commodities is done away with, and, simultaneously, the mastery of the product over the producer. Anarchy in social production is replaced by systematic, definite organisation. The struggle for individual existence disappears. Then for the first time man, in a certain sense, is finally marked off from the rest of the animal kingdom, and emerges from mere animal conditions of existence into really human ones. The whole sphere of the conditions of life which environ man, and which have hitherto ruled man, now comes under the dominion and control of man, who for the first time becomes the real, conscious lord of nature, because he has now become master of his own social organisation. The laws of his own social action, hitherto standing face to face with man as laws of Nature foreign to, and dominating him, will then be used with full understanding, and so mastered by him. Man's own social organisation, hitherto confronting him as a necessity imposed by Nature and history, now becomes the result of his own free action. The extraneous objective forces that have, hitherto, governed history,pass under the control of man himself. Only from that time will man himself, more and more consciously, make his own history – only from that time will the social causes set in movement by him have, in the main and in a constantly growing measure, the results intended by him. It is the ascent of man from the kingdom of necessity to the kingdom of freedom.

Let us briefly sum up our sketch of historical evolution.

I. MEDIAEVAL SOCIETY

Individual production on a small scale. Means of production adapted for individual use; hence primitive, ungainly, petty, dwarfed in action. Production for immediate consumption, either of the producer himself or of his feudal lord. Only where an excess of production over this consumption occurs is such excess offered for sale, enters into exchange. Production of commodities, therefore, only in its infancy. But already it contains within itself, in embryo, *anarchy in the production of society at large.*

II. CAPITALIST REVOLUTION

Transformation of industry, at first be means of simple cooperation and manufacture. Concentration of the means of production, hitherto scattered, into great workshops. As a consequence, their transformation from individual to social means of production – a transformation which does not, on the whole, affect the form of exchange. The old forms of appropriation remain in force. The capitalist appears. In his capacity as owner of the means of production, he also appropriates the products and turns them into commodities. Production has become a *social* act. Exchange and appropriation continue to be *individual* acts, the acts of individuals. *The social product is appropriated by the individual capitalist.* Fundamental contradiction, whence arise all the contradictions in which our present-day society moves, and which modern industry brings to light.

A.

Severance of the producer from the means of production. Condemnation of the worker to wage-labour for life. *Antagonism between the proletariat and the bourgeoisie.*

B.

Growing predominance and increasing effectiveness of the laws governing the production of commodities. Unbridled competition. *Contradiction between socialised organisation in the individual factory and social anarchy in the production as a whole.*

C.

On the one hand, perfecting of machinery, made by competition compulsory for each individual manufacturer, and complemented by a constantly growing displacement of labourers. *Industrial reserve army.* On the other hand, unlimited extension of production, also compulsory under competition, for every manufacturer. On both sides, unheard-of development of productive forces, excess of supply over demand, overproduction, glutting of the markets, crises every ten years, the vicious circle: excess here, of means of production and products – excess there, of labourers, without employment and without means of existence. But these two levers of production and of social well-being are unable to work together, because the capitalist form of production prevents the productive forces from working and the products from circulating, unless they are first turned into capital – which their very super-abundance prevents. The contradiction has grown into an absurdity. *The mode of production rises in rebellion against the form of exchange.* The bourgeoisie are convicted of incapacity further to manage their own social productive forces.

D.

Partial recognition of the social character of the productive forces forced upon the capitalists themselves. Taking over of the great institutions for production and communication, first by joint-stock companies, later in by trusts, then by the state. The bourgeoisie demonstrated to be a superfluous class. All its social functions are now performed by salaried employees.

III. PROLETARIAN REVOLUTION

Solution of the contradictions. The proletariat seizes the public power, and by means of this transforms the socialised means of production, slipping from the hands of the bourgeoisie, into public property. By this act, the proletariat frees the means of production from the character of capital they have thus far borne, and gives their socialised character complete freedom to work itself out. Socialised production upon a predetermined plan becomes henceforth possible. The development of production makes the existence of different classes of society thenceforth an anachronism. In proportion as anarchy in social production vanishes, the political authority of the state dies out. Man, at last the master of his own form of social organisation, becomes at the same time the lord over Nature, his own master – free.

To accomplish this act of universal emancipation is the historical mission of the modern proletariat. To thoroughly comprehend the historical conditions and thus the very nature of this act, to impart to the now oppressed proletarian class a full knowledge of the conditions and of the meaning of the momentous act it is called upon to accomplish, this is the task of the theoretical expression of the proletarian movement, scientific socialism.

Classic Literature: Words and Phrases
adapted from the Collins English Dictionary

Accoucheur NOUN a male midwife or doctor ❑ *I think my sister must have had some general idea that I was a young offender whom an Accoucheur Policemen had taken up (on my birthday) and delivered over to her* (*Great Expectations* by Charles Dickens)

addled ADJ confused and unable to think properly ❑ *But she counted and counted till she got that addled* (*The Adventures of Huckleberry Finn* by Mark Twain)

admiration NOUN amazement or wonder ❑ *lifting up his hands and eyes by way of admiration* (*Gulliver's Travels* by Jonathan Swift)

afeard ADJ afeard means afraid ❑ *shake it–and don't be afeard* (*The Adventures of Huckleberry Finn* by Mark Twain)

affected VERB affected means to assume the appearance of ❑ *Hadst thou affected sweet divinity* (*Doctor Faustus 5.2* by Christopher Marlowe)

aground ADV when a boat runs aground, it touches the ground in a shallow part of the water and gets stuck ❑ *what kep' you?–boat get aground?* (*The Adventures of Huckleberry Finn* by Mark Twain)

ague NOUN a fever in which the patient has alternate hot and cold shivering fits ❑ *his exposure to the wet and cold had brought on fever and ague* (*Oliver Twist* by Charles Dickens)

alchemy ADJ false or worthless ❑ *all wealth alchemy* (*The Sun Rising* by John Donne)

all alike PHRASE the same all the time ❑ *Love, all alike* (*The Sun Rising* by John Donne)

alow and aloft PHRASE alow means in the lower part or bottom, and aloft means on the top, so alow and aloft means on the top and in the bottom or throughout ❑ *Someone's turned the chest out alow and aloft* (*Treasure Island* by Robert Louis Stevenson)

ambuscade NOUN ambuscade is not a proper word. Tom means an ambush, which is when a group of people attack their enemies, after hiding and waiting for them ❑ *and so we would lie in ambuscade, as he called it* (*The Adventures of Huckleberry Finn* by Mark Twain)

amiable ADJ likeable or pleasant ❑ *Such amiable qualities must speak for themselves* (*Pride and Prejudice* by Jane Austen)

amulet NOUN an amulet is a charm thought to drive away evil spirits. ❑ *uttered phrases at once occult and familiar, like the amulet worn on the heart* (*Silas Marner* by George Eliot)

amusement NOUN here amusement means a strange and disturbing puzzle ❑ *this was an amusement the other way* (*Robinson Crusoe* by Daniel Defoe)

ancient NOUN an ancient was the flag displayed on a ship to show which country it belongs to. It is also called the ensign ❑ *her ancient and pendants out* (*Robinson Crusoe* by Daniel Defoe)

antic ADJ here antic means horrible or grotesque ❑ *armed and dressed after a very antic manner* (*Gulliver's Travels* by Jonathan Swift)

antics NOUN antics is an old word meaning clowns, or people who do silly things to make other people laugh ❑ *And point like antics at his triple crown* (*Doctor Faustus 3.2* by Christopher Marlowe)

appanage NOUN an appanage is a living allowance ❑ *As if loveliness were not the special prerogative of woman–her legitimate appanage and heritage!* (*Jane Eyre* by Charlotte Brontë)

appended VERB appended means attached or added to ❑ *and these words appended* (*Treasure Island* by Robert Louis Stevenson)

approver NOUN an approver is someone who gives evidence against someone he used to work with ❑ *Mr Noah Claypole: receiving a free pardon from the Crown in consequence of being admitted approver against Fagin* (*Oliver Twist* by Charles Dickens)

areas NOUN the areas is the space, below street level, in front of the basement of a house ❑ *The Dodger had a vicious propensity, too, of pulling the caps from the heads of small boys and tossing them down areas* (*Oliver Twist* by Charles Dickens)

argument NOUN theme or important idea or subject which runs through a piece of writing ❑ *Thrice needful to the argument which now* (*The Prelude* by William Wordsworth)

artificially ADV artfully or cleverly ❑ *and he with a sharp flint sharpened very artificially* (*Gulliver's Travels* by Jonathan Swift)

artist NOUN here artist means a skilled workman ❑ *This man was a most ingenious artist* (*Gulliver's Travels* by Jonathan Swift)

assizes NOUN assizes were regular court sessions which a visiting judge was in charge of ❑ *you shall hang at the next assizes* (*Treasure Island* by Robert Louis Stevenson)

attraction NOUN gravitation, or Newton's theory of gravitation ❑ *he predicted the same fate to attraction* (*Gulliver's Travels* by Jonathan Swift)

aver VERB to aver is to claim something strongly ❑ *for Jem Rodney, the mole catcher, averred that one evening as he was returning homeward* (*Silas Marner* by George Eliot)

baby NOUN here baby means doll, which is a child's toy that looks like a small person ❑ *and skilful dressing her baby* (*Gulliver's Travels* by Jonathan Swift)

bagatelle NOUN bagatelle is a game rather like billiards and pool ❑ *Breakfast had been ordered at a pleasant little tavern, a mile or so away upon the rising ground beyond the green; and there was a bagatelle board in the room, in case we should desire to unbend our minds after the solemnity.* (*Great Expectations* by Charles Dickens)

bah EXCLAM Bah is an exclamation of frustration or anger ❑ *'Bah,' said Scrooge.* (*A Christmas Carol* by Charles Dickens)

bairn NOUN a northern word for child ❑ *Who has taught you those fine words, my bairn?* (*Wuthering Heights* by Emily Brontë)

bait VERB to bait means to stop on a journey to take refreshment ❑ *So, when they stopped to bait the horse, and ate and drank and enjoyed themselves, I could touch nothing that they touched, but kept my fast unbroken.* (*David Copperfield* by Charles Dickens)

balustrade NOUN a balustrade is a row of vertical columns that form railings ❑ *but I mean to say you might have got a hearse up that staircase, and taken it broadwise, with the splinter-bar towards the wall, and the door towards the balustrades: and done it easy* (*A Christmas Carol* by Charles Dickens)

bandbox NOUN a large lightweight box for carrying bonnets or hats ❑ *I am glad I bought my bonnet, if it is only for the fun of having another bandbox* (*Pride and Prejudice* by Jane Austen)

barren NOUN a barren here is a stretch or expanse of barren land ❑ *a line of upright stones, continued the* *length of the barren* (*Wuthering Heights* by Emily Brontë)

basin NOUN a basin was a cup without a handle ❑ *who is drinking his tea out of a basin* (*Wuthering Heights* by Emily Brontë)

battalia NOUN the order of battle ❑ *till I saw part of his army in battalia* (*Gulliver's Travels* by Jonathan Swift)

battery NOUN a Battery is a fort or a place where guns are positioned ❑ *You bring the lot to me, at that old Battery over yonder* (*Great Expectations* by Charles Dickens)

battledore and shuttlecock NOUN The game battledore and shuttlecock was an early version of the game now known as badminton. The aim of the early game was simply to keep the shuttlecock from hitting the ground. ❑ *Battledore and shuttlecock's a wery good game vhen you an't the shuttlecock and two lawyers the battledores, in which case it gets too excitin' to be pleasant* (*Pickwick Papers* by Charles Dickens)

beadle NOUN a beadle was a local official who had power over the poor ❑ *But these impertinences were speedily checked by the evidence of the surgeon, and the testimony of the beadle* (*Oliver Twist* by Charles Dickens)

bearings NOUN the bearings of a place are the measurements or directions that are used to find or locate it ❑ *the bearings of the island* (*Treasure Island* by Robert Louis Stevenson)

beaufet NOUN a beaufet was a sideboard ❑ *and sweet-cake from the beaufet* (*Emma* by Jane Austen)

beck NOUN a beck is a small stream ❑ *a beck which follows the bend of the glen* (*Wuthering Heights* by Emily Brontë)

bedight VERB decorated ❑ *and bedight with Christmas holly stuck into the top.* (*A Christmas Carol* by Charles Dickens)

Bedlam NOUN Bedlam was a lunatic asylum in London which had statues carved by Caius Gabriel Cibber at its entrance ❑ *Bedlam, and those carved maniacs at the gates* (*The Prelude* by William Wordsworth)

beeves NOUN oxen or castrated bulls which are animals used for pulling vehicles or carrying things ❑ *to deliver in every morning six beeves* (*Gulliver's Travels* by Jonathan Swift)

begot VERB created or caused ❑ *Begot in thee* (*On His Mistress* by John Donne)

behoof NOUN behoof means benefit ❑ *'Yes, young man,' said he, releasing the handle of the article in question, retiring a step or two from my table, and speaking for the behoof of the landlord and waiter at the door* (*Great Expectations* by Charles Dickens)

berth NOUN a berth is a bed on a boat ❑ *this is the berth for me* (*Treasure Island* by Robert Louis Stevenson)

bevers NOUN a bever was a snack, or small portion of food, eaten between main meals ❑ *that buys me thirty meals a day and ten bevers* (*Doctor Faustus 2.1* by Christopher Marlowe)

bilge water NOUN the bilge is the widest part of a ship's bottom, and the bilge water is the dirty water that collects there ❑ *no gush of bilge-water had turned it to fetid puddle* (*Jane Eyre* by Charlotte Brontë)

bills NOUN bills is an old term meaning prescription. A prescription is the piece of paper on which your doctor writes an order for medicine and which you give to a chemist to get the medicine ❑ *Are not thy bills hung up as monuments* (*Doctor Faustus 1.1* by Christopher Marlowe)

black cap NOUN a judge wore a black cap when he was about to sentence a prisoner to death ❑ *The judge assumed the black cap, and the prisoner still stood with the same air and gesture.* (*Oliver Twist* by Charles Dickens)

boot-jack NOUN a wooden device to help take boots off ❑ *The speaker appeared to throw a boot-jack, or some such article, at the person he addressed* (*Oliver Twist* by Charles Dickens)

booty NOUN booty means treasure or prizes ❑ *would be inclined to give up their booty in payment of the dead man's debts* (*Treasure Island* by Robert Louis Stevenson)

Bow Street runner PHRASE Bow Street runners were the first British police force, set up by the author Henry Fielding in the eighteenth century ❑ *as would have convinced a judge or a Bow Street runner* (*Treasure Island* by Robert Louis Stevenson)

brawn NOUN brawn is a dish of meat which is set in jelly ❑ *Heaped up upon the floor, to form a kind of throne, were turkeys, geese, game, poultry, brawn, great joints of meat, suckling-pigs* (*A Christmas Carol* by Charles Dickens)

bray VERB when a donkey brays, it makes a loud, harsh sound ❑ *and she doesn't bray like a jackass* (*The Adventures of Huckleberry Finn* by Mark Twain)

break VERB in order to train a horse you first have to break it ❑ *'If a high-mettled creature like this,' said he, 'can't be broken by fair means, she will never be good for anything'* (*Black Beauty* by Anna Sewell)

bullyragging VERB bullyragging is an old word which means bullying. To bullyrag someone is to threaten or force someone to do something they don't want to do ❑ *and a lot of loafers bullyragging him for sport* (*The Adventures of Huckleberry Finn* by Mark Twain)

but PREP except for (this) ❑ *but this, all pleasures fancies be* (*The Good-Morrow* by John Donne)

by hand PHRASE by hand was a common expression of the time meaning that baby had been fed either using a spoon or a bottle rather than by breast-feeding ❑ *My sister, Mrs. Joe Gargery, was more than twenty years older than I, and had established a great reputation with herself . . . because she had bought me up 'by hand'* (*Great Expectations* by Charles Dickens)

bye-spots NOUN bye-spots are lonely places ❑ *and bye-spots of tales rich with indigenous produce* (*The Prelude* by William Wordsworth)

calico NOUN calico is plain white fabric made from cotton ❑ *There was two old dirty calico dresses* (*The Adventures of Huckleberry Finn* by Mark Twain)

camp-fever NOUN camp-fever was another word for the disease typhus ❑ *during a severe camp-fever* (*Emma* by Jane Austen)

cant NOUN cant is insincere or empty talk ❑ *'Man,' said the Ghost, 'if man you be in heart, not adamant, forbear that wicked cant until you have discovered What the surplus is, and Where it is.'* (*A Christmas Carol* by Charles Dickens)

canty ADJ canty means lively, full of life ❑ *My mother lived til eighty, a canty dame to the last* (*Wuthering Heights* by Emily Brontë)

canvas VERB to canvas is to discuss ❑ *We think so very differently on this point Mr Knightley, that there can be no use in canvassing it* (*Emma* by Jane Austen)

capital ADJ capital means excellent or extremely good ❑ *for it's capital, so shady, light, and big* (*Little Women* by Louisa May Alcott)

capstan NOUN a capstan is a device used on a ship to lift sails and anchors ❑ *capstans going, ships going out to sea, and unintelligible sea creatures roaring curses over the* *bulwarks at respondent lightermen* (*Great Expectations* by Charles Dickens)

case-bottle NOUN a square bottle designed to fit with others into a case ❑ *The spirit being set before him in a huge case-bottle, which had originally come out of some ship's locker* (*The Old Curiosity Shop* by Charles Dickens)

casement NOUN casement is a word meaning window. The teacher in *Nicholas Nickleby* misspells window showing what a bad teacher he is ❑ *W-i-n, win, d-e-r, der, winder, a casement.* (*Nicholas Nickleby* by Charles Dickens)

cataleptic ADJ a cataleptic fit is one in which the victim goes into a trancelike state and remains still for a long time ❑ *It was at this point in their history that Silas's cataleptic fit occurred during the prayer-meeting* (*Silas Marner* by George Eliot)

cauldron NOUN a cauldron is a large cooking pot made of metal ❑ *stirring a large cauldron which seemed to be full of soup* (*Alice's Adventures in Wonderland* by Lewis Carroll)

cephalic ADJ cephalic means to do with the head ❑ *with ink composed of a cephalic tincture* (*Gulliver's Travels* by Jonathan Swift)

chaise and four NOUN a closed four-wheel carriage pulled by four horses ❑ *he came down on Monday in a chaise and four to see the place* (*Pride and Prejudice* by Jane Austen)

chamberlain NOUN the main servant in a household ❑ *In those times a bed was always to be got there at any hour of the night, and the chamberlain, letting me in at his ready wicket, lighted the candle next in order on his shelf* (*Great Expectations* by Charles Dickens)

characters NOUN distinguishing marks ❑ *Impressed upon all forms the characters* (*The Prelude* by William Wordsworth)

chary ADJ cautious ❑ *I should have been chary of discussing my guardian too freely even with her* (*Great Expectations* by Charles Dickens)

cherishes VERB here cherishes means cheers or brightens ❑ *some philosophic song of Truth that cherishes our daily life* (*The Prelude* by William Wordsworth)

chickens' meat PHRASE chickens' meat is an old term which means chickens' feed or food ❑ *I had shook a bag of chickens' meat out in that place* (*Robinson Crusoe* by Daniel Defoe)

chimeras NOUN a chimera is an unrealistic idea or a wish which is unlikely to be fulfilled ❑ *with many other wild impossible chimeras* (*Gulliver's Travels* by Jonathan Swift)

chines NOUN chine is a cut of meat that includes part or all of the backbone of the animal ❑ *and they found hams and chines uncut* (*Silas Marner* by George Eliot)

chits NOUN chits is a slang word which means girls ❑ *I hate affected, niminy-piminy chits!* (*Little Women* by Louisa May Alcott)

chopped VERB chopped means come suddenly or accidentally ❑ *if I had chopped upon them* (*Robinson Crusoe* by Daniel Defoe)

chute NOUN a narrow channel ❑ *One morning about day-break, I found a canoe and crossed over a chute to the main shore* (*The Adventures of Huckleberry Finn* by Mark Twain)

circumspection NOUN careful observation of events and circumstances; caution ❑ *I honour your circumspection* (*Pride and Prejudice* by Jane Austen)

clambered VERB clambered means to climb somewhere with difficulty, usually using your hands and your feet ❑ *he clambered up and down stairs* (*Treasure Island* by Robert Louis Stevenson)

clime NOUN climate ❑ *no season knows nor clime* (*The Sun Rising* by John Donne)

clinched VERB clenched ❑ *the tops whereof I could but just reach with my fist clinched* (*Gulliver's Travels* by Jonathan Swift)

close chair NOUN a close chair is a sedan chair, which is an covered chair which has room for one person. The sedan chair is carried on two poles by two men, one in front and one behind ❑ *persuaded even the Empress herself to let me hold her in her close chair* (*Gulliver's Travels* by Jonathan Swift)

clown NOUN clown here means peasant or person who lives off the land ❑ *In ancient days by emperor and clown* (*Ode to a Nightingale* by John Keats)

coalheaver NOUN a coalheaver loaded coal onto ships using a spade ❑ *Good, strong, wholesome medicine, as was given with great success to two Irish labourers and a coalheaver* (*Oliver Twist* by Charles Dickens)

coal-whippers NOUN men who worked at docks using machines to load coal onto ships ❑ *here, were colliers by the score and score, with the coal-whippers plunging off stages on deck* (*Great Expectations* by Charles Dickens)

cobweb NOUN a cobweb is the net which a spider makes for catching insects ❑ *the walls and ceilings were all hung round with cobwebs* (*Gulliver's Travels* by Jonathan Swift)

coddling VERB coddling means to treat someone too kindly or protect them too much ❑ *and I've been coddling the fellow as if I'd been his grand-mother* (*Little Women* by Louisa May Alcott)

coil NOUN coil means noise or fuss or disturbance ❑ *What a coil is there?* (*Doctor Faustus 4.7* by Christopher Marlowe)

collared VERB to collar something is a slang term which means to capture. In this sentence, it means he stole it [the money] ❑ *he collared it* (*The Adventures of Huckleberry Finn* by Mark Twain)

colling VERB colling is an old word which means to embrace and kiss ❑ *and no clasping and colling at all* (*Tess of the D'Urbervilles* by Thomas Hardy)

colloquies NOUN colloquy is a formal conversation or dialogue ❑ *Such colloquies have occupied many a pair of pale-faced weavers* (*Silas Marner* by George Eliot)

comfit NOUN sugar-covered pieces of fruit or nut eaten as sweets ❑ *and pulled out a box of comfits* (*Alice's Adventures in Wonderland* by Lewis Carroll)

coming out VERB when a girl came out in society it meant she was of marriageable age. In order to 'come out' girls were expecting to attend balls and other parties during a season ❑ *The younger girls formed hopes of coming out a year or two sooner than they might otherwise have done* (*Pride and Prejudice* by Jane Austen)

commit VERB commit means arrest or stop ❑ *Commit the rascals* (*Doctor Faustus 4.7* by Christopher Marlowe)

commodious ADJ commodious means convenient ❑ *the most commodious and effectual ways* (*Gulliver's Travels* by Jonathan Swift)

commons NOUN commons is an old term meaning food shared with others ❑ *his pauper assistants ranged themselves behind him; the gruel was served out; and a long grace was said over the short commons.* (*Oliver Twist* by Charles Dickens)

complacency NOUN here complacency means a desire to please others. To-day complacency means feeling pleased with oneself without good reason. ❑ *Twas thy power that raised the first complacency in me* (*The Prelude* by William Wordsworth)

complaisance NOUN complaisance was eagerness to please ❑ *we cannot wonder at his complaisance* (*Pride and Prejudice* by Jane Austen)

complaisant ADJ complaisant means polite ❑ *extremely cheerful and complaisant to their guest* (*Gulliver's Travels* by Jonathan Swift)

conning VERB conning means learning by heart ❑ *Or conning more* (*The Prelude* by William Wordsworth)

consequent NOUN consequence ❑ *as avarice is the necessary consequent of old age* (*Gulliver's Travels* by Jonathan Swift)

consorts NOUN concerts ❑ *The King, who delighted in music, had frequent consorts at Court* (*Gulliver's Travels* by Jonathan Swift)

conversible ADJ conversible meant easy to talk to, companionable ❑ *He can be a conversible companion* (*Pride and Prejudice* by Jane Austen)

copper NOUN a copper is a large pot that can be heated directly over a fire ❑ *He gazed in stupefied astonishment on the small rebel for some seconds, and then clung for support to the copper* (*Oliver Twist* by Charles Dickens)

copper-stick NOUN a copper-stick is the long piece of wood used to stir washing in the copper (or boiler) which was usually the biggest cooking pot in the house ❑ *It was Christmas Eve, and I had to stir the pudding for next day, with a copper-stick, from seven to eight by the Dutch clock* (*Great Expectations* by Charles Dickens)

counting-house NOUN a counting-house is a place where accountants work ❑ *Once upon a time–of all the good days in the year, on Christmas Eve–old Scrooge sat busy in his counting-house* (*A Christmas Carol* by Charles Dickens)

courtier NOUN a courtier is someone who attends the king or queen–a member of the court ❑ *next the ten courtiers;* (*Alice's Adventures in Wonderland* by Lewis Carroll)

covies NOUN covies were flocks of partridges ❑ *and will save all of the best covies for you* (*Pride and Prejudice* by Jane Austen)

cowed VERB cowed means frightened or intimidated ❑ *it cowed me more than the pain* (*Treasure Island* by Robert Louis Stevenson)

cozened VERB cozened means tricked or deceived ❑ *Do you remember, sir, how you cozened me* (*Doctor Faustus 4.7* by Christopher Marlowe)

cravats NOUN a cravat is a folded cloth that a man wears wrapped around his neck as a decorative item of clothing ❑ *we'd 'a' slept in our cravats to-night* (*The Adventures of Huckleberry Finn* by Mark Twain)

crock and dirt PHRASE crock and dirt is an old expression meaning soot and dirt ❑ *and the mare catching cold at the door, and the boy grimed with crock and dirt* (*Great Expectations* by Charles Dickens)

crockery NOUN here crockery means pottery ❑ *By one of the parrots was a cat made of crockery* (*The Adventures of Huckleberry Finn* by Mark Twain)

crooked sixpence PHRASE it was considered unlucky to have a bent sixpence ❑ *You've got the beauty, you see, and I've got the luck, so you must keep me by you for your crooked sixpence* (*Silas Marner* by George Eliot)

croquet NOUN croquet is a traditional English summer game in which players try to hit wooden balls through hoops ❑ *and once she remembered trying to box her own ears for having cheated herself in a game of croquet* (*Alice's Adventures in Wonderland* by Lewis Carroll)

cross PREP across ❑ The two great streets, which run cross and divide it into four quarters (*Gulliver's Travels* by Jonathan Swift)

culpable ADJ if you are culpable for something it means you are to blame ❑ *deep are the sorrows that spring from false ideas for which no man is culpable.* (*Silas Marner* by George Eliot)

cultured ADJ cultivated ❑ *Nor less when spring had warmed the cultured Vale* (*The Prelude* by William Wordsworth)

cupidity NOUN cupidity is greed ❑ *These people hated me with the hatred of cupidity and disappointment.* (*Great Expectations* by Charles Dickens)

curricle NOUN an open two-wheeled carriage with one seat for the driver and space for a single passenger ❑ *and they saw a lady and a gentleman in a curricle* (*Pride and Prejudice* by Jane Austen)

cynosure NOUN a cynosure is something that strongly attracts attention or admiration ❑ *Then I thought of Eliza and Georgiana; I beheld one the cynosure of a ballroom, the other the inmate of a convent cell* (*Jane Eyre* by Charlotte Brontë)

dalliance NOUN someone's dalliance with something is a brief involvement with it ❑ *nor sporting in the dalliance of love* (*Doctor Faustus Chorus* by Christopher Marlowe)

darkling ADV darkling is an archaic way of saying in the dark ❑ *Darkling I listen* (*Ode to a Nightingale* by John Keats)

delf-case NOUN a sideboard for holding dishes and crockery ❑ *at the pewter dishes and delf-case* (*Wuthering Heights* by Emily Brontë)

determined ■ VERB here determined means ended ❑ *and be out of vogue when that was determined* (*Gulliver's Travels* by Jonathan Swift) ■ VERB determined can mean to have been learned or found especially by investigation or experience ❑ *All the sensitive feelings it wounded so cruelly, all the shame and misery it kept alive within my breast, became more poignant as I thought of this; and I determined that the life was unendurable* (*David Copperfield* by Charles Dickens)

Deuce NOUN a slang term for the Devil ❑ *Ah, I dare say I did. Deuce take me, he added suddenly, I know I did. I find I am not quite unscrewed yet.* (*Great Expectations* by Charles Dickens)

diabolical ADJ diabolical means devilish or evil ❑ *and with a thousand diabolical expressions* (*Treasure Island* by Robert Louis Stevenson)

direction NOUN here direction means address ❑ *Elizabeth was not surprised at it, as Jane had written the direction remarkably ill* (*Pride and Prejudice* by Jane Austen)

discover VERB to make known or announce ❑ *the Emperor would discover the secret while I was out of his power* (*Gulliver's Travels* by Jonathan Swift)

dissemble VERB hide or conceal ❑ *Dissemble nothing* (*On His Mistress* by John Donne)

dissolve VERB dissolve here means to release from life, to die ❑ *Fade far away, dissolve, and quite forget* (*Ode to a Nightingale* by John Keats)

distrain VERB to distrain is to seize the property of someone who is in debt in compensation for the money owed ❑ *for he's threatening to distrain for it* (*Silas Marner* by George Eliot)

Divan NOUN a Divan was originally a Turkish council of state–the name was transferred to the couches they sat on and is used to mean this in English ❑ *Mr Brass applauded this picture very much, and the bed being soft and comfortable, Mr Quilp determined to use it, both as a sleeping place by night and as a kind of Divan by day.* (*The Old Curiosity Shop* by Charles Dickens)

divorcement NOUN separation ❑ *By all pains which want and divorcement* *hath* (*On His Mistress* by John Donne)

dog in the manger, PHRASE this phrase describes someone who prevents you from enjoying something that they themselves have no need for ❑ *You are a dog in the manger, Cathy, and desire no one to be loved but yourself* (*Wuthering Heights* by Emily Brontë)

dolorifuge NOUN dolorifuge is a word which Thomas Hardy invented. It means pain-killer or comfort ❑ *as a species of dolorifuge* (*Tess of the D'Urbervilles* by Thomas Hardy)

dome NOUN building ❑ *that river and that mouldering dome* (*The Prelude* by William Wordsworth)

domestic NOUN here domestic means a person's management of the house ❑ *to give some account of my domestic* (*Gulliver's Travels* by Jonathan Swift)

dunce NOUN a dunce is another word for idiot ❑ *Do you take me for a dunce? Go on?* (*Alice's Adventures in Wonderland* by Lewis Carroll)

Ecod EXCLAM a slang exclamation meaning 'oh God!' ❑ *'Ecod,' replied Wemmick, shaking his head, 'that's not my trade.'* (*Great Expectations* by Charles Dickens)

egg-hot NOUN an egg-hot (see also 'flip' and 'negus') was a hot drink made from beer and eggs, sweetened with nutmeg ❑ *She fainted when she saw me return, and made a little jug of egg-hot afterwards to console us while we talked it over.* (*David Copperfield* by Charles Dickens)

encores NOUN an encore is a short extra performance at the end of a longer one, which the entertainer gives because the audience has enthusiastically asked for it ❑ *we want a little something to answer encores with, anyway* (*The Adventures of Huckleberry Finn* by Mark Twain)

equipage NOUN an elegant and impressive carriage ❑ *and besides, the equipage did not answer to any of their neighbours* (*Pride and Prejudice* by Jane Austen)

exordium NOUN an exordium is the opening part of a speech ❑ *'Now, Handel,' as if it were the grave beginning of a portentous business exordium, he had suddenly given up that tone* (*Great Expectations* by Charles Dickens)

expect VERB here expect means to wait for ❑ *to expect his farther commands* (*Gulliver's Travels* by Jonathan Swift)

familiars NOUN familiars means spirits or devils who come to someone when they are called ❑ *I'll turn all the lice about thee into familiars* (*Doctor Faustus 1.4* by Christopher Marlowe)

fantods NOUN a fantod is a person who fidgets or can't stop moving nervously ❑ *It most give me the fantods* (*The Adventures of Huckleberry Finn* by Mark Twain)

farthing NOUN a farthing is an old unit of British currency which was worth a quarter of a penny ❑ *Not a farthing less. A great many back-payments are included in it, I assure you.* (*A Christmas Carol* by Charles Dickens)

farthingale NOUN a hoop worn under a skirt to extend it ❑ *A bell with an old voice–which I dare say in its time had often said to the house, Here is the green farthingale* (*Great Expectations* by Charles Dickens)

favours NOUN here favours is an old word which means ribbons ❑ *A group of humble mourners entered the gate: wearing white favours* (*Oliver Twist* by Charles Dickens)

feigned VERB pretend or pretending ❑ *not my feigned page* (*On His Mistress* by John Donne)

fence ■ NOUN a fence is someone who receives and sells stolen goods ❑ *What are you up to? Ill-treating the boys, you covetous, avaricious, in-sa-ti-a-ble old fence?* (*Oliver Twist* by

Charles Dickens) **2** NOUN defence or protection ❑ *but honesty hath no fence against superior cunning* (*Gulliver's Travels* by Jonathan Swift)

fess ADJ fess is an old word which means pleased or proud ❑ *You'll be fess enough, my poppet* (*Tess of the D'Urbervilles* by Thomas Hardy)

fettered ADJ fettered means bound in chains or chained ❑ *'You are fettered,' said Scrooge, trembling. 'Tell me why?'* (*A Christmas Carol* by Charles Dickens)

fidges VERB fidges means fidgets, which is to keep moving your hands slightly because you are nervous or excited ❑ *Look, Jim, how my fingers fidges* (*Treasure Island* by Robert Louis Stevenson)

finger-post NOUN a finger-post is a sign-post showing the direction to different places ❑ *'The gallows,' continued Fagin, 'the gallows, my dear, is an ugly finger-post, which points out a very short and sharp turning that has stopped many a bold fellow's career on the broad highway.'* (*Oliver Twist* by Charles Dickens)

fire-irons NOUN fire-irons are tools kept by the side of the fire to either cook with or look after the fire ❑ *the fire-irons came first* (*Alice's Adventures in Wonderland* by Lewis Carroll)

fire-plug NOUN a fire-plug is another word for a fire hydrant ❑ *The pony looked with great attention into a fire-plug, which was near him, and appeared to be quite absorbed in contemplating it* (*The Old Curiosity Shop* by Charles Dickens)

flank NOUN flank is the side of an animal ❑ *And all her silken flanks with garlands dressed* (*Ode on a Grecian Urn* by John Keats)

flip NOUN a flip is a drink made from warmed ale, sugar, spice and beaten egg ❑ *The events of the day, in combination with the twins, if not with the flip, had made Mrs Micawber hysterical, and she shed tears as she replied* (*David Copperfield* by Charles Dickens)

flit VERB flit means to move quickly ❑ *and if he had meant to flit to Thrushcross Grange* (*Wuthering Heights* by Emily Brontë)

floorcloth NOUN a floorcloth was a hard-wearing piece of canvas used instead of carpet ❑ *This avenging phantom was ordered to be on duty at eight on Tuesday morning in the hall (it was two feet square, as charged for floorcloth)* (*Great Expectations* by Charles Dickens)

fly-driver NOUN a fly-driver is a carriage drawn by a single horse ❑ *The fly-drivers, among whom I inquired next, were equally jocose and equally disrespectful* (*David Copperfield* by Charles Dickens)

fob NOUN a small pocket in which a watch is kept ❑ *'Certain,' replied the man, drawing a gold watch from his fob* (*Oliver Twist* by Charles Dickens)

folly NOUN folly means foolishness or stupidity ❑ *the folly of beginning a work* (*Robinson Crusoe* by Daniel Defoe)

fond ADJ fond means foolish ❑ *Fond worldling* (*Doctor Faustus 5.2* by Christopher Marlowe)

fondness NOUN silly or foolish affection ❑ *They have no fondness for their colts or foals* (*Gulliver's Travels* by Jonathan Swift)

for his fancy PHRASE for his fancy means for his liking or as he wanted ❑ *and as I did not obey quick enough for his fancy* (*Treasure Island* by Robert Louis Stevenson)

forlorn ADJ lost or very upset ❑ *you are from that day forlorn* (*Gulliver's Travels* by Jonathan Swift)

foster-sister NOUN a foster-sister was someone brought up by the same nurse or in the same household ❑ *I had been his foster-sister* (*Wuthering Heights* by Emily Brontë)

fox-fire NOUN fox-fire is a weak glow that is given off by decaying, rotten wood ❑ *what we must have was a lot of them rotten chunks that's called fox-fire* (*The Adventures of Huckleberry Finn* by Mark Twain)

frozen sea PHRASE the Arctic Ocean ❑ *into the frozen sea* (*Gulliver's Travels* by Jonathan Swift)

gainsay VERB to gainsay something is to say it isn't true or to deny it ❑ *'So she had,' cried Scrooge. 'You're right. I'll not gainsay it, Spirit. God forbid!'* (*A Christmas Carol* by Charles Dickens)

gaiters NOUN gaiters were leggings made of a cloth or piece of leather which covered the leg from the knee to the ankle ❑ *Mr Knightley was hard at work upon the lower buttons of his thick leather gaiters* (*Emma* by Jane Austen)

galluses NOUN galluses is an old spelling of gallows, and here means suspenders. Suspenders are straps worn over someone's shoulders and fastened to their trousers to prevent the trousers falling down ❑ *and home-knit galluses* (*The Adventures of Huckleberry Finn* by Mark Twain)

galoot NOUN a sailor but also a clumsy person ❑ *and maybe a galoot on it chopping* (*The Adventures of Huckleberry Finn* by Mark Twain)

gayest ADJ gayest means the most lively and bright or merry ❑ *Beth played her gayest march* (*Little Women* by Louisa May Alcott)

gem NOUN here gem means jewellery ❑ *the mountain shook off turf and flower, had only heath for raiment and crag for gem* (*Jane Eyre* by Charlotte Brontë)

giddy ADJ giddy means dizzy ❑ *and I wish you wouldn't keep appearing and vanishing so suddenly; you make one quite giddy.* (*Alice's Adventures in Wonderland* by Lewis Carroll)

gig NOUN a light two-wheeled carriage ❑ *when a gig drove up to the garden gate: out of which there jumped a fat gentleman* (*Oliver Twist* by Charles Dickens)

gladsome ADJ gladsome is an old word meaning glad or happy ❑ *Nobody ever stopped him in the street to say, with gladsome looks* (*A Christmas Carol* by Charles Dickens)

glen NOUN a glen is a small valley; the word is used commonly in Scotland ❑ *a beck which follows the bend of the glen* (*Wuthering Heights* by Emily Brontë)

gravelled VERB gravelled is an old term which means to baffle or defeat someone ❑ *Gravelled the pastors of the German Church* (*Doctor Faustus 1.1* by Christopher Marlowe)

grinder NOUN a grinder was a private tutor ❑ *but that when he had had the happiness of marrying Mrs Pocket very early in his life, he had impaired his prospects and taken up the calling of a Grinder* (*Great Expectations* by Charles Dickens)

gruel NOUN gruel is a thin, watery cornmeal or oatmeal soup ❑ *and the little saucepan of gruel (Scrooge had a cold in his head) upon the hob.* (*A Christmas Carol* by Charles Dickens)

guinea, half a NOUN half a guinea was ten shillings and sixpence ❑ *but lay out half a guinea at Ford's* (*Emma* by Jane Austen)

gull VERB gull is an old term which means to fool or deceive someone ❑ *Hush, I'll gull him supernaturally* (*Doctor Faustus 3.4* by Christopher Marlowe)

gunnel NOUN the gunnel, or gunwale, is the upper edge of a boat's side ❑ *But he put his foot on the gunnel and rocked her* (*The Adventures of Huckleberry Finn* by Mark Twain)

gunwale NOUN the side of a ship ❑ *He dipped his hand in the water over the boat's gunwale* (*Great Expectations* by Charles Dickens)

Gytrash NOUN a Gytrash is an omen of misfortune to the superstitious, usually taking the form of a hound ❑ *I remembered certain of Bessie's tales, wherein figured a North-of-England spirit, called a 'Gytrash'* (*Jane Eyre* by Charlotte Brontë)

hackney-cabriolet NOUN a two-wheeled carriage with four seats for hire and pulled by a horse ❑ *A hackney-cabriolet was in waiting; with the same vehemence which she had exhibited in addressing Oliver, the girl pulled him in with her, and drew the curtains close.* (*Oliver Twist* by Charles Dickens)

hackney-coach NOUN a four-wheeled horse-drawn vehicle for hire ❑ *The twilight was beginning to close in, when Mr Brownlow alighted from a hackney-coach at his own door, and knocked softly.* (*Oliver Twist* by Charles Dickens)

haggler NOUN a haggler is someone who travels from place to place selling small goods and items ❑ *when I be plain Jack Durbeyfield, the haggler* (*Tess of the D'Urbervilles* by Thomas Hardy)

halter NOUN a halter is a rope or strap used to lead an animal or to tie it up ❑ *I had of course long been used to a halter and a headstall* (*Black Beauty* by Anna Sewell)

hamlet NOUN a hamlet is a small village or a group of houses in the countryside ❑ *down from the hamlet* (*Treasure Island* by Robert Louis Stevenson)

hand-barrow NOUN a hand-barrow is a device for carrying heavy objects. It is like a wheelbarrow except that it has handles, rather than wheels, for moving the barrow ❑ *his sea chest following behind him in a hand-barrow* (*Treasure Island* by Robert Louis Stevenson)

handspike NOUN a handspike was a stick which was used as a lever ❑ *a bit of stick like a handspike* (*Treasure Island* by Robert Louis Stevenson)

haply ADV haply means by chance or perhaps ❑ *And haply the Queen-Moon is on her throne* (*Ode to a Nightingale* by John Keats)

harem NOUN the harem was the part of the house where the women lived ❑ *mostly they hang round the harem* (*The Adventures of Huckleberry Finn* by Mark Twain)

hautboys NOUN hautboys are oboes ❑ *sausages and puddings resembling flutes and hautboys* (*Gulliver's Travels* by Jonathan Swift)

hawker NOUN a hawker is someone who sells goods to people as he travels rather than from a fixed place like a shop ❑ *to buy some stockings from a hawker* (*Treasure Island* by Robert Louis Stevenson)

hawser NOUN a hawser is a rope used to tie up or tow a ship or boat ❑ *Again among the tiers of shipping, in and out, avoiding rusty chain-cables, frayed hempen hawsers* (*Great Expectations* by Charles Dickens)

headstall NOUN the headstall is the part of the bridle or halter that goes around a horse's head ❑ *I had of course long been used to a halter and a headstall* (*Black Beauty* by Anna Sewell)

hearken VERB hearken means to listen ❑ *though we sometimes stopped to lay hold of each other and hearken* (*Treasure Island* by Robert Louis Stevenson)

heartless ADJ here heartless means without heart or dejected ❑ *I am not heartless* (*The Prelude* by William Wordsworth)

hebdomadal ADJ hebdomadal means weekly ❑ *It was the hebdomadal treat to which we all looked forward from Sabbath to Sabbath* (*Jane Eyre* by Charlotte Brontë)

highwaymen NOUN highwaymen were people who stopped travellers and robbed them ❑ *We are highwaymen* (*The Adventures of Huckleberry Finn* by Mark Twain)

hinds NOUN hinds means farm hands, or people who work on a farm ❑ *He called his hinds about him* (*Gulliver's Travels* by Jonathan Swift)

histrionic ADJ if you refer to someone's behaviour as histrionic, you are being critical of it because it is dramatic and exaggerated ❑ *But the histrionic muse is the darling* (*The Adventures of Huckleberry Finn* by Mark Twain)

hogs NOUN hogs is another word for pigs ❑ *Tom called the hogs 'ingots'* (*The Adventures of Huckleberry Finn* by Mark Twain)

horrors NOUN the horrors are a fit, called delirium tremens, which is caused by drinking too much alcohol ❑ *I'll have the horrors* (*Treasure Island* by Robert Louis Stevenson)

huffy ADJ huffy means to be obviously annoyed or offended about something ❑ *They will feel that more than angry speeches or huffy actions* (*Little Women* by Louisa May Alcott)

hulks NOUN hulks were prison-ships ❑ *The miserable companion of thieves and ruffians, the fallen outcast of low haunts, the associate of the scourings of the jails and hulks* (*Oliver Twist* by Charles Dickens)

humbug NOUN humbug means nonsense or rubbish ❑ *'Bah,' said Scrooge. 'Humbug!'* (*A Christmas Carol* by Charles Dickens)

humours NOUN it was believed that there were four fluids in the body called humours which decided the temperament of a person depending on how much of each fluid was present ❑ *other peccant humours* (*Gulliver's Travels* by Jonathan Swift)

husbandry NOUN husbandry is farming animals ❑ *bad husbandry were plentifully anointing their wheels* (*Silas Marner* by George Eliot)

huswife NOUN a huswife was a small sewing kit ❑ *but I had put my huswife on it* (*Emma* by Jane Austen)

ideal ADJ ideal in this context means imaginary ❑ *I discovered the yell was not ideal* (*Wuthering Heights* by Emily Brontë)

If our two PHRASE if both our ❑ *If our two loves be one* (*The Good-Morrow* by John Donne)

ignis-fatuus NOUN ignis-fatuus is the light given out by burning marsh gases, which lead careless travellers into danger ❑ *it is madness in all women to let a secret love kindle within them, which, if unreturned and unknown, must devour the life that feeds it; and, if discovered and responded to, must lead ignis-fatuus-like, into miry wilds whence there is no extrication.* (*Jane Eyre* by Charlotte Brontë)

imaginations NOUN here imaginations means schemes or plans ❑ *soon drove out those imaginations* (*Gulliver's Travels* by Jonathan Swift)

impressible ADJ impressible means open or impressionable ❑ *for Marner had one of those impressible, self-doubting natures* (*Silas Marner* by George Eliot)

in good intelligence PHRASE friendly with each other ❑ *that these two persons were in good intelligence with each other* (*Gulliver's Travels* by Jonathan Swift)

inanity NOUN inanity is silliness or dull stupidity ❑ *Do we not wile away moments of inanity* (*Silas Marner* by George Eliot)

incivility NOUN incivility means rudeness or impoliteness ❑ *if it's only for a piece of incivility like to-night's* (*Treasure Island* by Robert Louis Stevenson)

indigenae NOUN indigenae means natives or people from that area ❑ *an exotic that the surly indigenae will not recognise for kin* (*Wuthering Heights* by Emily Brontë)

indocible ADJ unteachable ❑ *so they were the most restive and indocible* (*Gulliver's Travels* by Jonathan Swift)

ingenuity NOUN inventiveness ❑ *entreated me to give him something as an encouragement to ingenuity* (*Gulliver's Travels* by Jonathan Swift)

ingots NOUN an ingot is a lump of a valuable metal like gold, usually shaped like a brick ❑ *Tom called the hogs 'ingots'* (*The Adventures of Huckleberry Finn* by Mark Twain)

inkstand NOUN an inkstand is a pot which was put on a desk to contain either ink or pencils and pens ❑ *throwing an inkstand at the Lizard as she spoke* (*Alice's Adventures in Wonderland* by Lewis Carroll)

inordinate ADJ without order. To-day inordinate means 'excessive'. ❑ *Though yet untutored and inordinate* (*The Prelude* by William Wordsworth)

intellectuals NOUN here intellectuals means the minds (of the workmen) ❑ *those instructions they give being too refined for the intellectuals of their workmen* (*Gulliver's Travels* by Jonathan Swift)

interview NOUN meeting ❑ *By our first strange and fatal interview* (*On His Mistress* by John Donne)

jacks NOUN jacks are rods for turning a spit over a fire ❑ *It was a small bit of pork suspended from the kettle hanger by a string passed through a large door key, in a way known to primitive housekeepers unpossessed of jacks* (*Silas Marner* by George Eliot)

jews-harp NOUN a jews-harp is a small, metal, musical instrument that is played by the mouth ❑ *A jews-harp's plenty good enough for a rat* (*The Adventures of Huckleberry Finn* by Mark Twain)

jorum NOUN a large bowl ❑ *while Miss Skiffins brewed such a jorum of tea, that the pig in the back premises became strongly excited* (*Great Expectations* by Charles Dickens)

jostled VERB jostled means bumped or pushed by someone or some people ❑ *being jostled himself into the kennel* (*Gulliver's Travels* by Jonathan Swift)

keepsake NOUN a keepsake is a gift which reminds someone of an event or of the person who gave it to them. ❑ *books and ornaments they had in their boudoirs at home: keepsakes that different relations had presented to them* (*Jane Eyre* by Charlotte Brontë)

kenned VERB kenned means knew ❑ *though little kenned the lamplighter that he had any company but Christmas!* (*A Christmas Carol* by Charles Dickens)

kennel NOUN kennel means gutter, which is the edge of a road next to the pavement, where rain water collects and flows away ❑ *being jostled himself into the kennel* (*Gulliver's Travels* by Jonathan Swift)

knock-knee ADJ knock-knee means slanted, at an angle. ❑ *LOT 1 was marked in whitewashed knock-knee letters on the brewhouse* (*Great Expectations* by Charles Dickens)

ladylike ADJ to be ladylike is to behave in a polite, dignified and graceful way ❑ *No, winking isn't ladylike* (*Little Women* by Louisa May Alcott)

lapse NOUN flow ❑ *Stealing with silent lapse to join the brook* (*The Prelude* by William Wordsworth)

larry NOUN larry is an old word which means commotion or noisy celebration ❑ *That was all a part of the larry!* (*Tess of the D'Urbervilles* by Thomas Hardy)

laths NOUN laths are strips of wood ❑ *The panels shrunk, the windows cracked; fragments of plaster fell out of the ceiling, and the naked laths were shown instead* (*A Christmas Carol* by Charles Dickens)

leer NOUN a leer is an unpleasant smile ❑ *with a kind of leer* (*Treasure Island* by Robert Louis Stevenson)

lenitives NOUN these are different kinds of drugs or medicines: lenitives and palliatives were pain relievers; aperitives were laxatives; abstersives caused vomiting; corrosives destroyed human tissue; restringents caused constipation; cephalalgics stopped headaches; icterics were used as medicine for jaundice; apophlegmatics were cough medicine, and acoustics were cures for the loss of hearing ❑ *lenitives, aperitives, abstersives, corrosives, restringents, palliatives, laxatives, cephalalgics, icterics, apophlegmatics, acoustics* (*Gulliver's Travels* by Jonathan Swift)

lest CONJ in case. If you do something lest something (usually) unpleasant happens you do it to try to prevent it happening ❑ *She went in without knocking, and hurried upstairs, in great fear lest she should meet the real Mary Ann* (*Alice's Adventures in Wonderland* by Lewis Carroll)

levee NOUN a levee is an old term for a meeting held in the morning, shortly after the person holding the meeting has got out of bed ❑ *I used to attend the King's levee once or twice a week* (*Gulliver's Travels* by Jonathan Swift)

life-preserver NOUN a club which had lead inside it to make it heavier and therefore more dangerous ❑ *and with no more suspicious articles displayed to view than two or three heavy bludgeons which stood in a corner, and a 'life-preserver' that hung over the chimney-piece.* (*Oliver Twist* by Charles Dickens)

lighterman NOUN a lighterman is another word for sailor ❑ *in and out, hammers going in ship-builders' yards, saws going at timber, clashing engines going at things unknown, pumps going in leaky ships, capstans going, ships going out to sea, and unintelligible sea creatures roaring curses over the bulwarks at respondent lightermen* (*Great Expectations* by Charles Dickens)

livery NOUN servants often wore a uniform known as a livery ❑ *suddenly a footman in livery came running out of the wood* (*Alice's Adventures in Wonderland* by Lewis Carroll)

livid ADJ livid means pale or ash coloured. Livid also means very angry ❑ *a dirty, livid white* (*Treasure Island* by Robert Louis Stevenson)

lottery-tickets NOUN a popular card game ❑ *and Mrs Philips protested that they would have a nice comfortable noisy game of lottery tickets* (*Pride and Prejudice* by Jane Austen)

lower and upper world PHRASE the earth and the heavens are the lower and upper worlds ❑ *the changes in the lower and upper world* (*Gulliver's Travels* by Jonathan Swift)

lustres NOUN lustres are chandeliers. A chandelier is a large, decorative frame which holds light bulbs or candles and hangs from the ceiling ❑ *the lustres, lights, the carving and the guilding* (*The Prelude* by William Wordsworth)

lynched VERB killed without a criminal trial by a crowd of people ❑ *He'll never know how nigh he come to getting lynched* (*The Adventures of Huckleberry Finn* by Mark Twain)

malingering VERB if someone is malingering they are pretending to be ill to avoid working ❑ *And you stand there malingering* (*Treasure Island* by Robert Louis Stevenson)

managing PHRASE treating with consideration ❑ *to think the honour of my own kind not worth managing* (*Gulliver's Travels* by Jonathan Swift)

manhood PHRASE manhood means human nature ❑ *concerning the nature of manhood* (*Gulliver's Travels* by Jonathan Swift)

man-trap NOUN a man-trap is a set of steel jaws that snap shut when trodden on and trap a person's leg

❑ *'Don't go to him,' I called out of the window, 'he's an assassin! A man-trap!'* (*Oliver Twist* by Charles Dickens)

maps NOUN charts of the night sky ❑ *Let maps to others, worlds on worlds have shown* (*The Good-Morrow* by John Donne)

mark VERB look at or notice ❑ *Mark but this flea, and mark in this* (*The Flea* by John Donne)

maroons NOUN A maroon is someone who has been left in a place which it is difficult for them to escape from, like a small island ❑ *if schooners, islands, and maroons* (*Treasure Island* by Robert Louis Stevenson)

mast NOUN here mast means the fruit of forest trees ❑ *a quantity of acorns, dates, chestnuts, and other mast* (*Gulliver's Travels* by Jonathan Swift)

mate VERB defeat ❑ *Where Mars did mate the warlike Carthigens* (*Doctor Faustus Chorus* by Christopher Marlowe)

mealy ADJ Mealy when used to describe a face meant pallid, pale or colourless ❑ *I only know two sorts of boys. Mealy boys, and beef-faced boys* (*Oliver Twist* by Charles Dickens)

middling ADV fairly or moderately ❑ *she worked me middling hard for about an hour* (*The Adventures of Huckleberry Finn* by Mark Twain)

mill NOUN a mill, or treadmill, was a device for hard labour or punishment in prison ❑ *Was you never on the mill?* (*Oliver Twist* by Charles Dickens)

milliner's shop NOUN a milliner's sold fabrics, clothing, lace and accessories; as time went on they specialized more and more in hats ❑ *to pay their duty to their aunt and to a milliner's shop just over the way* (*Pride and Prejudice* by Jane Austen)

minching un' munching PHRASE how people in the north of England used to describe the way people from the south speak ❑ *Minching un' munching!* (*Wuthering Heights* by Emily Brontë)

mine NOUN gold ❑ *Whether both th'Indias of spice and mine* (*The Sun Rising* by John Donne)

mire NOUN mud ❑ *Tis my fate to be always ground into the mire under the iron heel of oppression* (*The Adventures of Huckleberry Finn* by Mark Twain)

miscellany NOUN a miscellany is a collection of many different kinds of things ❑ *under that, the miscellany began* (*Treasure Island* by Robert Louis Stevenson)

mistarshers NOUN mistarshers means moustache, which is the hair that grows on a man's upper lip ❑ *when he put his hand up to his mistarshers* (*Tess of the D'Urbervilles* by Thomas Hardy)

morrow NOUN here good-morrow means tomorrow and a new and better life ❑ *And now good-morrow to our waking souls* (*The Good-Morrow* by John Donne)

mortification NOUN mortification is an old word for gangrene which is when part of the body decays or 'dies' because of disease ❑ *Yes, it was a mortification–that was it* (*The Adventures of Huckleberry Finn* by Mark Twain)

mought VERB mought is an old spelling of might ❑ *what you mought call me? You mought call me captain* (*Treasure Island* by Robert Louis Stevenson)

move VERB move me not means do not make me angry ❑ *Move me not, Faustus* (*Doctor Faustus 2.1* by Christopher Marlowe)

muffin-cap NOUN a muffin-cap is a flat cap made from wool ❑ *the old one, remained stationary in the muffin-cap and leathers* (*Oliver Twist* by Charles Dickens)

mulatter NOUN a mulatter was another word for mulatto, which is a person with parents who are from different races ❑ *a mulatter, most as white as a white man* (*The Adventures of Huckleberry Finn* by Mark Twain)

mummery NOUN mummery is an old word that meant meaningless (or pretentious) ceremony ❑ *When they were all gone, and when Trabb and his men–but not his boy: I looked for him–had crammed their mummery into bags, and were gone too, the house felt wholesomer.* (*Great Expectations* by Charles Dickens)

nap NOUN the nap is the woolly surface on a new item of clothing. Here the surface has been worn away so it looks bare ❑ *like an old hat with the nap rubbed off* (*The Adventures of Huckleberry Finn* by Mark Twain)

natural ■ NOUN a natural is a person born with learning difficulties ❑ *though he had been left to his particular care by their deceased father, who thought him almost a natural.* (*David Copperfield* by Charles Dickens) ■ ADJ natural meant illegitimate ❑ *Harriet Smith was the natural daughter of somebody* (*Emma* by Jane Austen)

navigator NOUN a navigator was originally someone employed to dig canals. It is the origin of the word 'navvy' meaning a labourer ❑ *She ascertained from me in a few words what it was all about, comforted Dora, and gradually convinced her that I was not a labourer–from my manner of stating the case I believe Dora concluded that I was a navigator, and went balancing myself up and down a plank all day with a wheelbarrow–and so brought us together in peace.* (*David Copperfield* by Charles Dickens)

necromancy NOUN necromancy means a kind of magic where the magician speaks to spirits or ghosts to find out what will happen in the future ❑ *He surfeits upon cursed necromancy* (*Doctor Faustus chorus* by Christopher Marlowe)

negus NOUN a negus is a hot drink made from sweetened wine and water ❑ *He sat placidly perusing the newspaper, with his little head on one side, and a glass of warm sherry negus at his elbow.* (*David Copperfield* by Charles Dickens)

nice ADJ discriminating. Able to make good judgements or choices ❑ *consequently a claim to be nice* (*Emma* by Jane Austen)

nigh ADV nigh means near ❑ *He'll never know how nigh he come to getting lynched* (*The Adventures of Huckleberry Finn* by Mark Twain)

nimbleness NOUN nimbleness means being able to move very quickly or skilfully ❑ *and with incredible accuracy and nimbleness* (*Treasure Island* by Robert Louis Stevenson)

noggin NOUN a noggin is a small mug or a wooden cup ❑ *you'll bring me one noggin of rum* (*Treasure Island* by Robert Louis Stevenson)

none ADJ neither ❑ *none can die* (*The Good-Morrow* by John Donne)

notices NOUN observations ❑ *Arch are his notices* (*The Prelude* by William Wordsworth)

occiput NOUN occiput means the back of the head ❑ *saw off the occiput of each couple* (*Gulliver's Travels* by Jonathan Swift)

officiously ADV kindly ❑ *the governess who attended Glumdalclitch very officiously lifted me up* (*Gulliver's Travels* by Jonathan Swift)

old salt PHRASE old salt is a slang term for an experienced sailor ❑ *a 'true sea-dog', and a 'real old salt'* (*Treasure Island* by Robert Louis Stevenson)

or ere PHRASE before ❑ *or ere the Hall was built* (*The Prelude* by William Wordsworth)

ostler NOUN one who looks after horses at an inn ❑ *The bill paid, and the waiter remembered, and the ostler not forgotten, and the chambermaid taken into consideration* (*Great Expectations* by Charles Dickens)

ostry NOUN an ostry is an old word for a pub or hotel ❑ *lest I send you into the ostry with a vengeance* (*Doctor Faustus 2.2* by Christopher Marlowe)

outrunning the constable PHRASE outrunning the constable meant spending more than you earn ❑ *but I shall by this means be able to check your bills and to pull you up if I find you outrunning the constable.* (*Great Expectations* by Charles Dickens)

over ADV across ❑ *It is in length six yards, and in the thickest part at least three yards over* (*Gulliver's Travels* by Jonathan Swift)

over the broomstick PHRASE this is a phrase meaning 'getting married without a formal ceremony' ❑ *They both led tramping lives, and this woman in Gerrard-street here, had been married very young, over the broomstick (as we say), to a tramping man, and was a perfect fury in point of jealousy.* (*Great Expectations* by Charles Dickens)

own VERB own means to admit or to acknowledge ❑ *It's my old girl that advises. She has the head. But I never own to it before her. Discipline must be maintained* (*Bleak House* by Charles Dickens)

page NOUN here page means a boy employed to run errands ❑ *not my feigned page* (*On His Mistress* by John Donne)

paid pretty dear PHRASE paid pretty dear means paid a high price or suffered quite a lot ❑ *I paid pretty dear for my monthly fourpenny piece* (*Treasure Island* by Robert Louis Stevenson)

pannikins NOUN pannikins were small tin cups ❑ *of lifting light glasses and cups to his lips, as if they were clumsy pannikins* (*Great Expectations* by Charles Dickens)

pards NOUN pards are leopards ❑ *Not charioted by Bacchus and his pards* (*Ode to a Nightingale* by John Keats)

parlour boarder NOUN a pupil who lived with the family ❑ *and somebody had lately raised her from the condition of scholar to parlour boarder* (*Emma* by Jane Austen)

particular, a London PHRASE London in Victorian times and up to the 1950s was famous for having very dense fog–which was a combination of real fog and the smog of pollution from factories ❑ *This is a London particular . . . A fog, miss* (*Bleak House* by Charles Dickens)

patten NOUN pattens were wooden soles which were fixed to shoes by straps to protect the shoes in wet weather ❑ *carrying a basket like the Great Seal of England in plaited straw, a pair of pattens, a spare shawl, and an umbrella, though it was a fine bright day* (*Great Expectations* by Charles Dickens)

paviour NOUN a paviour was a labourer who worked on the street pavement ❑ *the paviour his pickaxe* (*Oliver Twist* by Charles Dickens)

peccant ADJ peccant means unhealthy ❑ *other peccant humours* (*Gulliver's Travels* by Jonathan Swift)

penetralium NOUN penetralium is a word used to describe the inner rooms of the house ❑ *and I had no desire to aggravate his impatience previous to inspecting the penetralium* (*Wuthering Heights* by Emily Brontë)

pensive ADV pensive means deep in thought or thinking seriously about something ❑ *and she was leaning pensive on a tomb-stone on her right elbow* (*The Adventures of Huckleberry Finn* by Mark Twain)

penury NOUN penury is the state of being extremely poor ❑ *Distress, if not penury, loomed in the distance* (*Tess of the D'Urbervilles* by Thomas Hardy)

perspective NOUN telescope ❑ *a pocket perspective* (*Gulliver's Travels* by Jonathan Swift)

phaeton NOUN a phaeton was an open carriage for four people ❑ *often* *condescends to drive by my humble abode in her little phaeton and ponies* (*Pride and Prejudice* by Jane Austen)

phantasm NOUN a phantasm is an illusion, something that is not real. It is sometimes used to mean ghost ❑ *Experience had bred no fancies in him that could raise the phantasm of appetite* (*Silas Marner* by George Eliot)

physic NOUN here physic means medicine ❑ *there I studied physic two years and seven months* (*Gulliver's Travels* by Jonathan Swift)

pinioned VERB to pinion is to hold both arms so that a person cannot move them ❑ *But the relentless Ghost pinioned him in both his arms, and forced him to observe what happened next.* (*A Christmas Carol* by Charles Dickens)

piquet NOUN piquet was a popular card game in the C18th ❑ *Mr Hurst and Mr Bingley were at piquet* (*Pride and Prejudice* by Jane Austen)

plaister NOUN a plaister is a piece of cloth on which an apothecary (or pharmacist) would spread ointment. The cloth is then applied to wounds or bruises to treat them ❑ *Then, she gave the knife a final smart wipe on the edge of the plaister, and then sawed a very thick round off the loaf: which she finally, before separating from the loaf, hewed into two halves, of which Joe got one, and I the other.* (*Great Expectations* by Charles Dickens)

plantations NOUN here plantations means colonies, which are countries controlled by a more powerful country ❑ *besides our plantations in America* (*Gulliver's Travels* by Jonathan Swift)

plastic ADJ here plastic is an old term meaning shaping or a power that was forming ❑ *A plastic power abode with me* (*The Prelude* by William Wordsworth)

players NOUN actors ❑ *of players which upon the world's stage be* (*On His Mistress* by John Donne)

plump ADV all at once, suddenly ❑ *But it took a bit of time to get it well round, the change come so uncommon plump, didn't it?* (*Great Expectations* by Charles Dickens)

plundered VERB to plunder is to rob or steal from ❑ *These crosses stand for the names of ships or towns that they sank or plundered* (*Treasure Island* by Robert Louis Stevenson)

pommel ■ VERB to pommel someone is to hit them repeatedly with your fists ❑ *hug him round the neck, pommel his back, and kick his legs in irrepressible affection!* (*A Christmas Carol* by Charles Dickens) ■ NOUN a pommel is the part of a saddle that rises up at the front ❑ *He had his gun across his pommel* (*The Adventures of Huckleberry Finn* by Mark Twain)

poor's rates NOUN poor's rates were property taxes which were used to support the poor ❑ *'Oh!' replied the undertaker; 'why, you know, Mr. Bumble, I pay a good deal towards the poor's rates.'* (*Oliver Twist* by Charles Dickens)

popular ADJ popular means ruled by the people, or Republican, rather than ruled by a monarch ❑ *With those of Greece compared and popular Rome* (*The Prelude* by William Wordsworth)

porringer NOUN a porringer is a small bowl ❑ *Of this festive composition each boy had one porringer, and no more* (*Oliver Twist* by Charles Dickens)

postboy NOUN a postboy was the driver of a horse-drawn carriage ❑ *He spoke to a postboy who was dozing under the gateway* (*Oliver Twist* by Charles Dickens)

post-chaise NOUN a fast carriage for two or four passengers ❑ *Looking round, he saw that it was a post-chaise, driven at great speed* (*Oliver Twist* by Charles Dickens)

postern NOUN a small gate usually at the back of a building ❑ *The little servant happening to be entering the* *fortress with two hot rolls, I passed through the postern and crossed the drawbridge, in her company* (*Great Expectations* by Charles Dickens)

pottle NOUN a pottle was a small basket ❑ *He had a paper-bag under each arm and a pottle of strawberries in one hand . . .* (*Great Expectations* by Charles Dickens)

pounce NOUN pounce is a fine powder used to prevent ink spreading on untreated paper ❑ *in that grim atmosphere of pounce and parchment, red-tape, dusty wafers, ink-jars, brief and draft paper, law reports, writs, declarations, and bills of costs* (*David Copperfield* by Charles Dickens)

pox NOUN pox means sexually transmitted diseases like syphilis ❑ *how the pox in all its consequences and denominations* (*Gulliver's Travels* by Jonathan Swift)

prelibation NOUN prelibation means a foretaste of or an example of something to come ❑ *A prelibation to the mower's scythe* (*The Prelude* by William Wordsworth)

prentice NOUN an apprentice ❑ *and Joe, sitting on an old gun, had told me that when I was 'prentice to him regularly bound, we would have such Larks there!* (*Great Expectations* by Charles Dickens)

presently ADV immediately ❑ *I presently knew what they meant* (*Gulliver's Travels* by Jonathan Swift)

pumpion NOUN pumpkin ❑ *for it was almost as large as a small pumpion* (*Gulliver's Travels* by Jonathan Swift)

punctual ADJ kept in one place ❑ *was not a punctual presence, but a spirit* (*The Prelude* by William Wordsworth)

quadrille ■ NOUN a quadrille is a dance invented in France which is usually performed by four couples ❑ *However, Mr Swiveller had Miss Sophy's hand for the first quadrille (country-dances being low, were utterly proscribed)* (*The Old Curiosity Shop* by Charles Dickens) ■ NOUN quadrille was a card game for four people ❑ *to make up her pool of quadrille in the evening* (*Pride and Prejudice* by Jane Austen)

quality NOUN gentry or upper-class people ❑ *if you are with the quality* (*The Adventures of Huckleberry Finn* by Mark Twain)

quick parts PHRASE quick-witted ❑ *Mr Bennet was so odd a mixture of quick parts* (*Pride and Prejudice* by Jane Austen)

quid NOUN a quid is something chewed or kept in the mouth, like a piece of tobacco ❑ *rolling his quid* (*Treasure Island* by Robert Louis Stevenson)

quit VERB quit means to avenge or to make even ❑ *But Faustus's death shall quit my infamy* (*Doctor Faustus 4.3* by Christopher Marlowe)

rags NOUN divisions ❑ *Nor hours, days, months, which are the rags of time* (*The Sun Rising* by John Donne)

raiment NOUN raiment means clothing ❑ *the mountain shook off turf and flower, had only heath for raiment and crag for gem* (*Jane Eyre* by Charlotte Brontë)

rain cats and dogs PHRASE an expression meaning rain heavily. The origin of the expression is unclear ❑ *But it'll perhaps rain cats and dogs to-morrow* (*Silas Marner* by George Eliot)

raised Cain PHRASE raised Cain means caused a lot of trouble. Cain is a character in the Bible who killed his brother Abel ❑ *and every time he got drunk he raised Cain around town* (*The Adventures of Huckleberry Finn* by Mark Twain)

rambling ADJ rambling means confused and not very clear ❑ *my head began to be filled very early with rambling thoughts* (*Robinson Crusoe* by Daniel Defoe)

raree-show NOUN a raree-show is an old term for a peep-show or a fairground entertainment ❑ *A raree-show is here, with children gathered round* (*The Prelude* by William Wordsworth)

recusants NOUN people who resisted authority ❑ *hardy recusants* (*The Prelude* by William Wordsworth)

redounding VERB eddying. An eddy is a movement in water or air which goes round and round instead of flowing in one direction ❑ *mists and steam-like fogs redounding everywhere* (*The Prelude* by William Wordsworth)

redundant ADJ here redundant means overflowing but Wordsworth also uses it to mean excessively large or too big ❑ *A tempest, a redundant energy* (*The Prelude* by William Wordsworth)

reflex NOUN reflex is a shortened version of reflexion, which is an alternative spelling of reflection ❑ *To cut across the reflex of a star* (*The Prelude* by William Wordsworth)

Reformatory NOUN a prison for young offenders/criminals ❑ *Even when I was taken to have a new suit of clothes, the tailor had orders to make them like a kind of Reformatory, and on no account to let me have the free use of my limbs.* (*Great Expectations* by Charles Dickens)

remorse NOUN pity or compassion ❑ *by that remorse* (*On His Mistress* by John Donne)

render VERB in this context render means give. ❑ *and Sarah could render no reason that would be sanctioned by the feeling of the community.* (*Silas Marner* by George Eliot)

repeater NOUN a repeater was a watch that chimed the last hour when a button was pressed–as a result it was useful in the dark ❑ *And his watch is a gold repeater, and worth a hundred pound if it's worth a penny.* (*Great Expectations* by Charles Dickens)

repugnance NOUN repugnance means a strong dislike of something or someone ❑ *overcoming a strong repugnance* (*Treasure Island* by Robert Louis Stevenson)

reverence NOUN reverence means bow. When you bow to someone, you briefly bend your body towards them as a formal way of showing them respect ❑ *made my reverence* (*Gulliver's Travels* by Jonathan Swift)

reverie NOUN a reverie is a daydream ❑ *I can guess the subject of your reverie* (*Pride and Prejudice* by Jane Austen)

revival NOUN a religious meeting held in public ❑ *well I'd ben a-running' a little temperance revival thar' bout a week* (*The Adventures of Huckleberry Finn* by Mark Twain)

revolt VERB revolt means turn back or stop your present course of action and go back to what you were doing before ❑ *Revolt, or I'll in piecemeal tear thy flesh* (*Doctor Faustus 5.1* by Christopher Marlowe)

rheumatics/rheumatism NOUN rheumatics [rheumatism] is an illness that makes your joints or muscles stiff and painful ❑ *a new cure for the rheumatics* (*Treasure Island* by Robert Louis Stevenson)

riddance NOUN riddance is usually used in the form good riddance which you say when you are pleased that something has gone or been left behind ❑ *I'd better go into the house, and die and be a riddance* (*David Copperfield* by Charles Dickens)

rimy ADJ rimy is an adjective which means covered in ice or frost ❑ *It was a rimy morning, and very damp* (*Great Expectations* by Charles Dickens)

riper ADJ riper means more mature or older ❑ *At riper years to Wittenberg he went* (*Doctor Faustus chorus* by Christopher Marlowe)

rubber NOUN a set of games in whist or backgammon ❑ *her father was sure of his rubber* (*Emma* by Jane Austen)

ruffian NOUN a ruffian is a person who behaves violently ❑ *and when the ruffian had told him* (*Treasure Island* by Robert Louis Stevenson)

sadness NOUN sadness is an old term meaning seriousness ❑ *But I prithee tell me, in good sadness* (*Doctor Faustus 2.2* by Christopher Marlowe)

sailed before the mast PHRASE this phrase meant someone who did not look like a sailor ❑ *he had none of the appearance of a man that sailed before the mast* (*Treasure Island* by Robert Louis Stevenson)

scabbard NOUN a scabbard is the covering for a sword or dagger ❑ *Girded round its middle was an antique scabbard; but no sword was in it, and the ancient sheath was eaten up with rust* (*A Christmas Carol* by Charles Dickens)

schooners NOUN A schooner is a fast, medium-sized sailing ship ❑ *if schooners, islands, and maroons* (*Treasure Island* by Robert Louis Stevenson)

science NOUN learning or knowledge ❑ *Even Science, too, at hand* (*The Prelude* by William Wordsworth)

scrouge VERB to scrouge means to squeeze or to crowd ❑ *to scrouge in and get a sight* (*The Adventures of Huckleberry Finn* by Mark Twain)

scrutore NOUN a scrutore, or escritoire, was a writing table ❑ *set me gently on my feet upon the scrutore* (*Gulliver's Travels* by Jonathan Swift)

scutcheon/escutcheon NOUN an escutcheon is a shield with a coat of arms, or the symbols of a family name, engraved on it ❑ *On the scutcheon we'll have a bend* (*The Adventures of Huckleberry Finn* by Mark Twain)

sea-dog PHRASE sea-dog is a slang term for an experienced sailor or pirate ❑ *a 'true sea-dog', and a 'real old salt,'* (*Treasure Island* by Robert Louis Stevenson)

see the lions PHRASE to see the lions was to go and see the sights of London. Originally the phrase referred to the menagerie in the Tower of London and later in Regent's Park ❑ *We will go and see the lions for an hour or two–it's something to have a fresh fellow like you to show them to, Copperfield* (*David Copperfield* by Charles Dickens)

self-conceit NOUN self-conceit is an old term which means having too high an opinion of oneself, or deceiving yourself ❑ *Till swollen with cunning, of a self-conceit* (*Doctor Faustus chorus* by Christopher Marlowe)

seneschal NOUN a steward ❑ *where a grey-headed seneschal sings a funny chorus with a funnier body of vassals* (*Oliver Twist* by Charles Dickens)

sensible ADJ if you were sensible of something you are aware or conscious of something ❑ *If my children are silly I must hope to be always sensible of it* (*Pride and Prejudice* by Jane Austen)

sessions NOUN court cases were heard at specific times of the year called sessions ❑ *He lay in prison very ill, during the whole interval between his committal for trial, and the coming round of the Sessions.* (*Great Expectations* by Charles Dickens)

shabby ADJ shabby places look old and in bad condition ❑ *a little bit of a shabby village named Pikesville* (*The Adventures of Huckleberry Finn* by Mark Twain)

shay-cart NOUN a shay-cart was a small cart drawn by one horse ❑ *'I were at the Bargemen t'other night, Pip;' whenever he subsided into affection, he called me Pip, and whenever he relapsed into politeness he called me Sir; 'when there come up in his* *shay-cart Pumblechook.'* (*Great Expectations* by Charles Dickens)

shilling NOUN a shilling is an old unit of currency. There were twenty shillings in every British pound ❑ *'Ten shillings too much,' said the gentleman in the white waistcoat.* (*Oliver Twist* by Charles Dickens)

shines NOUN tricks or games ❑ *well, it would make a cow laugh to see the shines that old idiot cut* (*The Adventures of Huckleberry Finn* by Mark Twain)

shirking VERB shirking means not doing what you are meant to be doing, or evading your duties ❑ *some of you shirking lubbers* (*Treasure Island* by Robert Louis Stevenson)

shiver my timbers PHRASE shiver my timbers is an expression which was used by sailors and pirates to express surprise ❑ *why, shiver my timbers, if I hadn't forgotten my score!* (*Treasure Island* by Robert Louis Stevenson)

shoe-roses NOUN shoe-roses were roses made from ribbons which were stuck on to shoes as decoration ❑ *the very shoe-roses for Netherfield were got by proxy* (*Pride and Prejudice* by Jane Austen)

singular ADJ singular means very great and remarkable or strange ❑ *'Singular dream,' he says* (*The Adventures of Huckleberry Finn* by Mark Twain)

sire NOUN sire is an old word which means lord or master or elder ❑ *She also defied her sire* (*Little Women* by Louisa May Alcott)

sixpence NOUN a sixpence was half of a shilling ❑ *if she had only a shilling in the world, she would be very lilkely to give away sixpence of it* (*Emma* by Jane Austen)

slavey NOUN the word slavey was used when there was only one servant in a house or boarding-house–so she had to perform all the duties of a larger staff ❑ *Two distinct knocks, sir, will produce the slavey at any time* (*The Old Curiosity Shop* by Charles Dickens)

slender ADJ weak ❑ *In slender accents of sweet verse* (*The Prelude* by William Wordsworth)

slop-shops NOUN slop-shops were shops where cheap ready-made clothes were sold. They mainly sold clothes to sailors ❑ *Accordingly, I took the jacket off, that I might learn to do without it; and carrying it under my arm, began a tour of inspection of the various slop-shops.* (*David Copperfield* by Charles Dickens)

sluggard NOUN a lazy person ❑ *'Stand up and repeat "'Tis the voice of the sluggard",' said the Gryphon.* (*Alice's Adventures in Wonderland* by Lewis Carroll)

smallpox NOUN smallpox is a serious infectious disease ❑ *by telling the men we had smallpox aboard* (*The Adventures of Huckleberry Finn* by Mark Twain)

smalls NOUN smalls are short trousers ❑ *It is difficult for a large-headed, small-eyed youth, of lumbering make and heavy countenance, to look dignified under any circumstances; but it is more especially so, when superadded to these personal attractions are a red nose and yellow smalls* (*Oliver Twist* by Charles Dickens)

sneeze-box NOUN a box for snuff was called a sneeze-box because sniffing snuff makes the user sneeze ❑ *To think of Jack Dawkins–lummy Jack –the Dodger–the Artful Dodger–going abroad for a common twopenny-halfpenny sneeze-box!* (*Oliver Twist* by Charles Dickens)

snorted VERB slept ❑ *Or snorted we in the Seven Sleepers' den?* (*The Good-Morrow* by John Donne)

snuff NOUN snuff is tobacco in powder form which is taken by sniffing ❑ *as he thrust his thumb and forefinger into the proffered snuff-box of the undertaker: which was an ingenious little model of a patent* *coffin.* (*Oliver Twist* by Charles Dickens)

soliloquized VERB to soliloquize is when an actor in a play speaks to himself or herself rather than to another actor ❑ *'A new servitude! There is something in that,' I soliloquized (mentally, be it understood; I did not talk aloud)* (*Jane Eyre* by Charlotte Brontë)

sough NOUN a sough is a drain or a ditch ❑ *as you may have noticed the sough that runs from the marshes* (*Wuthering Heights* by Emily Brontë)

spirits NOUN a spirit is the nonphysical part of a person which is believed to remain alive after their death ❑ *that I might raise up spirits when I please* (*Doctor Faustus 1.5* by Christopher Marlowe)

spleen ■ NOUN here spleen means a type of sadness or depression which was thought to only affect the wealthy ❑ *yet here I could plainly discover the true seeds of spleen* (*Gulliver's Travels* by Jonathan Swift) ■ NOUN irritability and low spirits ❑ *Adieu to disappointment and spleen* (*Pride and Prejudice* by Jane Austen)

spondulicks NOUN spondulicks is a slang word which means money ❑ *not for all his spondulicks and as much more on top of it* (*The Adventures of Huckleberry Finn* by Mark Twain)

stalled of VERB to be stalled of something is to be bored with it ❑ *I'm stalled of doing naught* (*Wuthering Heights* by Emily Brontë)

stanchion NOUN a stanchion is a pole or bar that stands upright and is used as a building support ❑ *and slid down a stanchion* (*The Adventures of Huckleberry Finn* by Mark Twain)

stang NOUN stang is another word for pole which was an old measurement ❑ *These fields were intermingled with woods of half a stang* (*Gulliver's Travels* by Jonathan Swift)

starlings NOUN a starling is a wall built around the pillars that support a bridge to protect the pillars ❑ *There were states of the tide when, having been down the river, I could not get back through the eddy-chafed arches and starlings of old London Bridge* (*Great Expectations* by Charles Dickens)

startings NOUN twitching or night-time movements of the body ❑ *with midnight's startings* (*On His Mistress* by John Donne)

stomacher NOUN a panel at the front of a dress ❑ *but send her aunt the pattern of a stomacher* (*Emma* by Jane Austen)

stoop VERB swoop ❑ *Once a kite hovering over the garden made a stoop at me* (*Gulliver's Travels* by Jonathan Swift)

succedaneum NOUN a succedaneum is a substitute ❑ *But as a succedaneum* (*The Prelude* by William Wordsworth)

suet NOUN a hard animal fat used in cooking ❑ *and your jaws are too weak For anything tougher than suet* (*Alice's Adventures in Wonderland* by Lewis Carroll)

sultry ADJ sultry weather is hot and damp. Here sultry means unpleasant or risky ❑ *for it was getting pretty sultry for us* (*The Adventures of Huckleberry Finn* by Mark Twain)

summerset NOUN summerset is an old spelling of somersault. If someone does a somersault, they turn over completely in the air ❑ *I have seen him do the summerset* (*Gulliver's Travels* by Jonathan Swift)

supper NOUN supper was a light meal taken late in the evening. The main meal was dinner which was eaten at four or five in the afternoon ❑ *and the supper table was all set out* (*Emma* by Jane Austen)

surfeits VERB to surfeit in something is to have far too much of it, or to overindulge in it to an unhealthy degree ❑ *He surfeits upon cursed* *necromancy* (*Doctor Faustus chorus* by Christopher Marlowe)

surtout NOUN a surtout is a long close-fitting overcoat ❑ *He wore a long black surtout reaching nearly to his ankles* (*The Old Curiosity Shop* by Charles Dickens)

swath NOUN swath is the width of corn cut by a scythe ❑ *while thy hook Spares the next swath* (*Ode to Autumn* by John Keats)

sylvan ADJ sylvan means belonging to the woods ❑ *Sylvan historian* (*Ode on a Grecian Urn* by John Keats)

taction NOUN taction means touch. This means that the people had to be touched on the mouth or the ears to get their attention ❑ *without being roused by some external taction upon the organs of speech and hearing* (*Gulliver's Travels* by Jonathan Swift)

Tag and Rag and Bobtail PHRASE the riff-raff, or lower classes. Used in an insulting way ❑ *'No,' said he; 'not till it got about that there was no protection on the premises, and it come to be considered dangerous, with convicts and Tag and Rag and Bobtail going up and down.'* (*Great Expectations* by Charles Dickens)

tallow NOUN tallow is hard animal fat that is used to make candles and soap ❑ *and a lot of tallow candles* (*The Adventures of Huckleberry Finn* by Mark Twain)

tan VERB to tan means to beat or whip ❑ *and if I catch you about that school I'll tan you good* (*The Adventures of Huckleberry Finn* by Mark Twain)

tanyard NOUN the tanyard is part of a tannery, which is a place where leather is made from animal skins ❑ *hid in the old tanyard* (*The Adventures of Huckleberry Finn* by Mark Twain)

tarry ADJ tarry means the colour of tar or black ❑ *his tarry pig-tail* (*Treasure Island* by Robert Louis Stevenson)

thereof PHRASE from there ❑ *By all desires which thereof did ensue* (*On His Mistress* by John Donne)

thick with, be PHRASE if you are 'thick with someone' you are very close, sharing secrets–it is often used to describe people who are planning something secret ❑ *Hasn't he been thick with Mr Heathcliff lately?* (*Wuthering Heights* by Emily Brontë)

thimble NOUN a thimble is a small cover used to protect the finger while sewing ❑ *The paper had been sealed in several places by a thimble* (*Treasure Island* by Robert Louis Stevenson)

thirtover ADJ thirtover is an old word which means obstinate or that someone is very determined to do want they want and can not be persuaded to do something in another way ❑ *I have been living on in a thirtover, lackadaisical way* (*Tess of the D'Urbervilles* by Thomas Hardy)

timbrel NOUN timbrel is a tambourine ❑ *What pipes and timbrels?* (*Ode on a Grecian Urn* by John Keats)

tin NOUN tin is slang for money/cash ❑ *Then the plain question is, an't it a pity that this state of things should continue, and how much better would it be for the old gentleman to hand over a reasonable amount of tin, and make it all right and comfortable* (*The Old Curiosity Shop* by Charles Dickens)

tincture NOUN a tincture is a medicine made with alcohol and a small amount of a drug ❑ *with ink composed of a cephalic tincture* (*Gulliver's Travels* by Jonathan Swift)

tithe NOUN a tithe is a tax paid to the church ❑ *and held farms which, speaking from a spiritual point of view, paid highly-desirable tithes* (*Silas Marner* by George Eliot)

towardly ADJ a towardly child is dutiful or obedient ❑ *and a towardly child* (*Gulliver's Travels* by Jonathan Swift)

toys NOUN trifles are things which are considered to have little importance, value, or significance ❑ *purchase my life from them bysome bracelets, glass rings, and other toys* (*Gulliver's Travels* by Jonathan Swift)

tract NOUN a tract is a religious pamphlet or leaflet ❑ *and Joe Harper got a hymn-book and a tract* (*The Adventures of Huckleberry Finn* by Mark Twain)

train-oil NOUN train-oil is oil from whale blubber ❑ *The train-oil and gunpowder were shoved out of sight in a minute* (*Wuthering Heights* by Emily Brontë)

tribulation NOUN tribulation means the suffering or difficulty you experience in a particular situation ❑ *Amy was learning this distinction through much tribulation* (*Little Women* by Louisa May Alcott)

trivet NOUN a trivet is a three-legged stand for resting a pot or kettle ❑ *a pocket-knife in his right; and a pewter pot on the trivet* (*Oliver Twist* by Charles Dickens)

trot line NOUN a trot line is a fishing line to which a row of smaller fishing lines are attached ❑ *when he got along I was hard at it taking up a trot line* (*The Adventures of Huckleberry Finn* by Mark Twain)

troth NOUN oath or pledge ❑ *I wonder, by my troth* (*The Good-Morrow* by John Donne)

truckle NOUN a truckle bedstead is a bed that is on wheels and can be slid under another bed to save space ❑ *It rose under my hand, and the door yielded. Looking in, I saw a lighted candle on a table, a bench, and a mattress on a truckle bedstead.* (*Great Expectations* by Charles Dickens)

trump NOUN a trump is a good, reliable person who can be trusted ❑ *This lad Hawkins is a trump, I perceive* (*Treasure Island* by Robert Louis Stevenson)

tucker NOUN a tucker is a frilly lace collar which is worn around the neck ❑ *Whereat Scrooge's niece's sister–the plump one with the lace tucker: not the one with the roses–blushed.* (*A Christmas Carol* by Charles Dickens)

tureen NOUN a large bowl with a lid from which soup or vegetables are served ❑ *Waiting in a hot tureen!* (*Alice's Adventures in Wonderland* by Lewis Carroll)

turnkey NOUN a prison officer; jailer ❑ *As we came out of the prison through the lodge, I found that the great importance of my guardian was appreciated by the turnkeys, no less than by those whom they held in charge.* (*Great Expectations* by Charles Dickens)

turnpike NOUN the upkeep of many roads of the time was paid for by tolls (fees) collected at posts along the road. There was a gate to prevent people travelling further along the road until the toll had been paid. ❑ *Traddles, whom I have taken up by appointment at the turnpike, presents a dazzling combination of cream colour and light blue; and both he and Mr. Dick have a general effect about them of being all gloves.* (*David Copperfield* by Charles Dickens)

twas PHRASE it was ❑ *twas but a dream of thee* (*The Good-Morrow* by John Donne)

tyrannized VERB tyrannized means bullied or forced to do things against their will ❑ *for people would soon cease coming there to be tyrannized over and put down* (*Treasure Island* by Robert Louis Stevenson)

'un NOUN 'un is a slang term for one–usually used to refer to a person ❑ *She's been thinking the old 'un* (*David Copperfield* by Charles Dickens)

undistinguished ADJ undiscriminating or incapable of making a distinction between good and bad things ❑

their undistinguished appetite to devour everything (*Gulliver's Travels* by Jonathan Swift)

use NOUN habit ❑ *Though use make you apt to kill me* (*The Flea* by John Donne)

vacant ADJ vacant usually means empty, but here Wordsworth uses it to mean carefree ❑ *To vacant musing, unreproved neglect* (*The Prelude* by William Wordsworth)

valetudinarian NOUN one too concerned with his or her own health. ❑ *for having been a valetudinarian all his life* (*Emma* by Jane Austen)

vamp VERB vamp means to walk or tramp to somewhere ❑ *Well, vamp on to Marlott, will 'ee* (*Tess of the D'Urbervilles* by Thomas Hardy)

vapours NOUN the vapours is an old term which means unpleasant and strange thoughts, which make the person feel nervous and unhappy ❑ *and my head was full of vapours* (*Robinson Crusoe* by Daniel Defoe)

vegetables NOUN here vegetables means plants ❑ *the other vegetables are in the same proportion* (*Gulliver's Travels* by Jonathan Swift)

venturesome ADJ if you are venturesome you are willing to take risks ❑ *he must be either hopelessly stupid or a venturesome fool* (*Wuthering Heights* by Emily Brontë)

verily ADV verily means really or truly ❑ *though I believe verily* (*Robinson Crusoe* by Daniel Defoe)

vicinage NOUN vicinage is an area or the residents of an area ❑ *and to his thought the whole vicinage was haunted by her.* (*Silas Marner* by George Eliot)

victuals NOUN victuals means food ❑ *grumble a little over the victuals* (*The Adventures of Huckleberry Finn* by Mark Twain)

vintage NOUN vintage in this context means wine ❑ *Oh, for a draught of vintage!* (*Ode to a Nightingale* by John Keats)

virtual ADJ here virtual means powerful or strong ❑ *had virtual faith* (*The Prelude* by William Wordsworth)

vittles NOUN vittles is a slang word which means food ❑ *There never was such a woman for givin' away vittles and drink* (*Little Women* by Louisa May Alcott)

voided straight PHRASE voided straight is an old expression which means emptied immediately ❑ *see the rooms be voided straight* (*Doctor Faustus 4.1* by Christopher Marlowe)

wainscot NOUN wainscot is wood panel lining in a room so wainscoted means a room lined with wooden panels ❑ *in the dark wainscoted parlor* (*Silas Marner* by George Eliot)

walking the plank PHRASE walking the plank was a punishment in which a prisoner would be made to walk along a plank on the side of the ship and fall into the sea, where they would be abandoned ❑ *about hanging, and walking the plank* (*Treasure Island* by Robert Louis Stevenson)

want VERB want means to be lacking or short of ❑ *The next thing wanted was to get the picture framed* (*Emma* by Jane Austen)

wanting ADJ wanting means lacking or missing ❑ *wanting two fingers of the left hand* (*Treasure Island* by Robert Louis Stevenson)

wanting, I was not PHRASE I was not wanting means I did not fail ❑ *I was not wanting to lay a foundation of religious knowledge in his mind* (*Robinson Crusoe* by Daniel Defoe)

ward NOUN a ward is, usually, a child who has been put under the protection of the court or a guardian for his or her protection ❑ *I call the Wards in Jarndcye. They* *are caged up with all the others.* (*Bleak House* by Charles Dickens)

waylay VERB to waylay someone is to lie in wait for them or to intercept them ❑ *I must go up the road and waylay him* (*The Adventures of Huckleberry Finn* by Mark Twain)

weazen NOUN weazen is a slang word for throat. It actually means shrivelled ❑ *You with a uncle too! Why, I knowed you at Gargery's when you was so small a wolf that I could have took your weazen betwixt this finger and thumb and chucked you away dead* (*Great Expectations* by Charles Dickens)

wery ■ ADV very ❑ *Be wery careful o' vidders all your life* (*Pickwick Papers* by Charles Dickens) ■ *See* wibrated

wherry NOUN wherry is a small swift rowing boat for one person ❑ *It was flood tide when Daniel Quilp sat himself down in the wherry to cross to the opposite shore.* (*The Old Curiosity Shop* by Charles Dickens)

whether PREP whether means which of the two in this example ❑ *we came in full view of a great island or continent (for we knew not whether)* (*Gulliver's Travels* by Jonathan Swift)

whetstone NOUN a whetstone is a stone used to sharpen knives and other tools ❑ *I dropped pap's whetstone there too* (*The Adventures of Huckleberry Finn* by Mark Twain)

wibrated VERB in Dickens's use of the English language 'w' often replaces 'v' when he is reporting speech. So here 'wibrated' means 'vibrated'. In *Pickwick Papers* a judge asks Sam Weller (who constantly confuses the two letters) "Do you spell it with a 'v' or a 'w'?' to which Weller replies 'That depends upon the taste and fancy of the speller, my Lord' ❑ *There are strings . . . in the human heart that had better not be wibrated* (*Barnaby Rudge* by Charles Dickens)

wicket NOUN a wicket is a little door in a larger entrance ❑ *Having rested here, for a minute or so, to collect a good burst of sobs and an imposing show of tears and terror, he knocked loudly at the wicket* (*Oliver Twist* by Charles Dickens)

without CONJ without means unless ❑ *You don't know about me, without you have read a book by the name of* The Adventures of Tom Sawyer (*The Adventures of Huckleberry Finn* by Mark Twain)

wittles ■ NOUN wittles is a slang word which means food ❑ *I live on broken wittles–and I sleep on the coals* (*David Copperfield* by Charles Dickens) ■ *See* wibrated

woo VERB courts or forms a proper relationship with ❑ *before it woo* (*The Flea* by John Donne)

words, to have PHRASE if you have words with someone you have a disagreement or an argument ❑ *I do not want to have words with a young thing like you.* (*Black Beauty* by Anna Sewell)

workhouse NOUN workhouses were places where the homeless were given food and a place to live in return for doing very hard work ❑ *And the Union workhouses? demanded Scrooge. Are they still in operation?* (*A Christmas Carol* by Charles Dickens)

yawl NOUN a yawl is a small boat kept on a bigger boat for short trips. Yawl is also the name for a small fishing boat ❑ *She sent out her yawl, and we went aboard* (*The Adventures of Huckleberry Finn* by Mark Twain)

yeomanry NOUN the yeomanry was a collective term for the middle classes involved in agriculture ❑ *The yeomanry are precisely the order of people with whom I feel I can have nothing to do* (*Emma* by Jane Austen)

yonder ADV yonder means over there ❑ *all in the same second we seem to hear low voices in yonder!* (*The Adventures of Huckleberry Finn* by Mark Twain)